PREGNANCY IN THE VICTORIAN NOVEL

PREGNANCY IN THE VICTORIAN NOVEL

Livia Arndal Woods

THE OHIO STATE UNIVERSITY PRESS
COLUMBUS

Copyright © 2023 by The Ohio State University.
All rights reserved.

Library of Congress Cataloging-in-Publication Data
Names: Woods, Livia Arndal, author.
Title: Pregnancy in the Victorian novel / Livia Arndal Woods.
Description: Columbus : The Ohio State University Press, [2023] | Includes bibliographical references and index. | Summary: "Traces the connections between the medicalization of pregnancy and childbirth occurring over the Victorian era and lived experiences through somatic readings of the works of Emily Brontë, George Eliot, Lucas Malet, Elizabeth Gaskell, and Thomas Hardy"—Provided by publisher.
Identifiers: LCCN 2023021889 | ISBN 9780814215531 (hardback) | ISBN 081421553X (hardback) | ISBN 9780814283004 (ebook) | ISBN 0814283004 (ebook)
Subjects: LCSH: Brontë, Emily, 1818–1848—Criticism and interpretation. | Eliot, George, 1819–1880—Criticism and interpretation. | Malet, Lucas, 1852–1931—Criticism and interpretation. | Gaskell, Elizabeth Cleghorn, 1810–1865—Criticism and interpretation. | Hardy, Thomas, 1840–1928—Criticism and interpretation. | English fiction—19th century—History and criticism. | Pregnancy in literature. | Childbirth in literature.
Classification: LCC PR878.P695 W66 2023 | DDC 823/.809354—dc23/eng/20230809
LC record available at https://lccn.loc.gov/2023021889

Other identifiers: ISBN 978-0-8142-5887-3 (paper) | ISBN 0-814-25887-5 (paper)

Cover design by Alexa Love
Text design by Juliet Williams
Type set in Minion Pro

CONTENTS

Acknowledgments		vii
AN INTRODUCTION	Somatic Reading	1
CHAPTER 1	Judgment	25
CHAPTER 2	Sympathy	49
AN INTERLUDE	Sensation	75
CHAPTER 3	Diagnosis	91
CHAPTER 4	Impression	124
A VERY SHORT CONCLUSION	The Very Long Nineteenth Century	156
Works Cited		161
Index		171

ACKNOWLEDGMENTS

This book would not have come to be without Talia Schaffer. My gratitude also to Anne Humphreys, Richard Kaye, and Caroline Reitz for their help with the beginnings of this project. Thanks to Tanya Agathocleous, Alyson Cole, Dennis Denisoff, Mario DiGangi, Duncan Faherty, Stanley Friedman, Margaret Galvan, Ashleigh Harris, Carrie Hintz, Amanda Hughett, Gerhard Joseph and the participants in the CUNY Graduate Center's Victorian Seminar, Anne McCarthy, Tanya Pollard, Nancy Silverman, Maria Stracke, Megan Sweeney, and Nancy Yousef.

I am grateful to Mia Chen, Christine Choi, Colleen Cusick, Miciah Hussey, Taylor Kennamer, Lindsay Lehman, Rose O'Malley, Jon Rachmani, Erin Spampinato, and Anastasia Valassis for generous feedback on chapter drafts. Particular thanks to Meechal Hoffmann and Julie Fuller.

I appreciated research support for this project provided by Jay Barksdale, Carolyn Broomhead, and Melanie Locay at the New York Public Library and the resources of the Wertheim Room there. More broadly, my scholarship has been supported in vital ways by the CUNY Graduate Center and the professional and pedagogical generosity of Glenn Burger, Annmarie Drury, Gloria Fisk, Kim Smith, Amy Wan, Karen Weingarten, and the Queens College Department of English; Sarah Bilston, Chloe Wheatley, and the Trinity College Department of English; and Akash Belsare, Donna Bussell, Meg Cass, Lan Dong, Stephanie Hedge, Tena Helton, Sara Lupita Olivares, Sarah Webb, the University of Illinois at Springfield's (UIS) Department of English, and the Caryl Towsley Moy, PhD, Endowed Fund for Collaborative Research at UIS.

Rebecca Bostock's editorial support and generous feedback from two readers for The Ohio State University Press helped me immensely in making meaningful revisions to this project. Their support for a book that foregrounds a personal approach to criticism was invaluable. Thanks also to Rebecca S. Bender, Douglas Easton, Samara Rafert, Olivia Sergent, and Elizabeth Zaleski.

My gratitude to my parents, Leigh Woods and Ágústa Gunnarsdóttir, and to Yitz, Lilja Meital, and Amalia Ósk Savit-Woods. Most of all: Gavriel Savit.

Portions of this book appeared in earlier forms in the following: "Generations in, Generations Of: Pregnancy in Jane Austen," *Women's Writing*, vol. 26, no. 2, spring 2019, pp. 1–17; "Hints to Mothers, 1837/2018," *Synapsis: A Health Humanities Journal*, 9 Apr. 2018; "Now You See It: Concealing and Revealing Pregnant Bodies in *Wuthering Heights* and *The Clever Woman of the Family*," *Victorian Network*, vol. 6, no. 1, summer 2015, pp. 32–53; and "Not-So-Great Expectations: Pregnancy and Syphilis in Sarah Grand's *The Heavenly Twins*," *Syphilis and Subjectivity: From the Victorians to the Present*, edited by M. Kari Nixon and Lorenzo Servitje, Palgrave Macmillan, 2018, pp. 115–36.

AN INTRODUCTION

Somatic Reading

Victorian novels treat pregnancy modestly. Description of pregnancy as an embodied experience is—unsurprisingly—the exception rather than the rule. Insofar as pregnancy is hinted at as a somatic condition in these texts, it is alongside moralizing and/or medical judgment. These moralizing and medically inflected representations of pregnancy should be understood in the long and wide historical arc of Anglo-American modernity and its aftershocks, connecting the narration of, say, Rosamond Lydgate's miscarriage in George Eliot's British Victorian *Middlemarch* both backward to early modern witch trials and forward to the criminalization of women—mostly working-class women and women of color—for their pregnancy outcomes in twenty-first-century America. So, although this book uses close reading to chart a more or less chronological path through mostly canonical Victorian texts and familiar medico-historical contexts, it does so alongside less traditional and less historically or geographically bounded meditations on the cultural significances of bodies and critical attitudes. These meditations contribute to a call for somatic reading, an analytical attitude attuned to impressions of the body on the page and in our own messy lived experience. It's an approach that grows out of vibrant conversations about critical practice and the body in literary studies. The somatic reading I argue for as particularly valuable to engaging pregnancy in the Victorian novel helps us read bodies better by reading them modestly, attuned to uncertainty despite ever-present judgmental scaffolding.

Victorian textual logic demands bodily modesty from its pregnant characters if they wish to avoid harsh narrative judgment, but I hope—in the vein of many such calls in recent years—that scholars will choose intellectually modest approaches to narrations of embodiment and that such approaches can open out onto different perspectives on pregnant characters and, perhaps, pregnancy. I want to access modesty as an intellectual mode by treating some of the traditional bodily territory of modesty more openly. Let's be modest critics by employing more of our immodest bodies in criticism.

Pregnancy, like the body in general, often demands ways of not quite knowing. If, as Pardis Dabashi recently posited, "the status of critical claims about literature occupies an undefined territory between knowledge and belief, something on the order of a hunch," so—until very recently in human history—did pregnancy (951). Until well into the twentieth century, the pregnant body was a suggestive cipher. Applying what I know about pregnancy from my own experience and from observing the experiences of others, I assume that most pregnant people have at some point known themselves to be so in somatic ways: sudden nausea, a growing belly, fetal movements. But, until the middle of the twentieth century, such knowledge was difficult or impossible to verify. Though we now measure hormone levels in urine to confirm pregnancy, use ultrasounds to estimate a "due date," and track maternal and fetal heart rates to monitor risk, something like certainty about reproductive bodies (or about the body in general, though this is a much more complicated topic across histories and cultures) is radically new. Even the enlarged midsection so suggestive of pregnancy is easily misinterpreted, as, for example, was Lady Flora Hastings's abdominal tumor by a young Queen Victoria in 1839.[1] As aggressive paparazzi-style "bump watching" of the twenty-first century demonstrates, such uncertainty still clings insistently to our desire to know and control women's bodies.[2] Though reading literary representations of those bodies prompts this twenty-first-century reader to quantify and diagnose, we should not read those bodies without also building in room for that uncertainty; we can't read the description of reproductive bodies in the nineteenth century without heightened attention to the challenge pregnancy posed not only to novelistic conventions that eschewed the frank depiction of

---

1. Lady Flora Hastings, a lady-in-waiting to Queen Victoria's mother, died of a cancerous liver tumor in 1839 after months of pregnancy speculation fueled by Victoria.

2. The desire to control bodies is hardly limited to women, of course, and women are not the only people who can become pregnant. Because reproductive capacity was so central to Victorian ideologies of sex and gender, I often refer to pregnancy as particularly associated with women in this book. I affirm trans identities and the experiences of pregnant people who are not women.

embodied sexuality but also to emerging scientific and moral epistemologies. By joining calls for more space for the personal and anecdotal in scholarship, somatic reading helps us analyze with uncertainty rather than against it. In so doing, somatic reading builds on the critical practice debates of the last twenty years and joins what Dabashi calls an "emerging generation of scholars[hip] ... more interested in seeing the moment of argumentative utterance as one of trial and experiment ... a moment of speculation" (951).

We need speculation when we read pregnancy in the Victorian novel. This project focuses on representations of pregnancy in the novel rather than in Victorian literature writ large because of the particular texture of readerly and narrative conversation and collaboration that marks this form in this period. Victorian novels elide pregnancy as an embodied condition—somatically, tactilely, and haptically specific—in narrating the plots of women who more or less conform to feminine ideals. Reading these pregnancies as representations of embodied experience requires "reading rigorously in the absence of explicit evidence" in order to tell "an impossible story ... and amplify the impossibility of its telling" (Thierauf 480; Hartman 11).³ In reading the pregnancies of women who don't conform to Victorian feminine ideals—women who are poor, who are pregnant and unmarried, who are unfaithful or disobedient to their husbands—it is sometimes possible to catch glimpses of pregnant embodiment: in Cathy Linton's hectic cheeks, in Hetty Sorrel's difficult walk away from her home, or in Sue Bridehead's being turned away from rooms to let, for example. Focusing on these pregnancies—as this book does—involves readerly participation in implicit and explicit narrative judgments that seem to offer the possibility of moral certainty. But bodies often work outside of moral certainty, and so does somatic reading.

Somatic reading of pregnancy in Victorian novels doesn't necessarily revise established critical approaches to the pregnancies I analyze. Rather, somatic reading fleshes out established critical approaches to these pregnancies with prompts to pointedly invite the personal into the analytical as a means of countering (rather than escaping) insistent cues to judge pregnant bodies. Somatic reading sometimes travels along paths similar to those worn by sympathy and empathy, but it requires neither. I don't particularly sympathize with the character of Rosamond Lydgate, but I recognize that pregnancy loss beyond the first trimester is always physically painful and very often emo-

---

3. This project owes much to Hartman's theorization of "critical fabulation" as an analytical method for reading what the record omits. The Victorian novelistic record of pregnancy, full of elisions as it is, very markedly elides any explicit awareness of pregnancy as significant to the story of enslavement and oppression enacted on Black and Brown bodies by the British empire.

tionally difficult. I know that Rosamond has no real body and experiences no real pain. But I want the recognition that the circumstances she is described as experiencing without suffering almost always entail suffering to inform the way we approach *Middlemarch* in our scholarship. I also want such recognition to inform the way we treat pregnant people undergoing late-term abortions or struggling with addiction in our courts of law and public opinion. In sketching a space for somatic reading, this book pursues that first desire insistently and sometimes gestures toward the second; literary criticism doesn't often change the world, but scholarship must engage the world.

PREGNANCY IN DICKENS: A CASE STUDY

Is there pregnancy in Dickens? There are pregnant characters, certainly, but is pregnancy as an embodied condition represented? In asking a similar question about sex, William Cohen draws for his answer ("there is sex in Dickens") on cultural phenomenology:

> This critical strategy pays close attention to embodied experience, to affects, emotions and senses, to bodily transformations across dimensions of time and space, all the while understanding such experience to be socially, culturally and historically situated. . . . An attention to corporeal "micropractices" and the experiential dimension of the body . . . need not come at the cost of a historical or political account of power differentials. ("Interiors" 7)

This account of the affordances of cultural phenomenology rhymes with my descriptions of somatic reading and offers a helpful articulation that a focus on the body is always "socially, culturally and historically situated." In asking whether there is pregnancy in Dickens—in asking where and how there is pregnancy in the Victorian novel—and in using lived experience to frame my answers, I assume neither that these texts offer "evidence of women's lived experience" nor that lived experience offers ultimate truths (Stone and Sanders 88).[4] But the phenomena of lived experience make up much of the data

---

4. I draw here on Stone and Sanders. In their chapter "The Good Mother and the Proper Wife: Marriage, Pregnancy, and Motherhood," they emphasize that they "look to literary texts not for evidence of women's lived experience, but rather as evidence of the ways in which literature both reflects and produces cultural narratives around proper femininity in the Victorian era" (88). Though I use Victorian literary texts to think about lived experience, it is in the way those texts can sometimes point us to encounters with our own lived experiences.

that informs our partial ways of knowing pregnancy, and pregnancy—as a tradition of feminist thinking particularly indebted to Iris Marion Young's work demonstrates—offers a particularly compelling challenge to any phenomenological or, indeed, philosophical approach to existence that relies on notions of a Discrete Individual or Universal Truth. This tradition marks "hybrid responses" to pregnancy and maternity among contemporary feminist scholars and autotheorists (Feder xv). In the 2018 *Harvester of Hearts: Motherhood under the Sign of Frankenstein*, for example, Rachel Feder reports on a conversation with Anne Mellor about feminist ways of (un)knowing: "*Male autobiographers tend to think that lives have beginnings, middles, and ends* while a feminist counterargument says that life is *more random than repetitious, arbitrary, that lives don't have clear shapes*" (xii). The experiences of bodies loosened just a bit from efforts at sense-making can also seem more random than repetitious. Clearly, certain plots do repeat in individual bodies and across social bodies, but bodily experience is not made up only or even mostly of such shapes, made salient by their repetitions or recognized significances; bodily experience is made up, in large part, of little tickles and itches and stubbed toes that end up seeming meaningless in their randomness, almost as though it were uncertain whether they had ever happened at all.

My experience and observations of the phenomena of pregnancy—both its plottable, salient phenomena and also all the strange, small tuggings that may have been just my own imagination—teach me uncertainty. In what I've called their "thrumming, almost unspoken suggestion that there are thousands of threads of existence that cannot or will not get gathered up tidily," Victorian novels—though so often associated with rigid certainties—also teach me uncertainty (Woods, "Flashes"). While Cohen notes that "despite . . . the supposed squeamishness of the Victorians . . . a material, embodied understanding of the inner self, its aspirations, and desires, pervades nineteenth-century writing about the senses," such an embodied understanding does not pervade nineteenth-century novelistic dealings with pregnancy ("Interiors" 7).

In *Our Mutual Friend*, Bella Wilfer/Rokesmith/Harmon tells her new husband that they are expecting their first child elliptically and euphemistically: "I think . . . there is a ship upon the ocean . . . bringing . . . to you and me . . . a little baby" (Dickens 672). If Bella were a "real" person, there would be embodied reasons for her to make this declaration: She might have missed a menstrual cycle; she might be experiencing painful, swollen, and/or enlarged breasts; she might have mood swings, unusual exhaustion, strong cravings for and/or aversions to certain foods; and so forth. But the Bella who makes this declaration is not a real person in that way, and the reasons for her announcement seem to have more to do with the vicissitudes of wealth, want, and a much-studied volume of the *Complete British Housewife* than with blood, breasts, or bellies.

But those of us who study Bella *are* real people with bodies, real people who know other real people with bodies. Not all of us know the somatic specifics of pregnancy, but we are not inclined to believe that babies arrive via "ship upon the ocean." Though Mary Elizabeth Leighton and Lisa Surridge have recently demonstrated the ways that the terminology used to report on Queen Victoria's public reproductive body (terms as clear as "in a delicate condition") are not "euphemisms [but] well accepted expressions that clearly convey Victoria's state," this "ship" and "ocean" are novelistic euphemisms for Bella's private maternal body (425). Whether the language of pregnancy is clinical ("pregnant"), gently knowing ("interesting condition"), or highly euphemized ("ship," "ocean"), it carries meaning because we flesh out what we read with what we know about the flesh. In our conference papers or classrooms, we are unlikely to announce, "After I had intercourse with a sexual partner, I had only slight, spotty bleeding during the course of what was usually a heavy menstrual flow. That's how I came to suspect myself to be pregnant, and I think it's possible that an experience like that is implied—especially to other people who have been pregnant or very close to a pregnant person—in what Bella says to her husband." Nonetheless, our critical practices occur in conversation with specific fleshly experiences from which we draw conclusions. Whether or not our critical practices make much room for the articulation of somatic experience, most of us understand that our colleagues have feeling bodies too and that the experiences of those bodies inform their judgments about texts and contexts.

If you're reading this right now, you probably already know that the Victorian novel made even less room for the articulation of reproductive somatic experience than does criticism. Though I share a contemporary Victorianist understanding of the body as "omnipresent in Victorian discourse," it is nonetheless the case that Bella's elliptical, euphemistic reference to a ship bringing her a baby is paradigmatic of the tendencies of early and mid-Victorian *novelistic* treatments of pregnancy specifically (Leighton and Surridge 425). As a general rule, these texts conceal the somatic details of reproduction, particularly as regards the representation of female characters who conform to normative expectations for feminine behavior. Bella's halting mention of this "ship"—made obliquely to her husband in the safety of their domestic space—is *Our Mutual Friend*'s only reference to the reproductive possibilities of Bella's body until the arrival of her child. If Bella were a "real" person, only extreme effort would make it possible for those close enough to know her domestic arrangements and overhear her conversations—as the critic does—to remain unaware of her changing body; though not everyone can intuit changes in menstrual cycles and nipple sensitivity in others, most seeing people notice a protruding pregnant belly. This is true even when the exact contours of a belly are concealed by fashions as modest as Victorian maternity wear, which—like Victorian fiction—aimed to veil the pregnant body. Though the tendency of Victorian fiction to veil the pregnant body has been, heretofore, only lightly explored in literary criticism (most notably by Cynthia Northcutt Malone and Clare Hanson), fashion studies has over fifty years of established scholarly conversation on Victorian maternity wear. Norah Waugh's 1968 *The Cut of Women's Clothes: 1600–1930*, Zuzanna Shonfield's 1972 "The Expectant Victorian: Late 19th Century Maternity Clothes," Harriet Waterhouse's 2007 "A Fashionable Confinement: Whaleboned Stays and the Pregnant Woman," and, most recently and most connected to my own concerns here, Catriona Fisk's 2019 "Looking for Maternity: Dress Collections and Embodied Knowledge" all treat the tendency of mid- and late nineteenth-century fashions to mute pregnancy. Indeed, as Fisk notes, maternity wear itself is muted in archives of material culture by the multiple uses to which garments suitable for wear during pregnancy were put in the period; Fisk points to the resulting need for "wider scholarly reconsideration of fashion, materiality and bodily knowledge as entwined strands of lived historical experience" (403). This call is part of a broader scholarly turn toward the body with which this book is in conversation.

A growing investment in the medical humanities helps locate much of the recent work in body studies, and the field is one that often but not always intersects with medicine and medical history. In looking at the meanings bodies carry and resist in culture, body studies—particularly vibrant Victorianist scholarship on bodies in the last fifteen years—is a field out of which my ideas about somatic reading have grown. Kathryn Hughes's 2017 *Victorians Undone: Tales of the Flesh in the Age of Decorum* treats the somatic experiences of the Victorians as inherently interesting. Pamela K. Stone and Lise Shapiro Sanders's 2021 *Bodies and Lives in Victorian England: Science, Sexuality, and the Affliction of Being Female* reads pregnancy in medical and literary records. Cohen's 2009 *Embodied: Victorian Literature and the Senses*, the "The Victorian Tactile Imagination" issue of *Interdisciplinary Studies in the Long Nineteenth Century* edited by Hilary Fraser and Carolyn Burdett, Peter J. Capuano's 2015 *Changing Hands: Industry, Evolution, and the Reconfiguration of the Victorian Body*, Pamela K. Gilbert's 2019 *Victorian Skin: Surface,*

Self, History,[5] and David Sweeney Coombe's 2019 *Reading with the Senses in Victorian Literature and Science* all speak to a contemporary interest in the relationship between the body, history, and historical nodes of self and experience and explore these interests in readings of the Victorian novel.[6] This interest and its prevalence in Victorian studies demonstrates a desire to position the body and the ideas of body that live in text as salient points on something like what—beyond the Victorianist conversation—Julie Orlemanski calls the "scales of reading" that "render palpable the phenomenological determinants of experiencing texts." "Texts 'happen,'" Orlemanski argues, "when they are read. Texts' scale thus depends upon, and takes shape in, the interactions of readers and words" (218). The interactions between twenty-first century readers of Victorian novels and the words they encounter are shaped both by the very large scales of history and the small scale of the body—as described in text, as affected by modernity, and as experienced by the critic.

In a cultural moment marked by rising cries for acknowledgment of the ways bodies matter, this insistent focus on the small scale of the body whispers our desire for scholarship to *matter*. Somatic reading helps me articulate more carefully how Victorian novels matter to me and how the matter of me participates in this. But I hope that somatic reading also speaks to how Victorian and literary studies more broadly can articulate how what we do matters, precisely by refusing to limit ways of knowing that start with the personal to the personal alone. Like Lauren Fournier's recent *Autotheory as Feminist Practice in Art, Writing, and Criticism,* this book's approach "mov[es] among close reading, feminist analysis, self-reflective anecdotes, and reparative forms of critique" (1). Fournier sees autotheory as an ascendant mode in literary studies; recent Victorianist literary criticism, notably Rachel Ablow's *The Feeling of Reading* and Deirdre Lynch's *Loving Literature,* has argued that rather than denying or obscuring the feelings and experiences that undergird literary study, we can incorporate those personal motivations explicitly in our analysis; we can treat them as questions worthy of analysis. In "rel[ying] on embodiment as evidence" or something like evidence, perhaps somatic read-

---

5. For more work on skin and skin as a stand-in for a self variously understood as impermeable and vulnerable, see Michie, "Under." Pamela Gilbert's *Victorian Skin* places recent interest in consciousness in Victorian literature in direct conversation with the body. Though the science and vocabulary of "consciousness" are generally beyond the direct scope of this project, my interest in how and what we know and don't know does run alongside this line of enquiry. For more recent Victorianist scholarship concerned with consciousness, see Ward; Hayles; Jaffe, *Victorian Novel*; Kramnick.

6. For work in the medical humanist tradition of particular relevance to Victorian literary scholars, see, for example, Rothfield; Tougaw; Caldwell; Kennedy, *Revising* and "Victorian Novel."

ing can—like Twitter and other spaces in the academic borderlands—"make standpoint theorists of us all" (Spampinato 966).

But in thinking about the personal, the embodied, and the perspectival, I am still thinking about Dickens. Also thinking about bodies and Dickens, Anne Schwan offers a helpful reminder about the epistemological and political limits of "attention to individualized . . . corporeal practices":

> A critique of social experiences that is conceptualised through attention to individualised, or intersubjective, corporeal practices, is necessarily limited. A critical focus on the affective or performative self potentially colludes with a political agenda that privileges the bourgeois concept of individuality over that of collectivity, and performative micropractices over the transformation of social relationships on a structural level. . . . The fact that the text imagines resistance as enacted through the body suggests that a concern with embodied micropractices . . . could have positive implications for the study of social power relations. . . . Yet, the narrative [of *Dombey and Son*] does not fully realise the possibilities of such embodied resistance. . . . This failure by Dickens to imagine a systemic transformation points to the limits in similarly configured models of contemporary criticism. (92–93)

By placing representations of pregnancy in the Victorian novel in conversation with idiosyncratic and anecdotal experiences of the body and twenty-first-century cultures of reproduction, somatic reading doesn't imagine any "systemic transformation . . . [in] contemporary criticism." But it does work to keep "social relationships on a structural level" in sight. Because they matter.

Does Dickens's Bella matter? Is Bella matter? I casually claimed above that she isn't a real person in the way people with bodies—like the critics who read her—are. But is Bella a "real" person in any other way? Does that question, asked about a fictional white upper-middle-class heroine at the center of the British Empire from an America where "black women have a pregnancy-related mortality ratio approximately three times as high as that of white women," matter (Petersen et al. 423)? Which is to ask: Does this book matter?

In some ways, all of these questions are evidence that what Stephen Best called a "period of disciplinary navel-gazing" is ongoing ("Obvious"). Certainly, this project began in 2010 with my desire to put surface reading into conversation with literary representations of pregnancy by asking how literary studies can know something about bodies that the surface of the Victorian novel seems to exclude and that, in lived experience, announces itself as a notable, protruding surface. This began as a project about the degree to which it was possible to navel-gaze, literally and figuratively, at and on this topic. But in the intervening years, literary studies, national discourse, and my own life have changed. Discussions in literary studies have shifted from asking whether we can read literature in ways less bound up in the more destructive aspects of critique to asking—building from Saidiya Hartman's work on "critical fabulation"—whether we can incorporate explicitly subjective attitudes in our analytical processes. Work on reproductive bodies and maternity from historians often models the embodied texture such subjectivity can take; "Perhaps the best way to explore the pasts of having a baby is to put grand narratives aside," Sarah Knott argues in her 2019 *Mother Is a Verb*, "to build a trellis of tiny scenes . . . [that] make up the visceral ongoingness, the blood and guts of being 'with child'" (7).[7]

Over the past decade, many pregnant people in America have lost access to reproductive choice. Statistics regarding our nation's high rates of death during pregnancy, childbirth, and the postpartum period have also made clear the markedly worse pregnancy outcomes for people of color, and demands to reckon with the violence to which bodies of color are subject has been met with increasingly overt and racist nationalisms. Through this, I have been a white woman in my thirties: My friends have been getting pregnant, struggling to get pregnant, deciding that they will not become pregnant or carry pregnancies to term. I was pregnant or breastfeeding during most of 2016 through 2021. I was also on the academic job market for four years. My own precarity and uncertainty has been an ongoing, embodied experience occurring alongside a reckoning with the ways my culture wields embodied experiences of precarity and uncertainty as tools for violence against people of color in ways I can only imagine and that I believe scholars must imagine. So, over the past decade, I have worked hard to clear a little more space for this book to pause with the textual matter of Bella, put it into conversation with what I take to be real life as I know it and as I imagine it, turn that conversation outward toward the real and imagined lives of others, and return to thinking closely about the state of Bella's navel (has it "popped?") with more uncertainty about the distinction between reality and fiction rather than less.

There is something about a tight focus on the body in literary criticism that summons questions about "reality." Victorianist scholarship on bodies and the real has done careful work thinking through the ways literature refracts the period's medical and scientific understandings of the somatic and sensory. Athena Vrettos's work on what she calls "somatic fictions" and Coombs's work on reading and the senses are particular influences on the ways I think

---

7. For more recent historical scholarship on maternity grounded in the personal experiences I associated with critical modesty, see Withycombe's writing for *Nursing Cleo*, for example.

through questions of reality and "the problems of somatic representation" (Vrettos 18). In "examin[ing] what it meant to 'talk of diseases' in the second half of the nineteenth century," Vrettos argues that Victorian understandings of "the somatic consequences of narrative place the literary or medical 'text' ... between imaginative and corporeal categories of experience" (2). The title of an article by Coombs, "Does Grandcourt Exist?," puts an even sharper focus on the question of reality than does the book project from which it is drawn. In seeking an answer to that question, Coombs cites Heather Love's call for a method of "thin description" with which "one might undertake *rigorously empirical analyses of objects that do not exist*" (Love, "Close Reading" 429 qtd. in Coombs, "Does Grandcourt Exist?" 393; emphasis added). This particular thread of influence speaks to a relationship between a "postcritical" reassessment of humanist modes and contemporary scholarly ways of thinking about the textual body. My exploration of somatic reading as literary practice in the context of a project about representations of pregnancy in the Victorian novel seems, to me, intuitive. In tracing these threads of influence, it's worth noting that this book works in conversation with these contexts, but my most careful attention is paid not—as in Vrettos's and Coombs's work—to the details of Victorian understanding but, rather, to the mysteries of our own.

These issues of reality and matter also connect a nineteenth-century racial imaginary with this book's focus on how the significance of women's bodies is constructed in relationship to their conformity to social norms. If Dickens's Bella were not Bella, but were instead—say—the enslaved speaker of Elizabeth Barrett Browning's "The Runaway Slave at Pilgrim's Point," details about her body *as a body* would likely be more explicit.[8] Though Barrett Browning elides her speaker's pregnancy (jumping from "the white men [who] brought the shame" to "I wore a child upon my breast"), her descriptions of enslaved experiences of romantic love, rape, maternity, and infanticide are markedly embodied (lines 101, 107). Indeed, as Sasha Turner demonstrates, British

---

8. Though few British literary representations of pregnancy during the Victorian period offer as direct an intersection as Barrett Browning's 1848 poem, English speakers on both sides of the Atlantic were reading slave narratives, like Harriet Jacobs's 1861 *Incidents in the Life of a Slave Girl*, that treated women's reproductive bodies in conversation with questions of race. The tendency of Victorian literature to conceal, reveal, and pathologize pregnancy often speaks implicitly to Victorian ideologies and representations of racial difference. One might read the proximity of revealed pregnancy to racialized/imperial Others in Emily Brontë's *Wuthering Heights*, George Eliot's *Adam Bede*, and Olive Schreiner's *Story of an African Farm* as speaking to the work of pregnancy in the period's literary racial/imperial discourse. Meyer writes about a "general metaphor [in Victorian fiction] linking, and likening, white women [particularly white women who do not conform to domestic feminine ideals] and people of what were in nineteenth-century British texts variously termed the lower, inferior, or dark races" (2).

"abolitionists linked abolition and colonial reform to the reproductive lives of enslaved women" (4). Though racist nineteenth-century ideologies often posited that people of color felt pain differently or less than white Europeans, those same ideologies also categorized people of color as more "savage" and associated savagery with embodiment, particularly female embodiment.[9] The display in Britain and Europe of Sara Baartman as the "Hottentot Venus" from 1810 to 1815 (followed—after her death—by the display in France of her skeleton and a body cast emphasizing her buttocks until the 1970s) typifies the entitlement with which British and European people approached and sexualized the bodies of Black women.[10] Across the Atlantic, the experiments conducted by James Marion Sims on the unanesthetized bodies of enslaved women and his subsequent application of those techniques on sedated white women earned him the title of "father of American gynecology." Though obstetrics and gynecology developed in different ways in nineteenth-century Britain and America, Sims's international reputation and the application of his inventions and treatments in Britain demonstrates the significance of Black women's bodies to Victorian ways of knowing the reproductive body. The hypervisibility of Black bodies in the public and medical imaginations of the nineteenth century cleaves along their relative invisibility in Victorian fiction. Though Barrett Browning's poem joined popular British and American abolitionist slave narratives in linking the available and vulnerable Black woman's body to questions of reproduction, Victorian novelistic mentions or depictions of pregnancy do not explore Black experience. Deidre Cooper Owens's recent argument that "black women remained flesh-and-blood contradictions, vital to . . . research yet dispensable once their bodies and labor were no longer required" speaks beyond the nineteenth-century American medical context and into both Victorian Britain and the American present (3).

Among Victorian novelistic depictions of pregnancy, however, the pregnant bodies of working or ambiguously classed women make up a notable percentage. If Bella were not Bella but a nameless, ambiguously classed, unmarried mother of an Oliver Twist, say, it is much more likely that the novel's machinery would employ the revelation of her embodied experience of pregnancy as a narrative lesson. Without the covers of a father, guardian, or husband, without money or social standing, and without access to the domestic protections that such things make possible, conventional Victorian femininity is difficult for working-class characters to achieve. Nineteenth-century working-class bodies were exposed to weather, terrible factory conditions, the

---

9. For more on how this contributed to the medical experimentation on Black women's bodies, see Briggs; Owens.

10. For more on Sara Baartman, see, for example, Crais and Scully.

workhouse, postmortem dissections, and the dangers of early hospital care; the bodies of working-class women in Victorian novels are exposed to our gaze.

If Bella were still Bella but ill as well as pregnant, perhaps her somatic experiences might receive more attention, though Vrettos reminds us of the danger Victorians found in such narration. Nonetheless, perhaps Bella's physical illness would suggest a moral illness that would seem to license her exposure. Perhaps her physical illness would suggest a Victorian brand of spiritualized suffering with which the reader might be encouraged to sympathize, and then, perhaps the narrative treatment of her illness would map suggestively onto the symptoms of pregnancy. Perhaps the threat of death might demand a narrative reckoning of the fetal life also at risk. If Bella were ill, perhaps she would be treated by a medical doctor licensed to speak in something other than euphemism and hesitance about women's bodies. Of course, such license to speak was more available beyond the bounds of medicine before the medicalization of middle-class women's reproductive bodies that occurred over the course of the nineteenth century. Perhaps if Bella were a character in an eighteenth-century novel, her pregnancy—whether or not it coincided with illness—would be treated with direct and casual narration. And, perhaps, if Bella were a character of the fin de siècle, her illness would be that mandatory psychological one common to the modern condition and the narrative might treat pregnancy as another aspect of troubled interiority and dangerous futurity.

As she is—penned and published in the 1860s, white, middle class, married, feminine, in good physical and mental health—Bella's tendency to treat her pregnancy metaphorically demonstrates the widespread Victorian tendency to understand pregnancy as a node in something like what Nora Doyle refers to, in the American context, as "sentimental motherhood":

> a vision of women's role [as mother] as the ideal of sentimental motherhood, a term that encompasses the traits of the moral mother, republican motherhood, and imperial motherhood, while also recognizing the ways in which sentimental expression and the power of feeling became central to the definition of the good mother. (4)

The ideology of sentimental motherhood so significant to nineteenth-century ways of knowing women's social roles on both sides of the Atlantic was one in which Mother was expressed as idea and spiritual vocation. Victorian fictional pregnancy is not a representation of a bodily condition but a symbol of "something else," even if that "something else" is something as metonymically linked to pregnancy as, say, futurity or creation, two of the more familiar pregnant metaphors. Pregnancy is often thought of not as swollen nipples or round-ligament pain, but as a vague and difficult-to-decipher sign of what the future holds, as a metaphor for divine or artistic will and creation, as the symbolic measure of the health of a bloodline or society, as a marker of feminine compliance with expectations that encompass and exceed matters of reproduction.

In this book I sometimes trace the ways that metonymic, metaphorical, and symbolic approaches to pregnancy shape Victorian novels. However, my primary focus is on reading the literary representation of pregnancy as it relates to embodied experience, on trying to read pregnancy in Victorian novels in conversation with pregnancy in lived experience. That this focus is often thwarted by the novels themselves bespeaks a tension already inherent in pregnancy as a physical and philosophical condition: With pregnancy, we suspect that there is something going on beneath the surface of the body, and we suspect this with increasing clarity over the course of the normative nine months' gestation in part because something is also going on *on* the surface of the body. But our knowledge about just what that something going on *is* is circumscribed. Because we can never fully know how to read the surface of the bodies of others, even when the signs seem clear, because we can never fully know the interiority—mental or bodily—of others, conventional manners would have us avoid casual comments or questions to someone we expect is expecting unless we've been authoritatively informed about a pregnancy; we don't just go around congratulating women with big bellies. And, of course—though the twentieth-century advent of the prenatal ultrasound complicates the equation—even the holders of pregnant bellies (and their partners and care providers) never quite know how to read these surfaces and interiorities. Pregnancy pushes at a modern notion of the knowable, knowing, and singular individual in ways that make questions about the knowability, knowledge, and singularity of pregnancy particularly compelling.

PROGENITORS; OR, THE ANALYTICAL IS PERSONAL

In arguing for somatic reading as a mode for reading pregnancy in the Victorian novel, I'm inviting the uncertainty that inheres in our personal experiences of the body to the literary critical table. Something akin to this impulse has been ascendant in twenty-first-century literary criticism, first in certain threads of "postcritique" and what Jeffrey J. Williams has called "the New Modesty in Literary Criticism" and now in "'the generational dialectic' of 'modesty'" having as much to do with our scholarly relationships with one another as with text (Dabashi qtd. in Lavery 978). *Pregnancy in the Victorian*

Novel participates in these strains of scholarship produced by my generation. Dabashi's work in the *PMLA* "Theories and Methodologies" cluster on "Cultures of Argument" that I have already referenced stemmed from the heated debate following her 2019 MLA presentation on "The Pressure to Intervene: A Case for the Modest (Young) Critic." In that presentation, as in her *PMLA* introduction, Dabashi argues for modesty as a relational mode between scholars; those of us who have come of age in what Michael Bérubé succinctly terms "the desiccated post-2008 (and especially post-2015) job market" (and to which we might now add "the even more especially desiccated post-COVID job market") value this mode with the particular force of an academic cohort for whom there has been so little room (970). The critical modesty that motivates this book's inclusion of the kind of anecdotal experience more familiar to conversations among close friends than to conferences, articles, and scholarly manuscripts works in this realm; my investment in the intellectual modesty of my generation's phrase "I feel" is as connected to my experiences being pregnant while fighting for this book through five years in a deeply uncertain job market and through a global pandemic without childcare as it is to a decade-long meditation on what it means to read immodest pregnancy in Victorian novels.

"Because all pregnancies . . . follow their own rules and take on their own lives [and] . . . fictional pregnancy suggests the unknown and unknowable to us," fictional pregnancy offers an effective canvas for exploring the scope and affordances of uncertainty (Boswell 3). In her recent work on the phenomenology of reading and experiences of reality, Elaine Auyoung declares that "the absence of a sophisticated vocabulary for talking about literary experience [is not] a sign that it cannot or need not be examined in a serious way, but rather [is] evidence of how desperately we need more effective methods for investigating it" (2). Pregnancy is a central site of narrative in human cultures, and embodied experience is an initial source of knowledge in our lives. How desperately, then, if literary scholarship is to conceive of pregnancy and embodied experiences, do we need more effective methods for investigation than those offered by a cultural inheritance that positions narratives of pregnancy as narratives of disobedience and discussion of the personal as a threat to the rigors of analysis? As Coombs's work and, for just one other particularly notable recent example, Rachel Ablow's *Victorian Pain*, testify, the practices of reading run in experiential grooves cut by embodied feeling and sensing. Somatic reading, reading for impressions rather than facts, helps this book read those grooves in my own encounters with Victorian novels and lets me sit with the uncertainty and epistemic modesty of the endeavor. The analytical is personal.

Of course, popular and academic interest in the cultural significances of pregnancy grew out of a related declaration from second-wave feminism's focus on the personal as political. These conversations, beginning with feminists from wildly different perspectives thinking about how discourses of pregnancy can empower, disempower, and function beyond power, have developed alongside social and intellectual movements as varied as queer theory, the "mommy wars," and Black Lives Matter. Female reproductive potential is so central to notions of sex, gender, and sexuality that the ways in which that potential shapes particular ideological structures can be easily obscured by a seeming clarity and ubiquity. Though hardly immune to essentialisms, feminist criticism and theory of the last fifty years has done much to suggest that the ideological role of women's reproductive potential is neither inevitable nor uninteresting but, rather, that reproductive bodies—invested with social meaning and expressive of biological processes—offer complex and compelling ways of thinking through the relationship of mind to body and self to other and reader to text.[11] In its insistence on the value of personal experience to rigorous critique and creation, feminist theoretical tradition has also contributed to the emergence of autotheory, "the integration of the auto or 'self' with philosophy or theory, often in ways that are direct, performative, or self-aware" (Fournier 6). Somatic reading as a critical attitude that engages subjective somatic experience in the analysis of textual representations of the body owes a debt to this vibrant field, particularly its points of intersection with pregnancy and the reproductive body, notably Maggie Nelson's 2015 *The Argonauts*.

Often well beyond autotheory, however, is a very long list of twenty-first-century "mommy memoirs" and the subcategories of pregnancy memoirs and guides; Emily Oster's 2014 *Expecting Better* and Angela Garbes's 2018 *Like a Mother* are notable for their close look at the way contemporary cultures of medicine and race, respectively, shape the ways we know pregnancy in twenty-first-century America. Scholarship has also seen an uptick in writing about pregnancy, though this has—heretofore—been more marked among scholars of history and media studies and among Americanists. Kelly Oliver's 2012 *Knock Me Up, Knock Me Down,* Nora Doyle's 2018 *Maternal Bodies: Redefining Motherhood in Early America,* and Sasha Turner's 2017 *Contested Bodies: Pregnancy, Childrearing, and Slavery in Jamaica* are all important contributions to the field. These sustained engagements with discourses of pregnancy have

---

11. For notable feminist scholarship on women's reproductive bodies, see Bordo; Ehrenreich and English; Irigaray; Cixous; Kristeva; Rich; Ruddick; Tuana; Chodorow. For notable feminist scholarship on pregnancy, see, for example, Oakley; Young.

had less impact on Victorianist literary scholarship than one might expect from an area that works in such close conversation with feminist theory and criticism and with the medical humanities.[12] Victorianists have done significant work on maternity.[13] Pregnancy remains underexplored in comparison, although the trickle of important scholarship on pregnancy in Victorian fiction—most notably Malone's 2000 "Near Confinement: Pregnant Women in the Nineteenth-Century British Novel," Clare Hanson's 2004 *A Cultural History of Pregnancy: Pregnancy, Medicine, and Culture, 1750–2000*, and Doreen Thierauf's 2014 "The Hidden Abortion Plot in George Eliot's *Middlemarch*"—is now accelerating.[14] *Pregnancy in the Victorian Novel* is part of this wave, participating in what Thierauf calls a process of the reader "adding in the intentionality underlying the course of events . . . retroactively" (486) or what Fisk calls "the process of 'filling in' what was once considered 'hidden from history'" (406–07).

Pregnancy is an undeniable physical fact of human life that exists across cultures and histories and around which ideologies are constructed. Pregnancy is also knowable only to one person and even then knowable primarily in ways that precede, exceed, and subvert language and the rational. When Love asks what it would mean "to speak about rather than for our subjects," she asks, in part, what it means to do humanist study and whether or how changeable the answers to that question might be ("Ecologies"). Though some particularly significant contributions to the postcritical conversation in literary studies (Sharon Marcus's 2007 *Between Women: Friendship, Desire, and Marriage in Victorian England*, for example, and her introduction with Stephen Best to the 2009 special issue of *Representations*) are now more than a decade old, work like Sarah Allison's 2018 *Reductive Reading: A Syntax of Victorian Moralizing* and the *Weak Theory* special issue of *Modernism/Modernity* edited by Paul Saint-Amour signal the ongoing interest not only in articulating and broadening the range of methods available to humanists but also in thinking about the particular affordances of "'weak' findings" (Allison 3) or "weak thought" in rigorous scholarship (Saint-Amour 3).

---

12. For more on the medicalization of women's bodies, see Carpenter; Cody; Foucault; Hanson; Jacobus et al.; Jordanova; Moscucci.

13. For more on women's reproductive bodies in Victorian literature, see Byrne; Hirsch; Homans; Matus; Michie, *Flesh*.

14. Cristina Mazzoni's *Maternal Impressions: Pregnancy and Childbirth in Literature and Theory* also treats pregnancy qua pregnancy directly in the context of nineteenth-century literature, though her focus is on the Italian fin de siècle. A peer-reviewed *Pregnancy and Childbirth in the Age of Victoria* cluster was published to *The Victorian Web* in 2022 as part of Mary Elizabeth Leighton and Lisa Surridge's Great Expectations Pregnancy Project. See also Regaignon.

IN HISTORY AND MEDICINE

Cynthia Northcutt Malone has observed that, while "eighteenth-century novels are peppered with women 'big with child': Moll Flanders, Molly Seagrim, Mrs. Pickle . . . nineteenth-century novels typically veil their pregnant characters" (368–69). Despite a strong tradition of "symptomatic reading"—reading that takes "meaning to be hidden, repressed, deep, and in need of detection and disclosure by an interpreter"—what Malone calls the veiling of pregnant characters in nineteenth-century fiction seems, for the most part, to have protected it from our critical gaze (Best and Marcus 1). Both in literature and criticism, pregnancy—as Marianne Hirsch says of maternity—remains largely an "unspeakable plot," and only a handful of Victorian literary scholars have addressed the treatment of pregnancy at any length (1). However, as Malone's work demonstrates, the narrative practice of veiling pregnancy was not an inheritance of the nineteenth-century novel, but an innovation.

Jane Austen's novels, for example—at once comedies of manners in a style reminiscent of the eighteenth century and also early domestic marriage-plot novels in a mode on which much Victorian literature riffs—stand as both chronological and generic midpoints between the easy treatment of embodied pregnancy in eighteenth-century fiction and the tight-lipped approach of Victorian novels to the matter.[15] Indeed, a very brief consideration of pregnancy in Jane Austen helps us to trace some of the mechanics of this shift.

Malone asserts that "Austen's *Sense and Sensibility* and *Persuasion* serve as a kind of fulcrum" between the easy representation of pregnancy in *Tom Jones* and the Victorian prudery of *Martin Chuzzlewit* and argues that "in *Sense and Sensibility* . . . no conduct is more certain to mark a character as rather vulgar than candid discussion of pregnancy" (370). In order to delineate the literary historical significance of Austen's treatment of pregnancy, it is important to observe that what Malone calls the tendency of "nineteenth-century novels . . . to veil their characters" has noteworthy exceptions in, for example, Ruth in Elizabeth Gaskell's *Ruth* (1853) and Hetty in George Eliot's *Adam Bede* (1859). These exceptions to the tendency of Victorian novels to conceal pregnancy are prompted by the pregnant characters' failure to uphold normative feminine standards of modesty and morality. As the power of middle-class mores in popular culture increased over the course of the nineteenth century, so, too, did genteel demands on feminine behavior. Immodest folly like that of Marianne in *Sense and Sensibility,* though it throws her into the dangerous company of the immoral Willoughby, does not damage her narrative poten-

---

15. I have written at more length about pregnancy in Austen in "Generations."

tial. Similar behavior from Maggie Tulliver half a century later, however, does. Although Austen employs pregnant bodies as sites at which we can measure a character's conformity to the conventions of genteel society—conventions that undergird linked Victorian ideologies of immodesty and immorality—the representation of pregnancy in Austen is a helpful contrast to the representations of pregnancy that the chapters of this book will read closely because it demonstrates the historical and cultural specificity of Victorian novelistic representations of pregnancy; in Austen, pregnancy is a matter of manners, not morals.

The morality that is so often the matter of Victorian novelistic representations of pregnancy is one that maps onto period notions of science and medicine. Katherine Byrne's work on tuberculosis in the Victorian novel offers a useful model for thinking about the ways that pregnancy is both a moral and medical marker. "Consumption's capacity," Byrne argues, "to act as a manifold metaphor made it a malleable vehicle for social expression and discussion in the art of a literature of the nineteenth century . . . [sometimes associated with] increased sexual appetites" (3). As Byrne notes, the "remarkable fluidity of meaning" associated with tuberculosis during the Victorian period sometimes encompasses pregnancy (2). But illness and pregnancy insistently converge in the novels this book reads in ways that extend far beyond consumption. In Victorian text, illness is often how pregnant embodiment speaks itself, the somatic language through which it becomes legible. That the authority to interpret this language rests, increasingly over the course of the nineteenth century, with the trained, credentialed, and gentrifying doctor steers critique on pregnancy in the Victorian novel.[16]

In what ways do we read "real" somatic experience into fictional representations? At the crossroads between our own specific embodied experience and the literary representation of bodies, analyses of pregnancy in the Victorian novel can tell us as much about the patterns of our own minds and cultures as they do about those of a text, author, character, or historical moment. Jill L. Matus has asked: "What are the consequences of knowing that 'within the body . . . there is an other'?" (3). What are the consequences of knowing that within the body there is an other when we read fictional representations of bodies in which there is nothing but text on a page? Can a character be pregnant before a novel narrates that pregnancy? If so, such a pregnancy is one of our own imagination. Though, of course, literary pregnancy is only ever imag-

---

16. For more on the doctor in Victorian literature and culture, see, for example, Sparks; Peterson, *Medical*. Jason Tougaw's *Strange Cases: The Medical Case History and the British Novel* is also significant to this project, particularly my second chapter, though Tougaw works, primarily, in the eighteenth- and early nineteenth-century context.

inary, and the extent to which pregnancy is a function of the mind as much as the body was of concern to the Victorians, increasingly so as the nineteenth century drew to a close. As the study of psychology gained momentum, novelistic representations of pregnancy shifted away from concerns about feminine morality toward broad concerns about the ways our minds, bodies, and futures shape and are shaped by one another.

Medical concern about the circulation of "irrational" reproductive epistemologies, however, has spanned modern obstetric history.[17] William Smellie's *Treatise on the Theory and Practice of Midwifery* (published from 1752 to 1764) ascribes poor outcomes in pregnancy and childbirth to irrational mothers disobedient to medical advice. Thomas Bull's 1837 *Hints to Mothers for the Management of Health during the Period of Pregnancy and in the Lying-in-Room* also emphasizes the importance of obedience to rational, male medical authority.[18] Published in the inaugural year of the Victorian period, *Hints to Mothers* is a notable example of the kind of medical advice for laypeople that became popular during the nineteenth century.[19] Unlike Smellie's *Treatise*, which was intended for a professional readership, *Hints to Mothers* spoke directly to a female audience and spoke, in part, about the dangers to which their unregulated minds might fall prey. Bull frames women's unwillingness to sufficiently communicate with and be calmed by their "medical advisers" in opposition to a tendency toward receiving advice from "ignorant persons" and, thereby, succumbing to "ignorant" worries:

> In the minds of married women, and especially in young females, those feelings of delicacy naturally and commendably exist which prevent a full disclosure of their circumstances, when they find it necessary to consult their medical advisers. To meet this difficulty, and also to counteract the ill-advised suggestions of ignorant persons during the period of confinement, is the chief object of the following pages.
>
> ... There are many little circumstances, too, in which it does not occur to seek for advice, of the nature and result of which she ought not to be ignorant. Young married women are especially liable to many needless, yet

---

17. My piece "Hints to Mothers, 1837/2018" draws on this material.

18. Historian Anne Huebel's recent "Managing Victorian Reproduction: Medical Authority over Childbirth in British Advice Literature" offers a helpful primer on nineteenth-century pregnancy and childbirth advice manuals and their role in ongoing negotiations of doctors' and women's power over reproductive bodies, though the site was unfortunately no longer available at the time of this book's publication.

19. See also, for example, Mears; Fox; Chavasse.

harassing fears, which it has been the anxious object of the author to remove, by showing that they have no foundation in truth. (3–4)

For Bull, the problem of feminine misinformation is one of an otherwise praiseworthy "delicacy" that disinclines "young females" to speak of their reproductive "circumstances" directly with their doctors. Combined with "the ill-advised suggestions of ignorant persons" who shall remain nameless, but whom we can assume to be female acquaintances, the result is "needless" anxiety that could be easily assuaged by "truth" that only the doctor can access and offer, though Dara Rossman Regaignon's 2021 *Writing Maternity: Medicine, Anxiety, Rhetoric and Genre* argues for the way advice literature participated in the creation of cultures of maternal anxiety they sought to dispel.

It's helpful to consider the tendency of nineteenth-century novels to narrate embodied articulations of pregnancy in conversation with feminine lack of self-control alongside a developing medical discourse that urges women to cede their control over reproduction to doctors. Indeed, Clare Hanson's 2004 *A Cultural History of Pregnancy* foregrounds the relationships between literary, medical, and popular texts. In *Pregnancy in the Victorian Novel*, however, I focus the majority of my analysis on novelistic representation because this book is most invested in sketching out the space for and stakes of somatic reading as an embodied way of (not) knowing that we fill in when the body is hinted at or elided in narrative.

ITINERARY

This book is organized in chapters that move through the thematic content of Victorian representations of pregnancy (judgment, poverty, diagnosis, and impression) in a roughly chronological march through the period. These chapters sketch a tightening of conventions in the narration of pregnancy in Victorian novels toward a control typified by the doctor and then the anxious breakdown of that control at the period's close. I pause midway for an interlude on pregnancy in novels of Sensation and pregnancy in twenty-first-century cultures of race and celebrity, and I close with a short reflection on the personal, political, and ethical afterlives of moralizing Victorian narrative representations of pregnant bodies.[20]

---

20. "Sensation," capitalized, is used here to refer to the literary genre and is distinct from lowercase "sensation," which refers to physical feeling.

The novels I read closely—Emily Brontë's 1847 *Wuthering Heights*, Anthony Trollope's 1864–65 *Can You Forgive Her?*, Charlotte Mary Yonge's 1865 *The Clever Woman of the Family*, Elizabeth Gaskell's 1853 *Ruth*, George Eliot's 1859 *Adam Bede*, Ellen Wood's 1861 *East Lynne*, George Eliot's 1871–72 *Middlemarch*, Sarah Grand's 1893 *The Heavenly Twins*, Thomas Hardy's 1894 *Jude the Obscure*, Lucas Malet's 1901 *The History of Sir Richard Calmady*, and Victoria Cross's 1901 *Anna Lombard*—demonstrate Victorian literary tendencies to make legible only the pregnant bodies of immodest characters who transgress gendered ideologies while the pregnant bodies of modest characters go undescribed. In addition to articulating the conventions for the novelistic depiction of pregnant bodies, I also push toward moments in which I can imagine myself alongside these revealed bodies, experimenting with the relevance and limits of my own somatic experience to understanding Victorian literary pregnancy. Tracing the medicalization of pregnancy and childbirth over the course of the long nineteenth century, my chapters demonstrate the functions of moralizing narrative conventions in the representation of pregnancy in mid-Victorian novels and of a self-conscious use of free indirect diagnosis in high-Victorian fiction before establishing a shift at the fin de siècle from pregnancy as a signifier of morality to a symbol of instability.

"Judgment," the first chapter of this book, reads the basic moralistic tendencies of the treatment of pregnancy in the mid-Victorian novel in order to demonstrate how modes of judgment are suggested to readers. I analyze how the revelation of Cathy's pregnancy in *Wuthering Heights* implies its preceding concealment in ways that can align readerly judgment of her reproductive body with moralizing narrative judgment of her sexualized relationship with Heathcliff. I then use *Can You Forgive Her?* to think through the relationship between the readerly judgment of pregnant bodies and the readerly pleasures of collaboration with narrative perspective. In a final reading of *Clever Woman of the Family*, however, I look at the ways that pregnancy can additionally serve to demonstrate not only the wages of sin for feminine characters but also the ways that readerly judgment can be brought to submit to narrative authority. I push toward some of the textual moments that suggest imaginative somatic possibilities for the pregnant characters in these novels that might exceed these judgmental ecosystems. Indeed, these judgmental ecosystems are what motivate my desire for a different readerly attitude in relationship to people's reproductive bodies.

A book on representations of reproductive bodies in Victorian fiction must engage *Ruth* and *Adam Bede*. These novels arguably contain the period's most notable depictions of pregnancy, and in so doing, both explore sympathy as a primary theme. Playing on familiar tropes for critical approaches to the literary treatment of social class, gender, and sexuality, I demonstrate the ways that Hetty Sorrel's pregnancy in *Adam Bede* is notable for Hetty's diagnostic exclusion from the sympathetic networks of the novel and the ways that exclusion emphasizes her hypervisibility, her body exposed to view under floodlights. The readerly corrective to such exclusion and objectification of a central reproductive body not only in the novel but in the period might seem to be more sympathy. Perhaps it might even seem as though somatic reading asks us to give just this: more sympathy. But this is not what somatic reading requires. Ruth's pregnancy is notable for the ways it transforms openly embodied descriptions of pregnancy into sympathetically veiled and idealized womanhood. This affinitive sympathy uses class and illness to foster a generous affective response in the reader. But somatic reading does *not* require generous affective responses to characters. It is possible to reserve space for the radical uncertainty that allows for the suspension of diagnostic judgment without affinity, and reserving such space is important to the work of untethering understandings of bodies from our frameworks for morality. In "Sympathy," I chart a path through diagnostic and affinitive readerly modes to argue that somatic readings of Ruth and Hetty open out onto possibilities beyond the limits of sympathy.

"Sensation" is an interlude that centers a reading of *East Lynne* to explore the personal and presentist texture of somatic reading in the context of the novels of Sensation so strongly associated with the body. Looking informally toward sensationalized reproductive bodies of color in twenty-first-century American culture, I sketch a broad, gestural connection between the narrative structures that give us troubled access to Lady Isabel's body and maternity in Wood's novel and the relationship between maternal loss and guilt. This interlude prioritizes loose meditations on the possibility that somatic reading can offer ways of drawing pointedly "weak" connections between Victorian moralizing narratives of embodied maternity and contemporary narratives about maternal loss and guilt that focus disproportionate blame on the people most likely to suffer such loss.

"Diagnosis" extends this book's interest in the nexus of illness and pregnancy in the Victorian novel. Analyzing the effects of narrative conventions for the representation of pregnancy on modes of reading by focusing in on the "narrative zone of the doctor-husband," this chapter engages the medical humanist stakes of this project most explicitly (Malone 368). I identify the workings of what I call "free indirect diagnosis" in George Eliot's *Middlemarch*. Articulating free indirect diagnosis as a narrative mode helps to signal the ways that diagnosis is positioned as a primary way of knowing pregnancy. My analysis of this mode prompts reflection on the ways that resistance to primarily diagnostic ways of knowing pregnancy in the Victorian novel requires more than simply shifting to literary diagnoses that see pregnancy as metaphor and symbol; it also requires making room for reading the narrative representation of bodies as bodies rather than symptoms. In reading Rosamond Lydgate's pregnancy loss, I push toward such somatic engagement.

My final chapter, "Impression," turns to the ways in which more explicit representations of pregnancy at the turn of the century shift toward a decadent emphasis on the significance of unstable minds to pregnancy and futurity. Drawing on disability studies' emphasis on engaging bodies as bodies rather than metaphors, this chapter reads representations of pregnancy that signify as pointed metaphors centering paternal influence for the hints of specific somatic experience that exceed the structures that frame narrative significance. I refer to the tendency of fin de siècle literature to figure paternity and futurity through women's reproductive bodies as "paternal impression." Paternal impression, a play on the more familiar "maternal impression," centers fears that masculine minds might be unstable in ways that imprint a dangerous futurity on the canvas of women's reproductive bodies. Readings of *Heavenly Twins, Jude the Obscure, The History of Sir Richard Calmady,* and *Anna Lombard* trace the play of paternal impression figured variously as disease, existential dissatisfaction, disability, and racial Otherness.

The conclusion reflects on the need for modes of reading that center uncertainty in the analysis of cultures of pregnancy. A felt sense of such uncertainty is often accessible in our experiences of the personal and present. Somatic reading foregrounds the personal and present in literary criticism to signal a felt relevance of Victorian novels to twenty-first-century ideologies and bodies.

CHAPTER 1

Judgment

This chapter moves through three mid-century novels in which reading pregnancy closely means participating with a moralizing gaze. This moralizing gaze isn't simply the narrative voice; it is refracted through narrators, characters, and elements of form and genre. We are primed to fall into step alongside this gaze when reading Cathy's pregnancy in Emily Brontë's *Wuthering Heights* (1848), Lady Glencora Palliser's infertility and pregnancy in Anthony Trollope's *Can You Forgive Her?* (1864), and Bessie Keith's pregnancy in Charlotte Mary Yonge's *The Clever Woman of the Family* (1865). Brontë's work shocked early Victorian readers with its amorality. The narrator of Trollope's Palliser series breaks the fourth wall periodically for lessons on women's true natures. Yonge's career was built on the goal of quietly inculcating Oxford movement mores in her receptive lady readers. Though these novelists represent a range of positions in the well-mapped "teaching morality" landscape, they each demonstrate the overarching and unsurprising tendency of Victorian fiction to catch the reader up in judgment of legible pregnancy.

The more readers focus on reproductive bodies in Victorian fiction, the easier it is to participate in moral judgment of those bodies. Though there is hardly consensus about the degree to which Victorian novels writ large and individually participate in moralizing discourse through support or resistance or an uneven admixture of the two, there is broad agreement that a connection between morality and the novel as a form informs the literary period.

This chapter maps representations of the reproductive body onto that familiar geography. However, this chapter also argues that reading these pregnant bodies differently is sometimes possible. By reading as much *in* our own critical bodies as we read *about* bodies critically, we can—as Pardis Dabashi would have it—loosen our critical garments, show our own scholarly seams, "unfasten the buttons, . . . and lean into our own uncertainty" (951).

CONCEALMENT AND REVELATION

In *Wuthering Heights,* one "human cuckoo" disrupts the nests of two families, the Earnshaws and Lintons (Sanger 287). Mr. Earnshaw comes home one night in the late eighteenth century with the orphan Heathcliff in tow. Although Heathcliff becomes instant enemies with Earnshaw's son, he forms a deep bond with Earnshaw's daughter, Cathy.[1] These elemental hates and loves eventually drive Cathy toward marriage with Edgar Linton, scion of the local gentry; Cathy's marriage, in turn, drives Heathcliff into conflict with, and a vengeful marriage into, the Linton family. These circumstances culminate in two pregnancies: Cathy Linton (née Earnshaw) dies giving birth to Catherine Linton, and Isabella Heathcliff (née Linton) gives birth to Linton Heathcliff after running away from her abusive husband. Hareton Earnshaw, the other child of the novel's second generation, is born to Hindley and Frances Earnshaw shortly before his mother's death. In the narration of both Frances and Cathy in periods during which the reader may later understand them to have been pregnant, their bodies are represented using vocabularies of illness. The play of concealment and revelation employed in the representation of pregnancy and pregnant bodies in *Wuthering Heights* suggests that a reader's options for understanding are all-or-nothing, either an absence of knowledge about how the experiences of reproductive bodies inform text and plot or clinical certainties wrapped up in moral judgment. I am invested in the possibility that we might wrest more room for uncertainty from this dynamic.

Reading Frances closely during what are likely the early months of her pregnancy demonstrates that the more closely we are able to read that body, the more complicit we become in the punishing retraction of textual cover as a response to the merest hint of feminine impropriety. That Frances's pregnant body is essentially concealed from the reader is not only testament to her relatively minor role in the plot but also a tribute to her gender confor-

---

1. I refer to Catherine Linton, née Earnshaw, as Cathy and her daughter, Catherine Heathcliff, née Linton, as Catherine.

mity. Frances's pregnancy in *Wuthering Heights* demonstrates the tendency of Victorian novels to treat modest characters modestly, protecting their sexual bodies from our readerly gaze. After the birth of Frances's son Hareton, however, it is possible to read pregnancy back into the language of illness and struggle that marks what the reader can now suspect to have been the first trimester of her pregnancy, a trimester often marked by exhaustion, nausea, and emotional intensity.

A little chronological guesswork suggests that Frances may well be pregnant in the sections of the novel I examine. Charles Percy Sanger's meticulous timeline of the events of *Wuthering Heights* demonstrates that Mr. Earnshaw dies and Hindley Earnshaw arrives with Frances in unspecified months of 1777. Nelly's narration does not make clear how much time elapses between their arrival and Cathy and Heathcliff's fateful trip to Thrushcross Grange, which Sanger places in the third week of November 1777; however, the elapsed time is passed over in about a page and a half of text, and it seems unlikely that Hindley and Frances arrive much more than a few months before their sister(-in-law)'s accident at the Grange. Sanger places Hareton Earnshaw's birth in early June of 1778. Unlike Catherine Linton's birth, no mention is made of Hareton arriving early. Therefore, it is most probable that Frances Earnshaw conceived in mid- to late September of 1777. If, as seems likely, no more than a few months elapse between her arrival at Wuthering Heights and Cathy's injury at Thrushcross Grange, then, whether or not this pregnancy predates her marriage, Frances is already pregnant when she first appears in the novel and when Nelly thinks her "half-silly, from her behavior" after the death of Mr. Earnshaw (45).

Nelly, unable or unwilling to see or narrate Frances's pregnancy, does narrate the signs of physical illness and emotional struggle that Frances experiences during Mr. Earnshaw's funeral:

[Frances] ran into her chamber, and made me come with her . . . : and there she sat shivering and clasping her hands, and asking repeatedly—
   "Are they gone yet?"
   Then she began describing with hysterical emotion the effect it produced on her to see black; and started and trembled, and, at last, fell a weeping—and when I asked what was the matter? answered, she didn't know; but she felt so afraid of dying.
   I imagined her as little likely to die as myself. She was rather thin, but young, and fresh complexioned, and her eyes sparkled as bright as diamonds. I did remark, to be sure, that mounting the stairs made her breathe quick, that the least sudden noise set her all in a quiver, and that she coughed

troublesomely sometimes: but, I knew nothing of what these symptoms portended, and had no impulse to sympathize with her. (45)

Certainly, "what these symptoms portend" most directly is Frances's consumptive illness.[2] Her manic behavior, sparkling eyes, difficulty breathing, and cough all speak to signs of tuberculosis that would have been readily recognized by Victorian readers. Indeed, interpreted only as evidence of Frances's consumption, the scene above demonstrates the ways in which a reader's somatic knowledge can shape textual significance. Nelly's narration of her own lack of awareness—she "knew nothing of what these symptoms portended"—hints that these symptoms indicate something significant but leaves that significance with the uncertain associations the reader may or may not bring to the scene.

A twenty-first-century reader is as likely to bring associations between young married women's physical struggles and pregnancy as between these symptoms and tuberculosis. Much as Nelly would have learned about Frances's consumption in the months that followed her original failure to read the significance of Frances's symptoms, so would she have learned about Frances's pregnancy. Pregnancy and consumption converge here. Much as Frances demonstrates familiar symptoms of tuberculosis, so, too, does she demonstrate familiar symptoms of pregnancy. Of course, people who are far along in pregnancy often report shortness of breath associated with the compression of one's internal organs to accommodate a growing fetus and the added weight one is moving through the world. But shortness of breath like Frances experiences "mounting the stairs" is also a common symptom of early pregnancy, one we now understand to be the result of increased progesterone production. Frances's "hysterical" state is suggestive of both our contemporary stereotype

---

2. As Byrne has argued in *Tuberculosis and the Victorian Literary Imagination*, tuberculosis (or consumption) was often depicted in medical and literary texts alike as an illness gendered feminine and classed genteel, considered to be brought on by sensual indulgence. However, the middle-class consumptive female body was also idealized and aestheticized, treated as both hypersexually attractive and yet purged of all sexual taint. Victorian literary representations of consumption, then, are particularly resonant with representations of pregnancy—a condition that remained largely unhidden among the aristocracy (see Lewis), whose willingness to appear at, for instance, balls in the third trimester of pregnancy offended middle-class sensibilities, and that was ideologically mandatory for a married angel of the house, clearly sexual and yet somehow desexualized by a woman's legitimate domestic role (social class and pregnancy will be more fully explored in chapter 2). Furthermore, the cleaving linguistic suggestions of consumption (the person suffering from the illness is both consumed and consuming) map onto the facts of pregnancy: A pregnant woman must consume more than her usual share of space and resources, and yet her body is likewise being consumed by the needs of another.

of the irrationally emotional pregnant woman and also Victorian stereotypes of behavior associated with the "puerperal madness" that could accompany pregnancy, childbirth, or the postpartum period.[3] That this behavior seems to cohere around anxiety over the threat and proximity of death speaks to Victorian concerns about death in childbirth. In imagining that Frances is "as unlikely to die" as herself, Nelly is failing to see or failing to acknowledge having seen Frances's deadly consumption, certainly, but also Frances's pregnancy. Even if she were not consumptive, Frances would be more likely to die than Nelly because she is pregnant. The reader's knowledge of this increased likelihood is one of the effects, certainly, of the narrative convergence of pregnancy and illness in general and pregnancy and consumption in particular: In reading pregnancy signified as illness, we understand the dangers of pregnancy narratively as well as historically, experientially, or viscerally.

Both contemporary and Victorian maternal mortality statistics vary significantly across geographical, class, and racial divides; the conditions faced by pregnant and birthing Victorian women being treated in their homes and those being treated in newly established hospitals, for example, were perhaps as different as the conditions faced by women today in different geological, social, racial, and economic positions. It is, however, generally true in the Western world that rates of maternal mortality in pregnancy and childbirth dropped significantly in the twentieth century.[4] Throughout the nineteenth century, despite increasing medical involvement and intervention in pregnancy and childbirth, pregnancy brought women into very real proximity to the possibility of death. Indeed, rates of maternal mortality in nineteenth-century hospitals were often as high as 1 per 100 births.[5] Whether the cause is tuberculosis, pregnancy, or a potent combination of the two, Frances is certainly more likely to die than Nelly. Her fears of death could as easily be a response to the dangers of pregnancy and childbirth as to the risks of tuberculosis.

As Frances's concerned repetition of the question "Are they gone yet?" in the previous passage signals, just being seen can be dangerous for any woman's reputation. Frances's reputation in the Gimmerton community—where she is a new arrival—is fetal: unformed and vulnerable to negative impressions. Indeed, reading the chronological likelihood that she is already pregnant when she arrives at Wuthering Heights sheds light on the speculation about

---

3. See Marland; Mangham.
4. In Britain, for example, from 1850–1970, "There was a period of irregular but general steady maternal death rates until about 1900. These then dipped slightly till the First World War and continued so till the late 1930s" (Chamberlain 560).
5. See Semmelweis.

her marriage to Hindley Earnshaw implicit in Nelly's narrative of the events surrounding Frances's arrival:

> Mr. Hindley came home to the funeral; and—a thing that amazed us, and set the neighbors gossiping right and left—he brought a wife with him.
> What she was, and where she was born he never informed us; probably, she had neither money nor name to recommend her, or he would scarcely have kept the union from his father. (45)

Certainly, one possibility is that Frances Earnshaw was unknown to Mr. Earnshaw while he lived because she was neither well-born nor wealthy—"had neither money nor name." However, another possibility is that Frances was unknown to Mr. Earnshaw during his life because Hindley and she were only married very shortly before his death. To have married quickly and in secret suggests the possibility of necessity, the possibility that Frances may have already been pregnant. The mention of neighborhood gossip surrounding her arrival gestures toward this possibility of impropriety. Nelly does not choose to elaborate upon the implications of the neighbors' gossip, but in reading Frances's pregnancy closely, we join their less restrained ranks.

The more closely we are able to read pregnant Victorian bodies, the more complicit we become—and the more aware of our complicity—in the retraction of textual cover that occurs in response to the merest hint of feminine immodesty or immorality. If we read Frances's body informed by a close consideration of the novel's chronology and the circumstances of her arrival at Wuthering Heights, we read the shadow of immodesty into her pregnancy. The more visible the pregnancy is to us, the more certainties we gather regarding Frances's body, the more immodest the pregnancy can seem. When we read pregnancy in the Victorian novel, it is easy to participate in the punishment of female sexuality. Though the structures of punishment are implicit in the novel's narration of Frances's pregnancy, Nelly frames Cathy's physical and mental suffering during pregnancy as punishment explicitly, as what "she deserved, for bringing [her illness] all on herself" (124).

A word on chronology, helped again by Sanger: Catherine Linton is born, premature, at "2am on Monday, 20th March, 1784," eleven months after Cathy and Edgar's marriage, about seven months after Heathcliff's return and about three months after Cathy locks herself up in her bedroom, inducing illness and insanity (292). Cathy herself dies two hours later. It is not until two months after the onset of her illness, likely early in her third trimester, that Cathy's pregnancy is explicitly revealed to the reader. However, it would very likely have been visible for months to at least Edgar, the doctor treating her during her illness, and Nelly, who serves as Lockwood's (and therefore the reader's) eyes and ears; the pregnancy would likely have been known to Cathy herself. Our somatic knowledge tells us that pregnant bodies most often become visible to even the casual observer during the second trimester. Taking into account historical differences in dress and decorum as well as Cathy's isolation during this section of the novel, it *is* possible that casual friends and family would not have been aware of her pregnancy. However, those with whom she is intimate at this time would have both been able to see and would likely have been informed by the doctor that she was expecting a child, but it is not until about a month before she gives birth and dies that Nelly informs us that "on [Cathy's] existence depended that of another" (133). This revelation of Cathy's pregnancy makes its concealment before this point apparent, highlighting Cathy's other secrets. Cathy's baby, "a seven month-child," is born seven months after the return of Heathcliff (137).[6] Though I am not arguing that Catherine Linton is Heathcliff's daughter, this timing is interesting in a novel as tightly organized as *Wuthering Heights*.

To punish Edgar and Heathcliff for clashing, Cathy—about four months pregnant—immures herself in her room for three days. She lives "on nothing but cold water and ill-temper," working herself into a consumptive illness and madness (123). Cathy's consumptive illness—like Frances's—is tangled up with pregnancy. Much as Nelly "knew nothing of what [Frances's] symptoms portended," so does she assert that she would "not have spoken so if [she] had known [Cathy's] true condition" (104). The implication in Cathy's case, as in Frances's, is that these "symptoms portend" the illness that is both women's "true condition." While Frances's pregnancy is likely only in its very early stages when Nelly fails to read her body, Cathy's condition is at least four months along, in the window of time when quickening becomes possible. Quickening, the maternal perception of fetal movement, usually occurs somewhere between the sixteenth and twentieth weeks of pregnancy, in the first half of the second trimester. Prior to the advent of medical methods for diagnosis, this was sometimes understood as the beginning of a pregnancy and almost always understood as the beginning of a more serious stage of pregnancy. Quickening played a key role, for example, in laws pertaining to abortion prior to 1837 (Hall). Whether Cathy's isolation marks a literal quickening is uncertain, but these three days certainly mark a figurative quickening, a delineation between *before* and *after* in which *after* moves her steadily closer to death in childbirth. Nelly's reference to Cathy's "true condition" also ges-

---

6. "Seven-month child" was also a common explanation for babies born too soon after a marriage. Though that is not the case here, we will see that premature birth carries the weight of potential immorality more generally in Victorian fiction.

tures toward a reading of this incident as a stage of pregnancy. "Condition" is a euphemistic mainstay for pregnancy, particularly in the nineteenth-century novel, much as the "confinement" of Cathy to her room employs the conventional vocabulary for late-term pregnancy, childbirth, and the postpartum period (114).

Cathy echoes Nelly's observation about the pregnant and ill Frances that "the least sudden noise set her all in a quiver" when she asks: "Why am I so changed? Why does my blood rush into a hell of tumult at a few words?" (124). This change, the hell of tumult that fuels Cathy's "strange exaggerated manner," is certainly suggestive of the emotional swings and conditions both Victorians and contemporary readers understand as risks of pregnancy. Andrew Mangham's *Violent Women and Sensation Fiction: Crime, Medicine, and Victorian Popular Culture* demonstrates the degree to which Victorian expectations about women's reproductive bodies included their particular potential for violence and madness. This is an expectation writ across Victorian medical and cultural forms that resonates with certain mental-health contexts in twenty-first-century America, where "perinatal depression affects 10%–20% of [pregnant] women" and perinatal anxiety is sometimes considered even more prevalent (Van Niel and Payne). Cathy wondering why her "blood rush[es] into a hell of tumult at a few words" calls to mind these Victorian and contemporary contexts both: She articulates a somatic source for her dis-ease (the movement of blood in her body) that suggests a racing heart; her framing of this sensation as "a hell" suggests the literal heat of a hot flash and the figurative heat of difficult emotion.

Throughout these scenes, Cathy is depicted in animalistic terms, "tossing" and "[tearing] with her teeth" (104). Such animalistic representations fit into long-standing associations between mental illness and the subhuman. That Cathy degenerates during her pregnancy also demonstrates the overlapping language used for swelling, pulsing, excreting female reproductive bodies and animality. This overlap between the pregnant woman's body and an animal's body would have been particularly disturbing to Victorian idealizations of ladies as ethereal; we see this tension at play in the oft-cited letter from Queen Victoria to her pregnant daughter warning her that "it is more like a rabbit or guinea-pig than anything else and really it is not very nice" (Fulford 195). Pregnancy, illness, and madness alike threatened to make beasts out of women.

During her illness, we see Cathy's whole body in troubled motion and are offered an image of that cutting away of layers of protection in "the frosty air that cut about her shoulders as keen as a knife" (108). This "knife" works something like our own sharp focus on Cathy's immodest body. Though we likely harbor more sympathy for Cathy than does Nelly, it is difficult for the reader to avoid at least considering whether Cathy has not brought her suffering upon herself with her "wicked waywardness" (109). Our ability, alongside Nelly, to see her half-undressed and disordered in her bedroom is a kind of narrative punishment that gives rise to Cathy's "glow of shame" at being observed in insanity (106).

Contemplating the contents of her ripped pillow, Cathy echoes Ophelia.[7] Encoded in an infantile sorting are anxieties about pregnancy and maternity:

> "That's a turkey's," she murmured to herself; "and this is a wild duck's; and this is a pigeon's. Ah, they put pigeons' feathers in the pillows—no wonder I couldn't die! Let me take care to throw it on the floor when I lie down. And here is a moor-cock's; and this—I should know it among a thousand—it's a lapwing's. Bonny bird; wheeling over our heads in the middle of the moor. It wanted to get to its nest, for the clouds had touched the swells, and it felt rain coming. This feather was picked up from the heath, the bird was not shot: we saw its nest in the winter, full of little skeletons. Heathcliff set a trap over it, and the old ones dared not come. I made him promise he'd never shoot a lapwing after that, and he didn't. Yes, here are more! Did he shoot my lapwings, Nelly? Are they red, any of them? Let me look." (105)

In this scene, Cathy both nests—in the sense that she gathers up her feathers and contemplates a literal nest—and fails to nest—in the sense of preparing for the birth of a child. That Nelly calls Cathy's feather collecting "baby work" deepens both the sense of this being a pregnant activity—work in preparation for a baby—and also a failure to prepare properly for a child (105). Indeed, it is a failure to care properly for babies that is at the heart of Cathy's feather scene; Cathy remembers the murder by forced neglect of the baby birds in the nest. Anxious about the possibility of further murder, Cathy checks the feathers of her pillow for the telltale "red" of blood. Cathy has just starved herself—and,

---

7. Clare Hanson and Katherine F. Fitzpatrick also each note this evocation of Ophelia. Ophelia's lines read:

> There's rosemary, that's for remembrance. Pray you, love, remember. And there is pansies, that's for thoughts. . . . There's fennel for you, and columbines. There's rue for you, and here's some for me. We may call it—herb of grace o' Sundays. O, you must wear your rue with a difference. There's a daisy. I would give you some violets, but they withered all when my father died. (sings) For bonny sweet Robin is all my joy. / And will he not come again? / And will he not come again? / No, no, he is dead, / Go to thy deathbed. / He never will come again. / His beard was as white as snow, / All flaxen was his poll. / He is gone, he is gone, / And we cast away moan, / God ha' mercy on his soul. And of all Christian souls, I pray God. God be wi' ye. (*Hamlet* act 4, sc. 5, lines 183–93)

by extension, the fetus she carries—for three days. She now recalls an instance of baby birds being starved to death and checks her bedding for blood; the blood of a shot bird is suggestive, here, of the blood of a miscarriage.

It is only when Cathy begins to recover from the physical illness (though not from the insanity) that her pregnancy is directly revealed to the reader. As Edgar "sit[s] beside her, tracing the gradual return of bodily health," tracing, in other words, changes in Cathy's body, the reader nears Nelly's announcement that "there was double cause to desire [Cathy's recovery], for on her existence depended that of another; we cherished the hope that in a little while Mr. Linton's heart would be gladdened . . . by the birth of an heir" (114, 115). The direct revelation of Cathy's pregnancy allows the reader, too, to trace Cathy's bodily condition, reading the pregnancy beneath her "loose, white dress" and "recovered flesh," and also to read pregnancy backward into the scenes of her madness (130–31). This familiar play of concealment and revelation engages the reader in a more intimate judgment of Cathy: We have had the full truth withheld from us.

In Cathy's final, frenzied meeting with Heathcliff before her death, Nelly observes "the violent, unequal throbbing of her heart, which beat visibly and audibly under this excess of agitation" (133). Again, Cathy's pregnant body overflows its own bounds. It is possible, though unlikely, that Nelly would see Cathy's heart beating under the layered covers of her clothing, her skin, and ribcage. It is, however, almost impossible that Nelly, an observer of rather than participant in the passionate scene between Cathy and Heathcliff, would be able to hear Cathy's heart beating. In *Wuthering Heights*, through Nelly's critical judgment, the reader is given a surreal, heightened access to Cathy's body. This models a kind of black-and-white approach to readerly knowledge of the body: Either its secrets are euphemized and concealed from us or they are fully accessible, as though our eyes on text were floodlights and sensitive stethoscopes in an examining room. Such rough somatic access can feel transgressive of Victorian novelistic mores, but it enforces rather than transgresses the Victorian novelistic tendency to engage the reader in moralizing judgment of pregnant bodies. Imagining the possibilities of Cathy's pregnant body (that she experiences heightened anxiety during pregnancy, she fears a miscarriage, etc.) opens space for more of the uncertainty that troubles judgment.

MORALS AND AMUSEMENT

One of the challenges of moving away from the kinds of harsh judgment so often trained on women and their bodies is that such judgment can be pleasurable. An instruction in morals that creates all the pathways for ogling the foibles and titillating transgressions of pretty faces and bodies (or looking with disdain on the not-so-pretty ones) can be amusing. When Trollope said that "it is the business of a novel to instruct in morals and to amuse," he both differentiated between moral instruction and the pleasure of amusement and also—in pairing the two—gestured toward a collaboration (*Thackeray*). And as in Victorian fiction more broadly, these two modes often collaborate in his novels. In *Can You Forgive Her?*, the pleasure of amused judgment marks the narration of Lady Glencora Palliser; I can't make it otherwise (perhaps I wouldn't even want to), but in tracing the unsurprising ways the novel trains this amused judgment on her infertility and pregnancy, I can also read the hazy places where her somatic plot seems to run in grooves I can imagine without any strong theory of Glencora. In reading for these plots, I am looking for points at which my object of study is as much my own experience and uncertainty as it is the representation of a young woman's reproductive capacity.

The pronouns in the title of *Can You Forgive Her?* pointedly enlist readerly judgment of women. The direct address to the second-person "You" establishes a relationship between the book and its reader in which the reader is appointed arbiter of feminine transgression. Trollope's narrators often step outside of the stories they tell to collude with readerly judgment; for example, I was just rereading *Barchester Towers* and was struck by the line "[Mr. Harding] did not hate the chaplain [Mr. Slope] as the archdeacon did, and as *we* do" (171; emphasis added). This "we" is the narrator and the reader sharing a negative judgment of a character. Though the pronouns of interest in the title of *Can You Forgive Her?* do not include this "we," the "You" nonetheless establishes the rhetorical situation of the entire novel as a conversation between narrator and reader focused on the exigency of reaching a verdict about "Her."[8] An implicit part of the exigency of this verdict lies in the question of whom the verdict is to judge; to whom does the "Her" of the title refer? Of course, the novel's protagonist is Alice Vavasor. Alice makes the mistake of ending an engagement to John Grey, a good man she loves, because she believes herself better suited to become the wife of her cousin, not at all a good man but a man with public, political ambitions that appeal to Alice. Certainly, the "Her" of the title can be read as Alice. Such a reading aligns the "You" of the reader not only with the narrator's judgment but also with her suitor's willingness to forgive her. Feminine behavior is positioned as needing to conform to readerly

---

8. I draw here on Regaignon's work on rhetorical situations in *Writing Maternity*. Regaignon, in turn, draws on Lloyd Bitzer's definition of rhetorical situation as "a complex of persons, events, objects, and relations presenting an actual or potential exigence" (qtd. in Regaignon 17).

expectations in the same way a man expects his fiancée to become his wife. Failure to conform to those expectations—established by social conventions, certainly, but also by the very form of marriage-plot novels—is synced with resistance to marriage. Alice owes the reader a wifely subservience.

Toward the novel's close, *Can You Forgive Her?* cashes its title in: "Oh! Reader," the narrator asks, "can you forgive her in that she had sinned against the softness of her feminine nature? I think that she may be forgiven, in that she had never brought herself to think lightly of her own fault" (311). It is, of course, Alice who has "sinned against the softness of her feminine nature" and Alice who "never brought herself to think lightly of her own fault." In judging herself, Alice, too, is aligned with narrator, reader, and husband. This allegiance suggests to the first-person "I" of the narrative voice that Alice "may be forgiven." Henry James agreed: "Can we forgive Miss Vavasor? Of course we can, and forget her too" (James 409 qtd. in Halperin 31).

Many readers of *Can You Forgive Her?*—from early reviewers like James to Deborah Morse in her recent "Mourning Glencora"—find themselves most drawn not to Alice but rather to the amusing, impulsive Glencora. The "Her" of the title can be read as Glencora. Can you forgive Glencora, bullied into marriage with the stiff and boring Plantagenet Palliser when she is in love with the handsome and fast Burgo Fitzgerald? Can you forgive her for admitting that she does not love her husband? For seriously considering running off with Burgo? Alice resists marriage to John Grey in part because she is concerned about her ability to subsume her own life into his. Glencora marries her husband in spite of an inability to subsume her own life into his. In the end, it is only to maternity that she proves capable of subservience; her pregnancy becomes the testing ground for the degree to which her husband, friends, and reader are able to forgive her, a forgiveness that requires such submission.

Glencora's pregnancy (and the infertility that precedes it) is raised with unusual frequency by Victorianist literary critics because of the plot "resolution" work it does in *Can You Forgive Her?*:

> In terms of narrative conventions, Glencora's pregnancy is a resolution, ending her rebellion and riveting her identity in the role of mother. As the narrator comments about both Alice's and Glencora's ambitions: "One was to become a wife and the other a mother, and that was to be their fate after each had made up her mind that no such lot was to be hers." (ch. 77 qtd. in Morse 21)

Though reading Glencora's pregnant body as the site of readerly judgment as I do does not run counter to such an understanding, it does shift our focus from what the pregnancy signifies to *how* the pregnancy signifies. I am most interested in the way Glencora's reproductive body is an arena of often pleasurable judgment from which we can try to step away, if only for moments. Such moments are most accessible to me in tracing small somatic possibilities that require little judgment.

The reader of *Can You Forgive Her?* often joins the narrator and sometimes Plantagenet Palliser in judgment of Glencora. This dynamic is established on the canvas of Glencora's infertile body. For much of the novel, the reproductive possibilities of Glencora's body and their failed realization form a twin organizing principle in her character alongside her thwarted (and sexual) love for Burgo. Much as the explicit narration of pregnancy as a bodily condition is unusual in Victorian fiction, it's unusual for infertility to be treated as directly and as so directly central to plot as is the case in *Can You Forgive Her?* Glencora is painfully aware that the purpose of Plantagenet Palliser's wife is to produce offspring. Indeed, as Judith Schneid Lewis notes in *In the Family Way: Childbearing in the British Aristocracy, 1760–1860*, the modesty norms that govern Victorian veiling of pregnancy were significantly more lax among the upper-crust families, for whom a pregnant belly signified a continuation of public power, and for whom sexual mores sometimes differed. Glencora has not been married long before she worries aloud to Alice that she is not fulfilling her public reproductive purpose: "It's a dreadful thing," she says, "not to have a child when so much depends on it!" That Glencora announces her infertility to Alice positions her perspective as characteristically lacking in reserve; we must not speak of matters touching on sexuality to young, unmarried ladies.

And though her husband would not "say an unkind word, not if his own position depended on it," Plantagenet is similarly troubled by the couple's childlessness (227). A subtle free indirect discourse marked by reserve and hesitation aligns the reader with a perspective on Glencora's body that seems to be shared by the narrator and her husband:

> One cause of unhappiness, or rather one doubt as to his entire good fortune, was beginning to make itself felt, as his wife had to her sorrow already discovered. He had hoped that before this he might have heard that she would give him a child. But the days were young yet for that trouble, and the care had not become a sorrow. (249)

Though this passage does name the issue (the hope for a child) directly, it does so under layers of the caution and prevarication so common to Plantagenet across the Palliser series. "One cause of unhappiness" is immediately revised to the less certain "or rather one doubt," and that one doubt itself is not a complete doubt but rather a partial doubt about the degree to which his "good fortune" is "entire." Even this is only "beginning to make itself felt," a feeling made new and, on that ground, less significant, though the "he had hoped" that follows suggests an earlier onset of this unhappiness. Even that hope is only that he "might" have been informed that Glencora thought herself to be pregnant. Though Plantagenet is not as endearing to generations of Trollope's readers as Glencora, his life is the spine that runs through the Palliser series, and his typical plodding thought process here moves in coordination with the novel's narrative perspective.

Plantagenet's perspective seems more measured and rational than Glencora's. But of course Glencora's perspective is immoderate and impassioned. Most people who have struggled to conceive—which is perhaps an unusually common experience among the demographic of people who get PhDs and establish careers in competitive job markets before doing so, the same demographic of people in twenty-first-century America most likely to read a lot of Trollope or this book—will feel a little panic at each of the novel's little reminders that Glencora is "possessed [of no] cradle upstairs" (261). I imagine that Glencora, aware of her duty as she is, is also aware of what it means when she starts bleeding each month, aware of what it means to wait and hope she won't start bleeding the next month. The significance of these intimate bodily matters is public, not just something Glencora's husband quickly starts to notice but something that a network of friends and relations discuss. One of the private matters Glencora's infertility seems to make public is her unhappiness with her marriage: As Lauren Cameron notes, "a plotline in which two likeable characters happily marry during prime reproductive years but do not have any children is unusual, especially for Anthony Trollope" (893). For Cameron, this observation stems from an interest in Phineas Finn and Madame Max, a Trollopian couple who remain infertile *despite* a happy marriage. Her reading of their infertility as a reflection of racialized ideas about evolutionary fitness suggests that the shadow of degeneration may also haunt Glencora's infertile body. Infertility triggers fears of "unfitness" that attach with more particular blame to women's bodies.

Glencora's striking embodiedness contributes to this shadowy threat of embodied degeneration. In Sophie Gilmartin's overview of criticism on "Trollope and the Body," she offers a helpful framing of Pamela Gilbert's reading of Glencora's "corrupt[able]" woman's body and Gilbert's engagement of Norbert Elias on Glencora's particularly marked and animalistic embodiment:

> Gilbert writes that in this period "Women's bodies . . . were the weak link in the social body; close to nature and the animal, women were thought to be

more susceptible to sensory impression, leading them to be more easily corrupted." She cites Norbert Elias as arguing that "the modern body emerges as a body concerned with closure and regulation of its openings." Glencora's mouth, nostrils and pores are opened by the exercise of dancing and her body is open to Burgo's touch. While there is sympathy for the lovers, the risk is clear: Burgo will drive her to destruction and "break her heart" as he did when he killed his horse. ("Nation" 129 qtd. in Gilmartin 128–29)

Glencora's body receives a notable amount of attention in Gilmartin's overview because, among Trollope's "meticulous . . . rendering[s] of the body," Glencora's is particularly so (121). And though Glencora's body—never having been concealed from the reader—is not revealed to heighten an impulse toward judgment, "there are . . . 'distancing codes': 'the distance between the heroine's body and the words used to describe it are . . . an aggravated and deeply political instance of culture intervening between a subject and its representation'" (Michie, *Flesh* 84 qtd. in Gilmartin 125). Representations of Glencora's body are unlikely to give the reader access to an intimate understanding of her subjectivity as shaped by experiences of bodily interiorities; modes of reading that fill that distance with judgment participate in both those "distancing codes" and also a prurient clawing toward somatic access without personal critical somatic engagement.

The novel puts such prurient pleasure on easy offer. While they are in Europe to escape the danger posed to Glencora by proximity to Burgo, Mr. Palliser becomes unreasonably offended with Alice for not more effectively checking his wife's impulses. As a result of his treatment, Alice wishes to return to England, but Glencora—without specifying why—asks Alice to stay because Glencora "wants [her] more than [she] ever wanted [her] before" (295). This reserve from a character marked by inappropriate directness calls some attention to itself and begins to suggest to a careful reader of her reproductive plot that she is or suspects herself to be early in a pregnancy.

A similar reserve marks the report Glencora gives to her husband as his own typical reticence is replaced by expansiveness at the news:

[Mr. Palliser] was sighing for Westminster . . . till on a sudden, there came to him tidings which upset all his plans, which rerouted the ponies, which made everything impossible, which made the Alps impassable and the railways dangerous, which drove Burgo Fitzgerald out of Mr. Palliser's head, and so confused him that he could no longer calculate the blunders of the present Chancellor of the Exchequer. All the Palliser world was about to be moved from its lowest depths, to the summits of its highest mountain. Lady

> Glencora had whispered into her husband's ear that she thought it probably—; she wasn't sure:—she didn't know. And then she burst into tears on his bosom as he sat by her on her bedside. (339)

This passage works like the sounding of horns ahead of a royal arrival, amplifying the announcement of Glencora's pregnancy that offers the reader the amusement of understanding what Glencora means better than she can say it. The news is hyperbolically communicated on an international scale ("the Alps [are] impassable and the railways dangerous") but in the language of "impossib[ility]," "impassab[ility]," and "[in]calcula[bility]." What seems most impossible here, however, is Glencora's direct articulation of her pregnancy, which her hesitations and gaps locate in a space that is unspeakable, as so many bodily experiences can be. The impossibilities of Plantagenet's reception of the news are absolute, the gestures toward speaking of her pregnancy from Glencora are partial and uncertain; she is "probably" something, but she "wasn't sure . . . didn't know." This uncertainty speaks evocatively to the uncertainties of early pregnancy: Late periods can signal conditions that limit fertility as well as pregnancy, tender nipples or little aches in the abdomen are often imprecise enough to seem imagined. I remember the strange suspicion that I might be imagining my own morning sickness in early pregnancy, despite my twenty-first-century access to pregnancy testing in those tentative early weeks. Though Glencora is herself uncertain about her pregnancy, her uncertain expressions offer the reader a clear judgment about her condition.

The passage above initiates the novel's default narration of Glencora's pregnancy as filtered through her husband's experience and judgment. That judgment rushes into ridiculous certainties, both moral and somatic:

> For the last eight or nine months, since his first hopes had begun to fade,—he had been a man degraded in his own sight amidst all his honors. What good was all the world to him if he had nothing of his own to come after him? We must give him his due, too, when we speak of this. He had not had wit enough to hide his grief from his wife; his knowledge of women and of men in social life had not been sufficient to teach him how this should be done; but he had wished to do it. He had never willingly rebuked her for his disappointment, either by a glance of his eye, or a tone of his voice; and now he had already forgiven everything. Burgo Fitzgerald was a myth. Mrs. Marsham should never again come near her. Mr. Bott was, of course, a thing abolished; —he had not even had the sense to keep his seat in Parliament. Dandy and Flirt should feed on gilded corn, and there should be an artificial moon always ready in the ruins. If only those d—able saddle ponies of

Lucerne had not come across his wife's path! He went at once into the yard and ordered that the ponies should be abolished; —sent away, one and all, to the furthest confines of the canton; and then he himself inspected the cushions of the carriage. Were they dry? As it was August in those days, and August at Lucerne is a warm month, it may be presumed that they were dry. (340)

In his relief that his fears of a notable "eight or nine months" of infertility are behind him, this narration of Plantagenet's consciousness gestures toward the novel's title ("he had already forgiven everything"). Rather than aligning the reader with his perspective, however, the play of pronouns ("we must give him his due when we speak of this") aligns the reader's perspective with a narrator both understanding of and amused by Plantagenet's sudden willingness to bow to Glencora's every whim ("abolish[ing]" her enemies Mr. Bott and Mrs. Marsham as well as innocent ponies, for example) and to protect her vulnerable body from imagined threats ("inspect[ing] the cushions of the carriage"). With "were they dry," the narration slips into a marked moment of free indirect discourse that sets the reader up to appreciate the dry, passive reply, "it may be presumed that they were dry." It may be so presumed by the reader, who accesses—from the distance of amusement—Glencora's bodily specificities through Plantagenet's highly specific concerns about that with which her body will come into contact. That amused distance works alongside the distance of a moral judgment that deems Glencora forgivable on the basis of her pregnancy. For Glencora too, despite a difficult labor, this baby "ma[kes] it all right" (415). Her own judgment on this matter finally aligns with her husband's, the narrator's, and the reader's.

PUNISHMENT

In *The Clever Woman of the Family,* Rachel Curtis is a compelling twenty-first-century heroine: rough around the edges and passionately invested in forgoing married life in order to improve living conditions for the working poor. But Rachel's "clever" attempts to enforce her will on her young male cousins as a tutor, her founding of S.P.E.W. (Society for the Professional Education of Women), and a subversion of masculine medical authority with her practice of allopathy are treated as parodic at best and deeply dangerous at worst. By placing herself in public view without masculine protection, Rachel sacrifices her femininized privacy and is obliged to testify in court, to acknowledge the miserable failures of her overreaching, and to submit meekly to a marriage with the cool, controlling Alick Keith, who directs her energies with a military efficiency that patrols not only his wife's behavior but also the implied readerly instinct to think too lightly of feminine misdemeanor. The lesson that submission rather than indulgence was what Rachel required is placed in relief against the tragic plot of her sister-in-law Bessie Keith's pregnancy. Where *Can You Forgive Her?* drew on a cohort of judges to pass verdicts on its ladies, the lesson *Clever Woman* seems to teach doesn't rely upon readerly collaboration with the narrative voice or Alick's husbandly perspective—which remains markedly inaccessible—but rather infuses the structure of the plot and a community of characters who each realizes aspects of failed understandings of women's true roles in a different way. Like many of these characters, the reader is at first charmed by Bessie. The novel instructs its reader in doubting the temptations of such charms and submitting feminine judgment to masculine authority.

The novel's conservative, didactic, third-person narrator teaches readers and characters alike what the wages of women's sin are, *very* broadly interpreted.[9] Focused primarily on humbling Rachel, the novel achieves the submission of her judgment to the inscrutable judgment of her husband, in part, through the examples of less redeemable women. Most notable among these is her charming, flirtatious, spendthrift sister-in-law, Bessie Keith. The dramatic revelation of Bessie's pregnancy via her death in childbirth is the direct result of her immodesty and leads to the exposure of her immorality. In context, Bessie's death reads as punishment for her failure to be a modest body and a subservient wife, sister, and niece. The novel emphasizes the visibility of Bessie's pregnant body acting in space and time, framing its accident and death as punishment for serious transgressions we had been unable to perceive but which Alick had always suspected. The revelation of Bessie's pregnancy serves to expose the extent of her transgressions of appropriate feminine behavior.

The narrative lays the foundations for this exposure in representing Bessie's charming but immodest behavior and heightened physicality. Bessie first appears in the novel in a semipublic scene of "saucy . . . cross fire" with her brother. That this private familial banter ought not to be open to more general view is indicated by Rachel's discomfort at witnessing it. Alick is, likewise, "in some anxiety at his sister's reckless talk." Bessie consistently draws attention to her own flirtations with immodesty; "I have not transgressed, have I?" she

---

9. Though my readings of Yonge differ in many regards from those of Gavin Budge, I find his discussion of the "strong mode" of reading that Yonge elicits compelling: "A formal consequence of this critical perspective to which I draw attention is the way in which Yonge's fiction solicits an active, or 'strong' mode of reading to a far greater degree than most Victorian novels. Explicit narratorial comment, of the kind exemplified by the moralizing authorial interventions of *East Lynne,* is almost entirely absent from Yonge's writing" (12).

asks in the midst of her "reckless talk," when—of course—she has (195, 196). Similarly, in speaking casually of her brother "as to an old friend," though she has known her interlocutor for no more than an hour or two, Bessie highlights, rather than conceals, her own impropriety: "I am afraid I was very naughty," she half-heartedly apologizes (197). In calling attention to her misbehavior, Bessie excuses her immodesty immodestly, building a sort of house of mirrors in which her hypervisibility makes it difficult to judge her actual transgressions. Similarly, in her eager pursuit of sport, Bessie announces her physical body rather than containing it. Her "one great pleasure [with Rachel is] bathing," and she experiences "ecstasies at the naiad performances they share[ ] together on the smooth bit of sandy shore, where they dabble[ ] and float[ ] fearlessly" (203–04). Though we are assured that Bessie's pagan ecstasy at physical freedom takes place in "absolute privacy," we are, nonetheless, treated to these textual displays of Bessie's enthusiastic body.

Bessie's public displays of enthusiastic embodiment take the form of play at croquet. One of the strangest aspects of *The Clever Woman of the Family* for the twenty-first-century reader is the unironic vilification of this seemingly tame lawn sport. Reading the novel, the croquet mallet and hoop come to seem like crudely obvious sexual symbols. The croquet field is the site of a promiscuous mixing of the sexes, feminine abnegation of duty, and the dangers that women's embodiment poses to their modesty, morality, and future well-being. It is Bessie who ushers croquet and all its evils onto the scene.

Upon first arriving in the neighborhood of Avonmouth, Bessie fondly remembers her summer at the instructively named Littleworthy, a summer spent playing at croquet and attendant "courtships . . . flirtations, and a house where all the neighbours were running in and out in a sociable way" (199). That her brother Alick was also at Littleworthy recovering from a serious injury and receiving little care from his otherwise occupied sister and some pain from the lack of peace and quiet does not seem to trouble Bessie much. Indeed, she finds those "who will not play at croquet . . . impracticable," this brother who would prefer she not play at croquet hardly excepted (200). Perhaps more troubling than her abnegation of sisterly duty are the hints that Bessie would rather play croquet than do her duty by her blind uncle, Mr. Clare. Again, Bessie attempts to conceal immodesty with immodesty, using the cover of her sporting body to shield her unfeminine desire to mingle casually with men, to inhabit a house without clear boundaries, and her lack of desire to care—in the private sphere—for the needs of male authority figures.

Bessie's enjoyment of her body twice leads other women directly into immodesty. In the first case, one of her "ecstatic" bathing adventures with Rachel leads to their encounter with Mr. Mauleverer, the ambiguously classed villain who enables Rachel's deadly attempts at charity. In the second case, the immodest mingling of the sexes and classes that occurs after Bessie exposes the Avonmouth community to "croquet fever" tarnishes even the novel's angelic widow, Fanny (258). Among the myriad "visitors, civil and military, [who] often did their part [at croquet,] the most fervent of all these was Mr. Touchett" (219). This fervor of the aptly named Mr. Touchett—a poor curate—is inseparable from his romantic feelings for Lady Fanny Temple. These feelings are fanned into an inappropriate ardor by the intimacies of croquet and by Bessie herself:

> Miss [Bessie] Keith's fun has been more encouragement than she knew; constantly summoning him the croquet-ground and giving him to understand that Lady Temple likes to have him there. Then came that unlucky day, it seems, when he found Bessie mounting her horse at the door, and she called out that it was too wet for croquet, but Lady Temple was in the garden, and would be glad to see him. . . . Somehow, in regretting the end of the croquet season, he was surprised into saying how much it had meant to him. (260)

In this passage, Bessie's responsibility for Mr. Touchett's improper attention to Fanny is emphasized. It is her physical fun that encourages him, and it is her prompting—as she "mounts her horse" for yet more physical expression—that directs him to Lady Temple. Croquet has worked for Mr. Touchett in something of the same way as Bessie's public announcements about her immodesty work—as a visible, public, and therefore seemingly "acceptable" immodesty that conceals deeper, unacceptable transgressions.

What proves most conclusively that Bessie ought to be ashamed of the superficial immodesties of the croquet ground and the very real transgressions it conceals is that croquet causes the textual exposure of her pregnancy. Bessie's own characterization of "the great charm of the sport [being] that one could not play it above eight months in the year" suggests an implicit connection between croquet and Bessie's reproductive body; Bessie's pregnancy, like croquet, does not play above eight months (255). Like Cathy in *Wuthering Heights*, Bessie gives birth prematurely. Bessie's pregnancy is hinted in the "minutely personal confidences about her habits, hopes, and fears" that she shares with Rachel. Within a month of offering those "personal confidences," Bessie's fears have come to pass: After tripping over a croquet hoop, her child makes a "sudden rush into the world," and though the child survives, Bessie does not (467). Like *Wuthering Heights*, *The Clever Woman of the Family* depicts an immodest pregnancy ending in premature birth. Though neither Cathy nor Bessie is likely to have been pregnant before marriage, premature labor is associatively freighted with the suggestion of immorality and immodesty.

It is the observation of Bessie's immodest body, tête-à-tête with a would-be lover, that triggers the accident that leads to her child's early arrival and her own death. Distressed at realizing she has been observed, Bessie is revealed trying to conceal for the first time in the novel. The scene of Bessie's exposure is marked by careful physical description that emphasizes the lifting of shields and the workings of shamed bodies:

> The terrace was prolonged into a walk beyond the screen of evergreens that shut in the main lawn, and, becoming a shrubbery path, led to a smooth glade, on whose turn preparations had been made for a second field of croquet. . . . No one was visible except a lady and gentleman on a seat under a tree about half-way down on the opposite side of the glade. The lady was in blue and white; the gentleman would hardly have been recognized by Rachel but for the start and thrill of her husband's arm, and the flush of colour on his usually pale cheek; but, ere he could speak or move, the lady sprang up, and came hastening towards them diagonally across the grass. Rachel saw the danger, and made a warning outcry, "Bessie, the hoop!" but it was too late, she had tripped over it, and fell prone, and entirely unable to save herself. (464)

Bessie's fall is both literal and figurative, of course. To be seen trying not to be seen, intentionally positioned behind a "screen of evergreens" alone with a young man who is not her husband—a young man, moreover, with whom she carried on a marked flirtation before her marriage—on the scandalous croquet ground that had been the site of those flirtations is beyond the Yongian pale. Bessie is not immediately espied as a person but rather as a body. The shame of the scene is legible on both Keith siblings' bodies: Alick starts, thrills, and flushes, and Bessie springs and hastens away from her admirer's expression of "ardent and lasting affection" (480).

The filmic, almost slow-motion narration of Bessie's fall communicates that this is no simple stumble. The dire reaction of all present is clearly a response to the particular dangers of a fall to Bessie's pregnant body, though there has still been no explicit mention of this pregnancy. Bessie's symptoms after rising heighten the hints about her pregnancy by mapping bodily struggle onto the labor we soon learn the accident has triggered. Bessie "move[s] with difficulty, breathing heavily," and a walk to the carriage "seemed very far and very hot, her alternately excited and shame-stricken manner, and sobbing breath, much alarm[ing] Rachel" (465, 466). Indeed, it seems that Bessie's baby is born within a few hours at most of her accident.

In her introduction to the Broadview edition of the novel, Clare A. Simmons mentions Georgina Battiscombe's frequently cited "joke" that, in *Clever Woman*, "'Bessie Keith falls over a croquet hoop . . . and immediately produces a baby' prompting the conclusion that Yonge 'resembled that legendary aboriginal tribe beloved of anthropologists in her ignorance of the connection between birth and sex'" (12). But Yonge's understanding of "the connection between birth and sex" is made clear in the use of Bessie's pregnancy as the mechanism by which her immorality is revealed. Rather than demonstrating authorial ignorance, the narration of Bessie's reproductive body demonstrates one of the ways that the novel teaches the reader to submit their judgment to masculine authority.

The play of concealment and revelation is heightened immediately after Bessie gives birth. Deploying her "double nature" in open view, Bessie insists on an immediate baptism for her son in order to avoid Lord Keith's arriving in time to veto the name she prefers. Indeed, when it is made clear to Bessie that she will not survive the birth of her child, this "double nature that had perplexed and chafed her brother was so integral that nothing could put it off. She fully comprehended [her impending death], but as if she and herself were two separate persons" (472). In death, Bessie is unable to cast off the habitual duplicity that only her brother has heretofore observed and that the novel only now names in confirmation of his suspicions. In her final delirium, Bessie struggles to justify her behavior to an Alick of her own imagination, turning—finally—toward his authority, though still unable to bow to it.

After Bessie's death, we learn of the careless cruelty and disloyalty of her flirtation with Mr. Carleton both before and after her marriage and of the debts she had incurred that even her marriage to the wealthy Lord Keith did not enable her to pay. The revelation of Bessie's pregnancy occurs amid a conflagration of revelations, all pointing back toward a lack of feminine modesty and morality that had been hinted all along. That the reader—along with every character in *The Clever Woman of the Family* excepting Alick Keith—has likely been unable to read the depths of Bessie's transgressions heretofore positions her pregnancy as a narrative lesson. Bessie's charmingly "naughty" lack of adherence to perfect feminine propriety has been as seductive to the reader as to the characters she deceives (197). Our realization that Alick—whom we may have suspected of being too harsh in his criticisms of his young, cheerful sister—was right all along has the effect of aligning his judgmental abilities with those of the quietly omniscient narrator. The revelations of Bessie's immodesty and immorality that follow the revelation of her pregnancy prompt the reader to bow to Alick's superior knowledge and judgment just as Rachel has: Let the revelation of Bessie's pregnancy serve as a lesson that the harsh punishment she receives teaches belief in Alick's masculine powers of perception and authority.[10] My sense of this dynamic between Alick and the reader has to do with the way the reader—prior to Bessie's accident and death—perceives Bessie primarily through the admiring but imperceptive perspectives of those she charms. Bessie charms everyone but her brother; "nobody protested but Alick," she acknowledges (198). Bessie charms womanly Lady Temple, wise Ermine Williams, and even the novel's most sage paternal figure, the clergyman uncle she neglects, Mr. Clare. Though admirable in various ways, none of these characters is able to achieve Alick's height of perception:

> It was Alick's fate never to meet with sympathy in his feeling of his sister's double-mindedness. . . . The most candid and transparent people in the world—his uncle [Mr. Clare] and his wife [Rachel]—never even succeeded in understanding his dissatisfaction with Bessie's doings. (460)

That Mr. Clare, in failing to understand Alick's "dissatisfaction with Bessie's doings," is actually blind draws emphatic attention to the lack of sight we—readers and characters alike—have all demonstrated with regard to Bessie's "double-mindedness." Once the limitation of our own vision is revealed, the reader is invited to join Rachel in reverencing Alick's male authority—even Bessie herself in a deathbed delirium thrice announces, "Alick was right!" (473).

Alick's "right" authority seems to emanate from his eyes, which he can hardly keep open when looking on the immodesties of women. Throughout

---

10. In the context of what she calls the "realist and non-realist" conventions in the novel, Kim Wheatly has argued that *The Clever Woman of the Family*, though tempting to recuperate on feminist grounds, advocates female domesticity and demonstrates that "a woman's cleverness requires both masculine and divine guidance" (896). In tracing critical approaches to these issues, Wheatley cites the tendency—relevant to my argument that the novel teaches its readers to respect Alick's masculine authority via Bessie's pregnancy—to read Bessie's fate as instructive:

> The same assumption was made in 1965 by a physician, Annis Gillie, who offered this alternative reading of Bessie's death: "If the injury following her fall over a croquet hoop had been severe enough to account for the fatal collapse I doubt if she could have had a living child. Here the author's shears were at work to eliminate a character. A motherless infant was needed to stimulate Rachel's latent maternal instinct—and poor Bessie had to go." According to this argument, the novelist bends reality where one character is concerned in order to render more credible the morally correct development of another. The notion of the "author's shears" implies an author who is fully in control of her creation, deliberately killing off a relatively minor character the better to invest in a central one. (897–98)

a novel rife with mentions of vision in general and Alick's in particular, his half-closed eyes signal judgment. After Rachel's thorough domestication, she signals that she has learned to submit to these intimations, checking herself in conversation when she "[finds her]self talking in the voice that always makes Alick shut his eyes" and reining in her passion for social reform when it leads Alick to "look[ ] meeker and meeker, and assent[ ] to all I said, as if he was half asleep" (541, 542). Alick's partially lidded eyes serve as a check on Rachel's propensity to rush into immodesty, a bodily demonstration of the need for cover and concealment. Certainly, in order to exercise full masculine authority, Alick must generally be able to look on the world with open eyes, but as Ermine, the novel's true clever woman, declares, "the happy medium is reached, that Alick should learn to open his eyes and Rachel to shut hers" (425). Rachel achieves modest femininity by ceding to her husband's perception and power to decide when she needs to be shielded from public view. Bessie's failure to cede her judgment to her brother before marriage or her husband afterward is sacrificed in service of the larger lesson.

Yonge's insistent antifeminism is on particularly clear display in the plot of *The Clever Woman of the Family*. And perhaps her relative lack of popularity among twenty-first-century readers beyond academics interested in the canonical borders and homeschooling parents interested in curricula that supports "traditional" Christian values indicates that readers are more likely to chafe against the type of moral judgments Yonge's novels encourage. However, though *The Clever Woman of the Family* fails to include the reader on its list of capable judges of women's behavior, this chapter has demonstrated that Yonge's prompting of judgment toward women's reproductive capacity is a feature in the representation of pregnancy in the Victorian novel rather than a didactic diversion from the norm. This feature motivates my inclination to push toward different readings of reproductive bodies, albeit uncertain, partial readings that are as much a reflection of my own engagement with cultures and experiences of the body as with literary text or history.

CHAPTER 2

Sympathy

Pregnancy that evidences immorality is a central plot point in Elizabeth Gaskell's *Ruth* (1853) and George Eliot's *Adam Bede* (1859). In both novels, a working-class girl unprotected by money or family falls prey to the sexual desires of an older, more privileged man and becomes pregnant out of wedlock. And though both novels use pregnancy as central points in plots that center sympathy and its limits, Gaskell's alignment of pregnancy with embodied illness and disembodied maternity prompts a readerly sympathy that relies on generous affective responses to female suffering, while Eliot employs infanticide as confirmation of the exclusion of Hetty Sorrel from the novel's sympathetic networks. In neither *Ruth* nor *Adam Bede* does sympathy offer generous uncertainty about the experiences of pregnant embodiment. By pushing toward somatic readings of the novels that invite the personal and subjective into the analytical, I hope to move beyond sympathy as the model for ethical engagement with pregnancy, especially pregnancies that occur outside of normative social expectations.

As readers of Ruth's pregnancy, we participate in her pathologization and redemption; as readers of Hetty's pregnancy, we participate in her narrative punishment. In critiquing the workings of pathologization and punishment, it is easy to slip into gendered, raced, and classed patterns of narrative logic that fetishize our texts. In resisting such slippage, it is easy to "chuckle amusedly."[1] In foregrounding "weak" knowledge and the insistent workings of the anecdotal and uncertain, somatic reading helps me to navigate a perspective on the structures of pathologization and punishment that centers the pulls toward engaged authority or disengaged bemusement in order to imagine how alternatives to such positions might feel.[2] What is the work of critical reading? How does that work participate in and also resist the literary and historical stakes of sympathy that structure the narratives of *Ruth* and *Adam Bede*? What questions and possibilities are opened by reading the nexus of that work and those patterns?

To read somatically, we must sometimes, like Keats, be "capable of being in uncertainties, mysteries, doubts, without any irritable reaching after fact and reason" (Rollins 193–94). The representation of illness (uncertainty embodied, even with the most authoritative diagnoses and treatments) in realist novels (narrative structures designed to quiet many of the active analytical impulses of the mind in favor of cultivating experience) often facilitates such negative capability. Indeed, Jason Tougaw has argued that the intersection of the novel and the medical case history allows "readers to concede the vulnerability they share with the suffering subjects that drive them, to examine the epistemo-

---

1. I refer here to the V21 Collective's ten-point manifesto posted in spring 2015, particularly the first of these points:

> Victorian Studies has fallen prey to *positivist historicism*: a mode of inquiry that aims to do little more than exhaustively describe, preserve, and display the past. Among its symptoms are a fetishization of the archival; an aspiration to definitively map the DNA of the period; an attempt to reconstruct the past *wie es eigentlich gewesen*; an endless accumulation of mere information. At its worst, positivist historicism devolves into show-and-tell epistemologies and bland antiquarianism. Its primary affective mode is the amused chuckle. Its primary institutional mode is the instrumentalist evisceration of humanistic ways of knowing. ("Manifesto")

One of the problems with this vantage point on our work to which I am particularly attuned is that its vocabulary of "symptoms" and "fetishization," for example, can be used to reductively position criticism and theory that deals with pathologization and desire as mere rehashings of what is already known, a "show-and-tell" that suggests that entire categories of investigation are locked in, fit only for the "display" granted them by the least compelling work in the field.

2. Here I join a number of scholars working in conversation with Eve Kosofsky Sedgwick's calls for "weak theory" in *Touching Feeling* (2002), notably Heather Love in "Close but Not Deep" (2010) and "Close Reading" (2013) and Sarah Allison in *Reductive Reading* (2018). Though Allison's interests in the digital humanities and style are very different from my own interests here in lived experiences of the body and realist form, her "defense of descriptive— call them 'weak'—findings" resonates, and her interest in locating the famous "moralizing" of Victorian novels in their style feels consonant to my own investment in locating that moralizing in bodies and their narrative avoidance (3). Also of note is the 2018 special issue of *Modernism/Modernity, Weak Theory/Weak Modernism*, particularly Paul Saint-Amour's introduction.

logical uncertainty and emotional flux that follows from our encounters with them" (26). In this chapter, I look not at the nexus of the novel and the medical case history but at the nexus of the novel and the feeling body. Both *Ruth* and *Adam Bede* foreground the visual and visible in their narrations of vulnerable reproductive bodies; in analyzing those bodies, I try to train my gaze as insistently on lived somatic experience and readerly attitudes as I do on narrations of women's transgressions and available paths toward forgiveness or punishment. In the opening section of this chapter, I sketch the gestures of diagnostic and affinitive modes of reading the narration of embodiment in order to explore the relationship between visibility, superiority, and sympathy as judgment.

In this chapter's second section, "Learn to Have a Little Sympathy," I read *Ruth*, Elizabeth Gaskell's sympathetic representation of a fallen woman. Ruth's pregnancy functions as both the mark of her conflict with conventional morality and also the path toward her rehabilitation. This aligns pregnancy's narrative function, here, with something like what Miriam Bailin demonstrates is a function of illness in the Victorian novel. Indeed, Ruth's pregnancy is narrated like an illness, and the novel's scandalous subject matter is tempered not only by its fallen heroine's complete renunciation of sensuality but also by her eventual self-sacrifice on the pyre of illness. Both this renunciation and sacrifice are made possible by Ruth's envelopment into a middle-class domesticity that confirms her belonging in the novel's sympathetic structures, engaging the reader in an affinitive relationship with her built on positive affective responses to her self-sacrifice.

The final section of this chapter, "In Which the Story Does Not Pause a Little," reads George Eliot's revision of the *Ruth* plot.[3] *Adam Bede*'s refusal to extend narrative sympathy—a refusal to pause a little for Hetty Sorrel's limited capacity to see and say herself—engages the reader in a diagnostic relationship with both her pregnancy and her interiority more generally. If we are to know Hetty, we must approach her with the suspicion that her textual and somatic surfaces are invitations to plumb her depths, even if we find nothing there. Because Hetty's pregnancy and its aftermath offer the most legible invitations to this mode of engagement, invitations that the reader answers with both the court of law and with the novel's modest, moral Dinah. Though Dinah is able to achieve an affinitive engagement with Hetty, her method is a mystery the reader cannot mimic. A somatic reading that uses even just our anecdotal knowledge about pregnancy to imagine something of the experience Hetty

---

3. It is also helpful to note that both novels work in conversation with what would have likely been the literary representation of pregnancy most familiar in the period, Sir Walter Scott's 1818 *The Heart of Midlothian*.

is represented as having is more accessible and less damning; such a reading certainly needs to work in conversation with the diagnostic mode the novel enables, but it can also help us wiggle free from a position of authority over Hetty into a more generous uncertainty that doesn't require any particular affective response to her character.

A LOOKER

Ruth and *Adam Bede* are the two works of mid-Victorian fiction that feature women's pregnant bodies most legibly. Ruth's pregnancy in Gaskell's novel is narrated during her first trimester in direct, accessible language and acknowledged repeatedly, though increasingly vaguely after Ruth earns the protections of a middle-class home; Hetty's pregnancy—though unstated in the most explicit sense—is emphasized by its inadequate concealment, the heightened narrative focus on her visibly altered body, a heavy use of euphemism and insinuation, and her own seeming inability to diagnose herself effectively.[4] The revelation of Hetty's pregnancy requires that the reader, whenever the truth dawns on them, rethink everything that has come before. This makes the

---

4. The extent to which Hetty's pregnancy is emphasized in *Adam Bede* is an open question. Early in the drafting of this project, I sat in on a graduate course on George Eliot in which trained readers expressed surprise at the revelation of Hetty's pregnancy after she has given birth. This would suggest that what I read as highly legible signs are the result, perhaps, of particular reading modes that focus attention on women's bodies. Indeed, as critics working on *Adam Bede* or on women's sexual bodies in the Victorian period—notably Jill L. Matus in the opening paragraph of *Unstable Bodies*—often note, an 1859 issue of the *Saturday Review* lambasted Eliot for what it considered an unacceptably frank and embodied depiction of pregnancy:

> There is also another feature in this part of the story on which we cannot refrain from making a passing remark. The author of *Adam Bede* has given in his adhesion to a very curious practice that is now becoming common among novelists, and it is a practice that we consider most objectionable. It is that of dating and discussing the several stages that precede the birth of a child. We seem to be threatened with a literature of pregnancy. . . . Hetty's feelings and changes are indicated with a punctual sequence that makes the account of her misfortunes read like the rough notes of a man-midwife's conversations with a bride. This is intolerable. Let us copy the old masters of the art, who, if they gave us a baby, gave it all at once. A decent author and a decent public may take the premonitory symptoms for granted. ("Adam Bede")

While I very much wish that the "literature of pregnancy" this reviewer fears were evidenced in the mid-Victorian period, it is likely that the "practice now becoming common" of speaking with something like bodily specificity about pregnancy required no more than *Ruth* and *Adam Bede* as evidence. Furthermore, as someone who has tried hard to pinpoint the exact chronology of Hetty's pregnancy, I find the reviewer's charges to be unfounded.

pregnancy the central fact of the novel, the point from which the plot hangs. Ruth's and Hetty's highly legible pregnant bodies are narrative focal points in *Ruth* and *Adam Bede*, respectively. Both of these novels explicitly engage readers in testing the limits of their sympathetic abilities and both thematize scenes and vocabularies of visuality, visibility, and perspective that encompass questions about our readerly gaze.

Victorianist literary criticism of the last quarter-century has frequently explored visuality, visibility, and perspective, and theorists of varying stripes have firmly established a concept of the gaze in our critical discourse.[5] The kind of gaze I analyze here is perhaps most closely descended from Foucault's medical gaze and feminist theory's male gaze but is more particular to the reading of embodied phenomena that resist being read. This is a gaze that notices and understands the possibly pregnant significance of a loose dress, a hand on the "side," a change in complexion or expression. This is a readerly gaze that apprehends pregnant bodies in the Victorian novel, a gaze attentive to the highly visible and salient surfaces of heavily pregnant bodies and to the bodily symptoms of the very bodies most marked by narrative reticence. This focus on bodies works with and against the punishing tendencies that structure the depiction of women's sexualized bodies in the Victorian novel. I read those bodies as having other plots, weak plots that come into focus with our application of idiosyncratic and anecdotal somatic knowledge and impression.[6]

Readerly engagement requires both literal and figurative staring. Reading pregnancy in the Victorian novel—reading, in other words, an embodied condition that we have the tools to know is there but that resists narrative legibility—heightens this requirement. In her 2009 *Staring*, Rosemarie Garland-Thomson offers a generous understanding of staring: "We stare," she says, "when ordinary seeing fails, when we want to know more. So staring is an interrogative gesture that asks what's going and on and demands a story" (3). Staring, then, though it has the potential to be a politically and ethically problematic act, is not necessarily one. It is an act akin to reading itself, particularly critical reading.

The year 2009 was a rich one for the investigation of these questions about the nature of looking, reading, and interrogating. In their introduction to a special issue of *Representations* that year, Stephen Best and Sharon Marcus explored challenges to the tradition of suspicious or symptomatic reading that

---

5. See, for example, Foucault; Mulvey; Pratt.
6. Similarly, of *Wuthering Heights,* Beth Newman has argued that "the gaze (and therefore the novel, which reproduces the gaze), however coercive, is never a locus of complete control—that the gaze even opens a space of resisting that control" (1036).

they see stemming from the roughly concurrent rise of psychoanalytic and Marxist literary theories in the 1970s and the emphasis placed by those theoretical approaches on buried meaning. I find this line of questioning compelling, and I find the vocabulary of illness ("symptom") that Best and Marcus employ particularly interesting in the context of the ways in which vocabularies of illness are expressive of pregnancy. There seems to me to be something about looking at the ways we look that dovetails thematically with looking at the ways bodies function in narrative forms that resist naming their functioning.

A diagnostic mode of engagement with bodies places the reader in a position of knowledge about and authority over a character's body that exceeds a character's, novel's, or author's knowledge and authority. We can discover traces of this superior diagnostic gaze on pregnant bodies in Victorian literature by thinking back, for instance, to Nelly's seeming maidenly ignorance about what Frances Earnshaw's "symptoms portend" (which leaves the critical reader to fill in their own "superior" knowledge about consumption and perhaps pregnancy) and Georgina Battiscombe's joking suggestion that Bessie's delivery after stumbling over a croquet hoop signals Charlotte Mary Yonge's ignorance about how babies are made. This diagnostic mode is both critically accessible—most readers can diagnose pregnancy in the Victorian novel if they choose—and useful for those who, like me, want to read implicit body plots. When these body plots are highly salient elements of fiction—what would *Ruth* and *Adam Bede* be without their unmarried, pregnant bodies?—this diagnostic mode also implicates the reader in a policing of sympathetic boundaries.

Audrey Jaffe's *Scenes of Sympathy: Identity and Representation in Victorian Fiction* (2000) explores connections between visible spectacle, sympathy, and class difference. These connections also frame the diagnostic readerly mode for engaging with Hetty's working-class pregnant body in *Adam Bede*. I follow Jaffe's interest in the ways sympathy often operates across the class barriers that make difference visible. But because sympathy imagines an extension of one's own interiority into the interiority of another and because a diagnostic mode of engagement with embodied experience assumes the limited interiority of the other, a diagnostic mode of engagement with pregnant bodies establishes a relationality in which sympathy is difficult. A diagnostic reading of Hetty's pregnancy in *Adam Bede* looks with an implicit superiority on the body of a woman made immodest as much by her social conditions as her sexual ones.

We look, Eliot's narrator famously tells us, in order to sympathize, to understand how and why. But a sympathetic understanding of Hetty is available only to Dinah, and though Dinah's engagement with Hetty's pregnancy models an alternative, the affinitive mode of perceiving bodily experience seems to be a symptom of extreme self-abnegation. For Rachel Ablow, the sympathy "by which we become subjects through our encounters with others" is theorized through the marital relationship (*Feeling* 8). Physically intimate sympathies between married couples are useful in thinking through an affinitive mode of perceiving pregnancy in the Victorian novel. Where diagnostic reading requires difference and distance, affinitive reading fleshes out the circumstances of textual pregnancy based on an affinity of proximity and intimacy that centers one's own position in conceiving of the embodied experience of the other. In contemplating how her own experiences of pregnancy reshaped her understanding of the role of Mary Shelley's reproductive biography in her work, for example, Rachel Feder returns again and again to Goethe's *Elective Affinities,* sympathy as harnessable alchemical mystery.

Neither the diagnostic nor the affinitive mode of engaging with bodies in Victorian novels offers a comfortable position from which to perceive pregnancy, however. Indeed, it is partly in our troubled resistance to these modes—in questioning, for example, why Ruth must be sacrificed in order to be fully redeemed or why Hetty must be abandoned altogether—that a readerly gaze that apprehends pregnancy in the Victorian novel functions. This gaze is not purely theoretical, simply an imagined "eye" on imagined "bodies." This gaze is also literal; when we read pregnancy in the Victorian novel, our actual eyes look at print on page and observe a shape and size to textual pregnancy, if often only in punctuation and white space. My engagement, across a visual divide, with that more defined shape and size of pregnancy in *Ruth* and *Adam Bede* gives shape and size to this book's ways of knowing pregnancy, certainly, but also to ways of knowing Victorian representations of class difference and illness. Both novels engage the reader's potential for "fellow feeling" with hardships faced by working-class characters (Eliot, *Adam Bede* 148). Ruth's and Hetty's bodies are immodestly available to our gaze and the gaze of men interested in their sexual bodies precisely because they work for their keep; they work for their keep because they are parentless and unmarried; because they work for their keep and are orphaned and unmarried, they are more easily led into immorality than women protected by parents or husbands; because they are led into immorality, the expansion of their sexual bodies into reproductive bodies is made diagnostically available to us; because the expansion of their sexual bodies is made diagnostically available, the limits of our sympathetic affinities are tested: Can we extend sympathy to Ruth to Hetty? Does our extension of such a sympathy make their suffering about us or require the intensification of their suffering? In other words, does sympathy with pregnancy in the nineteenth-century novel require dangerous superiority or illness? In the testing of the limits of our affinities, *Ruth* deploys illness as a final sympathetic offering for its fallen heroine. In *Adam Bede*, however, Hetty is unredeemed by illness, inviting our diagnosis but excluded from the sympathy of all but Dinah, whose tendency toward self-abnegation recalls *Ruth*. In my reading of both novels, then, I find sympathy and its affective demands insufficient to meet the narration of the body; I try to fill the gaps left by sympathy with a somatic imagination that doesn't require any particular affective position.

"LEARN TO HAVE A LITTLE SYMPATHY"

Ruth stands as a kind of halfway point between the textual treatment of married, upper-class characters whose immodesty draws novelistic and readerly judgment of revealed pregnancy and the unmarried, lower-class Hetty of *Adam Bede*, whose transgressions of accepted codes of modesty and morality result in a pregnancy that is perhaps more visible to the reader than to the character herself. The reader learns that Ruth "will have a child" within imaginative minutes of Ruth learning this herself and before the pregnancy would be readily visible to "real-life" observers (Gaskell 117). Though the revelation of Ruth's pregnancy comes directly and early, her remaining trimesters are narrated with increasing rather than decreasing modesty, as she is covered by the middle-class protection of the Bensons. This increasing textual cover inverts the concealment/revelation narration of the middle- and upper-class married bodies in *Wuthering Heights* and *Clever Woman*. While Cathy's and Bessie's pregnancies are concealed from direct notice by the text past the point at which they would be readily apparent to an observer and revealed in dramatic conflagrations shortly before the deaths that make the immoral bodies of both women more accessible to view rather than less, Ruth's body is more and more fully concealed by the novel as time goes by and "the fallen woman becomes the angel in the house" (S. Morgan 95). By the time a second serious illness finds Ruth, her sexual body has been fully sacrificed to a self-abnegating morality that undoes the Bensons' need to "to shield her from [public] censure" (Jaffe, *Scenes* 78).[7]

---

7. For Gaskell in *Ruth*, as in *Mary Barton* and *North and South*, unalloyed sympathy is "the solution to divisive social problems." Gaskell's focus on the problems of the fallen woman is displaced by the well-meaning Bensons' inventing for Ruth a respectable "cover" as the Widow Denbigh, "ostensibly to shield her from [public] censure" (Jaffe, *Scenes* 78). Jaffe argues that "in *Ruth*, Gaskell describes an identity so enmeshed in the projections of others, and in literary convention (her name [as a biblical allusion] tells us her story), that it becomes a kind of exposure of the power of the type—an assertion of the capacity of cultural identity to annihilate any sense of individual identity altogether" (Jaffe 92).

It is the doctor called in to treat illness who diagnoses Ruth's pregnancy. Indeed, both Ruth's pregnancy and later her death seem to be triggered by the illnesses she contracts from Bellingham. Our mode of engagement with Ruth in the novel is one in which we form an affinitive, sympathetic bond with her interiority in the context of our heightened awareness of her body in general and in illness in particular. Ruth's isolation in the novel's opening chapters encourages the reader to take her side and to observe the ways in which her physical beauty shapes her subjective experience. Her development of an interiority that can achieve a similar grasp of the interplay of experience and body grows alongside the child she carries. She understands the social and moral shape of her sin during her first trimester of pregnancy, learns that she must conceal the social shape of that sin during her second trimester, and resolves to establish cover for herself and her baby during her third. So, Ruth's psychic interiority develops alongside a literal interior development, coded positive. Our affinitive engagement with Ruth's pregnancy proves difficult to sustain as the cover of middle-class respectability is thrown over her by her inclusion in the Benson household. By this point, we can no longer use our narrative proximity to her body to read her. Affinitive connection is reestablished only by her final illness and a death in which the narrative structure of her pregnancy repeats itself with the sexuality edited out.

Ruth Hilton is a fifteen-year-old orphan working as a dressmaker's apprentice when we first meet her. The down-on-its-luck assize town with which the novel opens mirrors Ruth's own class position: She is the daughter of a lady and a well-to-do farmer whose fortunes are almost completely dissipated by the end of his life, leaving his orphaned daughter without the protections of family or social standing. Having had no mother to guide her through her transition from child to beautiful young woman, Ruth is vulnerable to seduction by the well-off Mr. Bellingham. This vulnerability results, we are gently informed, from Ruth's lack of an implicit education in moral sexuality that, like a fetus, takes root before we can see it:

> She was too young when her mother died to have received any cautions or words of advice respecting *the* subject of a woman's life—if, indeed, wise parents ever directly speak of what, in its depth and power, cannot be put into words—which is a brooding spirit with no definite form or shape that men should know it, but which is there, and present before we have recognized and realized its existence. (44)

"*The* subject of a woman's life" seems to be some amalgamation of the functions and customs governing women's use of their reproductive bodies: Ruth's mother died before she was able to impart any information about menstruation, sexuality, or maternity to her daughter. That this information—rightly imparted—would likely be imparted without speaking "directly . . . of what . . . cannot be put into words" later finds an echo in Faith Benson's ignorance about "how to word" Ruth's pregnancy (117). Mothers, it seems, erect a moral guard around their daughters best expressed in linguistic reserve, in not giving the "form or shape" of language to *the* things that take bodily forms and shapes. This kind of moral education, rather, communicates in something like an amniotic fluid that passes messages between two affinitively connected bodies without language and that demands a similarity and proximity between mother and child.

It is generally, however, the Victorian middle-class father who is tasked with erecting a physical guard around his daughters, a physical guard best expressed in providing the financial security that protects women from having to treat in the public world for their keep. Left without mother, father, or financial security, Ruth is left with a "shaky and tenuous sense of identity" (Chishty-Mujahid 58). From this shaky position, Ruth searches for connections with others: "The interval of blank, after her father's life-in-death, had made her all the more ready to value and cling to sympathy" (Gaskell 44). Ruth's search for the sympathetic "fibers . . . of nutriment" in Bellingham fails because his interest in her—a mocking echo of the masculine protection she lacks—is founded completely on her sexual beauty (39).

Sympathy requires not only that we look across the barrier of our own subjectivity but that when we recognize and imagine the subjectivities of others, we also experience "sympathy's reversibility, as if the other's identity might too easily become one's own" (Jaffe, *Scenes* 84). In her relationship with Mr. Bellingham, Ruth experiences this reversibility twice, in part because Mr. Bellingham never extends himself sympathetically. He is enchanted by Ruth's beauty only, perceiving it not as separate from himself but as a fitting extension of himself. Indeed, even Bellingham's desire to shield Ruth from view twists the covering function of the husband into a self-protective gesture, one that erects barriers rather than bridges. For example, though it means asking Ruth to walk six miles, Bellingham's seduction of Ruth avoids the use of "any of his carriages . . . [because] they must, to a certain degree, be encumbered by, and exposed to, the notice of servants" (43). Bellingham's furtive avoidance of being seen with her signals the failure of Ruth's search for sympathetic fibers in him. Uninterested in seeing Ruth's true physical or moral interests, Bellingham imagines being seen instead. Here Bellingham performs the movements of sympathy on himself, through the reflective surface offered by Ruth. This dynamic is thematized during Bellingham's first and second illness. During both, Ruth nurses him to her own detriment.

After his seduction of her, Bellingham asks Ruth to "have a little sympathy" for his interiority, his moods and wishes, and Ruth attempts to shape her behavior to Bellingham's wish for a lighthearted companion. But the whisper of an immorality she had not before understood reaches her, and Ruth struggles to maintain the bewitching aspect that appeals to him (72). Unconcerned by Ruth's struggles, it is Bellingham who lacks sympathy: "Her beauty was all that Mr. Bellingham cared for . . . it was all he recognized of her" (74). Bellingham's illness emerges out of their failures to establish mutual sympathy. Ruth rushes into caring for Bellingham in an affinitive move—"Let me put my cool hands on your forehead . . . that used to do mamma good"—in which she imagines the effect of her body on the feelings of his and draws on her proximity, and recollections of the maternal body that communicates affinitively in particular (75). But this mode doesn't serve Ruth; her affinitive engagement with Bellingham does not create an answering affinity in him. Her care of him during illness communicates illness to her—an illness that prompts the exposure of her pregnancy, an exposure that writes the evidence of her sin visibly on her body.

The stress of Bellingham's illness, through which Ruth first nurses him and is then forbidden from nursing him by the arrival of his mother, infects Ruth's mind with a "madness" that calls Mr. Benson to her aid (98). Bellingham's illness seems also to infect Ruth's body with a physical ailment that is at once illness and pregnancy. The declaration that "Ruth's condition ought to be known by those who were her friends" refers, of course, to her *true* condition, which is not the mental illness from which she suffers briefly, nor the physical illness she has literally contracted, but her pregnancy (104).

Pregnancy always occurs in a kind of physical isolation, working invisibly within the body of the mother; this makes the representation of pregnancy in text, particularly Victorian text, necessarily a vague impression of mysterious processes at work under a visible surface. Though Ruth's pregnancy is disclosed to the reader, it is with a disinclination to put specific language to the condition: "'Why, Thurstan,' Miss Benson says, 'there is something so shocking in the matter, that I cannot tell you.' . . . All things possible and impossible crossed [Thurstan's] mind, but the right one" (117). Miss Benson can know of the pregnancy, but she cannot yet "see" it (as the reader can in the text on the page), nor does she know how to say it, "how to word it." Miss Benson's hesitation, bordering on inability, to speak of Ruth's pregnancy seems to suggest some risk of literal infection by Ruth's "badge of . . . shame" (119). When she does manage to get the matter spoken, her declaration is diagnostic: "[Ruth] will have a child. The doctor says so" (117).

As was the case in *Wuthering Heights,* in *Ruth* the vocabularies for illness and pregnancy overlap. Before Ruth's pregnant "condition" is known to her friends or to Ruth herself, her "sick unconsciousness" and dizzy spells after Bellingham's abandonment of her speak simultaneously to her psychic anguish, physical illness, and prevalent first-trimester signs of pregnancy (81). In this state, food "revolted the appetite it was intended to provoke," a common symptom of the morning sickness of early pregnancy (82). It is worth noting that the revelation of Ruth's pregnancy and its incorporation into the Bensons' narrative of her as a respectable widow heightens rather than lessens the use of illness vocabulary to obscure or articulate pregnant specificities. During what is likely the early second trimester of her pregnancy, Ruth avoids a social function by pleading "delicacy of health" (159). This delicacy of health certainly speaks to her pregnancy at the period when that pregnancy would be beginning to be visible to those who see her; the language of illness here is not obfuscatory but euphemistic, gently hinting at her body as a site for consideration.

Even before her pregnancy, however, Ruth's body is sexually visible. Her beauty is the reason she is chosen from her fellow seamstresses to attend on the local gentry at a ball, is the reason she is noticed by Bellingham at that ball, is one of the reasons her relationship with Bellingham is remarked upon by the residents in the Welsh town to which they abscond. Without a guardian or economic privilege, there is no covering veil to cast over Ruth. That cover is only offered, belatedly and founded on deception, by the Bensons' decision to enfold her in their moral, middle-class home and family. In this way, the Bensons themselves work like Victorian maternity wear: Their protection conceals the markers of Ruth's sexuality. However, the Bensons also work as "maternity wear" in another sense, filling the maternal gap in the novel. As I have demonstrated, Ruth's fall is in large part figured by Gaskell as a result of her motherlessness, a result of the lack of a maternal sympathy that communicates primarily through unspoken, embodied vocabularies of affinity. In attempting to relegate Ruth's fall to the unspoken territory of secret, the Bensons mimic the structure of that sympathy. But it is the reader who best takes the place of Ruth's mother, affinitively sympathetic to her pregnant and ill body.

After failing to establish a functional affinitive connection with Bellingham and forging such a connection with the Bensons on the foundation of a lie about her identity, Ruth's most successful sympathetic connection is formed with the reader. Though the reader cannot share physical space with Ruth in the way a mother and child can, through gazing on her textual space, we mirror a physical behavior associated with affinitive maternity and associated with Ruth herself. As Rosemary Langridge points out, "Ruth is a 'looker,' in both the colloquial and the literal senses of the word . . . she is constantly engaged in acts of looking" (51).

Our ability to look at the specificities of Ruth's physical body, however, is limited once she joins the middle-class Benson home. This shift demands that Ruth pose as a respectable widow protected by various shields: a verbal shield—Ruth adopts the name Mrs. Denbigh—and physical shields—a black gown, a ring, "two widow's caps of the commonest make and coarsest texture," and a haircut (144). The Bensons decide to conceal the full social significance of Ruth's pregnancy. Though we know that they cannot conceal the highly visible later pregnancy itself, after Ruth's reincarnation as Mrs. Denbigh a gauzy veil is thrown over the physical facts of her reproductive body. This shifts a previously distinct timeline into hazier chronology and limits our affinitive access to Ruth.

Though this veil is effective in shielding Ruth's immorality from the gaze of the characters in the novel, we know that they are now seeing her pregnancy. Mrs. Bradshaw, for example, sends her "muslin in aid of any preparations Mrs. Denbigh might have to make" (156). This implicit visibility is odd, though, because it seems to spring up suddenly when Ruth arrives at the Bensons' home. Prior to that, a doctor had been needed to inform the Bensons, Ruth herself, and the reader that she was pregnant. But only a week after her arrival, it has become readily apparent to all. Though, of course, it does sometimes happen over the course of a pregnancy, particularly early in the second trimester, that a "bump" emerges rather suddenly, there is also an implication that Ruth's pregnancy can't be respectably seen or said when her body is coded as unmarried and that it becomes socially visible when she "becomes" a widow.

The chronology of Ruth's pregnancy, however, becomes less—not more—clear at this point in the narrative. Patsy Stoneman has written about "the disruptive factor of female sexuality, which cannot be acknowledged in the ideological surface of the novel, but is repressed, emerging as a subtext of imagery and dreams," causing what Stoneman calls "gaps, false leads, and inconsistencies in the narrative surface" (67–68). There is, if not quite an inconsistency, certainly an imprecision in the narration of Ruth's second and third trimester into which a somatic reading imagines specificities of the body. Though the narrator is explicit about the chronology of Ruth's early courtship with Bellingham (the novels opens in January, and their friendship is cemented in February) and their arrival (in July of that same year) in the Welsh town where Bellingham falls ill and Ruth meets Mr. Benson, a soft focus seems to fall over the timeline from that point on. Specific months—October and November—are mentioned after Ruth moves in with the Bensons, but without clear connection to Ruth's condition and more in the manner of a filmic montage that establishes the passage of time. Her baby arrives in a vague late winter ("the earth was still 'hiding her guilty front with innocent snow' when a little baby was laid by the side of the pale white mother"), and shortly after, Faith Benson brings her "the first snowdrops in the garden" (160). About a year before, Ruth and Mr. Bellingham had gone out walking together for the first time in late February, which Gaskell calls early spring. Most likely, then, Ruth's child is born in late February or early March. No mention is made of complications or of the child arriving early, so Ruth probably becomes pregnant in June and is early in her first trimester while she nurses Mr. Bellingham in Wales and perhaps about two months along when the doctor diagnoses her pregnancy. This timeline corresponds to his diagnosis, which would likely require that she report having missed a menstrual cycle or two. The level of conjecture required to establish this timeline, however, attests to the kind of soft focus with which the narration allows us to see her expanding body after her inclusion in the Benson family.

The novel's shift to a soft focus on Ruth coincides with her own transition into an idealized maternity that, in combination with the middle-class cover of the Benson family and the concealment of her immoral past, protects Ruth from the immodesty of heightened physical visibility. Her full social redemption is only achieved, however, by the repetition with a difference of her pregnancy narrative: Ruth's second "affair" with Mr. Bellingham—himself now covered by the false name Mr. Donne—has many of the markers of the first: illicit meetings, illness, her nursing of him and contraction of illness from him. But this time, Ruth doesn't fall, she ascends through chaste suffering. Her dying fever burns off the remnants of sin and reconnects the reader to our affinitive sense of her bodily experience.

The bodily, affinitive connection Ruth fostered during her affair with and care of Bellingham in Wales is figured by *Ruth* as a kind of permanent physical impression. Married by shared sin if not by law, both Mrs. Denbigh and Mr. Donne are impressed by the sexual bodies of Ruth Hilton and Mr. Bellingham. Ruth's body, of course, is literally impressed by the pregnancy that results from her affair with Mr. Bellingham, an embodied realization of the danger of sympathetic overidentification; during her pregnancy, Ruth literally fosters some of Mr. Bellingham inside of her own body. The link prompts her dangerously affinitive care of Mr. Donne during his fever at the novel's close. In nursing her former lover, Ruth experiences his bodily needs as her own in a sort of pregnant echo that sacrifices her health to his illness:

> Every sense had been strained in watching—every power of thought or judgment had been kept on the full stretch. . . . She could not remember that present time, or where she was. All times of her earliest youth—the days of her childhood—were in her memory with a minuteness and fullness of detail which was miserable . . . yet she could not remember who she was now, nor where she was, and whether she had now any interests in life to take the place of those which she was conscious had passed away, although their remembrance filled her mind with painful acuteness. (444–45)

Ruth's mind and body are at "full stretch" with pain, "filled" with a pregnant "fullness." This echo of pregnancy in illness is made more direct after her decline: "There she lay in the attic room in which her baby had been born" (447). In the passage above, the level of mental and bodily detail, the disjointed narrative, and a stream-of-consciousness texture allows the reader to engage affinitively with Ruth as we did in "the days of her childhood" at the novel's opening, when she was also narrated with heightened bodily "minuteness" and "acuteness."

The significance of the minute and acute details of Ruth's dying body and mind is fully realized in a passage marked by the language of visibility and looking:

> It so happened that the rays of the lamp fell bright and full upon Ruth's countenance, as she stood with her crimson lips parted with the hurrying breath, and the fever-flush brilliant on her cheeks. Her eyes were wide open, and their pupils distended. She looked on the invalid in silence, and hardly understood why Mr. David has summoned her there.
> "Don't you see the change? He is better!—the crisis is past!"
> But she did not speak; her looks were riveted on his softly-unclosing eyes, which met hers as they opened languidly. She could not stir or speak. She was held fast by that gaze of his, in which a faint recognition dawned, and grew to strength. (445)

The primary recognition that dawns and grows to strength here is our own knowledge of Ruth's impending death, figured through Ruth's hypervisible (the light of the lamp falls on her) fevered body. Ruth's eyes are the focal point of our recognition that "the crisis" is not "past" but yet to come. "Held fast by that gaze," her life has been sacrificed to the affinitive needs of Bellingham/Donne, certainly, but perhaps to the affinitive needs of the reader as well. The revealed pregnancies of Cathy and Bessie in *Wuthering Heights* and *Clever Woman* demonstrate the salience of their somatic experience to a narrative structure that demands punishment for certain transgressions of gender and class norms. The revelation of Ruth's illness—in combination with the affinitive experience fostered in the reader through its narration—satisfies a similar narrative requirement while sustaining and strengthening our ability to see her body, an ability that comes to seem complicit in her decline yet unable to ease it: As she dies, "the watchers [can]not touch her with their sympathy, or come near her in her dim world" (448).

And after her death, her erstwhile antagonist Mr. Bradshaw can "not speak . . . for the sympathy which choked up his voice and filled his eyes with tears" (458). Mr. Bradshaw's embodied, affinitive sympathy chokes up articulation. It is a mode of engagement that infects people with one another but does not, finally, offer escape.

IN WHICH THE STORY DOES NOT PAUSE A LITTLE

George Eliot's *Adam Bede* revises both the fallen-woman plot of *Ruth* and also the most accessible mode of narrative engagement with pregnant bodies.[8] There are few opportunities for the reader to develop the affinitive sympathy with Hetty Sorrel that Dinah Morris does. Indeed, it is Dinah, not Hetty, who most resembles Gaskell's angelic Ruth. It is only against the backdrop of Dinah that Hetty's interiority is even potentially legible. Hetty does not know herself; her inability to know her pregnancy is the novel's most direct lesson about the dangers of lack of self-knowledge. Lacking self-knowledge, Hetty lacks the ability to make active choices though her body moves her inexorably into a maternity she does not desire. Her rejection of that maternity is the passive rejection of an abandonment that becomes infanticide after the death of her newborn. Faced with courts of law and the judgment of everyone she encounters, she remains unable to claim agency or name her actions until she is persuaded by Dinah's spiritual guidance. Dinah is able to gain access to the locked room of Hetty's soul, prompting an acknowledgment of her crime before she's shuffled off of the narrative stage, a sentence to hang commuted to transportation. But Dinah's access to Hetty and Hetty's eventual acknowledgment of guilt doesn't grant the reader access to an interiority the novel insistently denies. Without such access, affective sympathy is foreclosed and access to Hetty is most easily gained in diagnostic access to her highly visible, sexualized, working-class body. *Adam Bede* uses pregnancy to position Hetty's lack of self-knowledge as a moral failing, but reading the uncertainties of her

---

8. See Beer 59. Matus also notes the relationship between *Adam Bede* and *Ruth*.

pregnancy as the uncertainties of the body rather than only the failings of the character can gesture toward ways to read her pregnancy that rely less on diagnostic judgment.

Hetty's pregnancy in *Adam Bede* is perhaps the most notable pregnancy in Victorian literature, but it is one that the pregnant woman herself seems not to note. Hetty's unknowingness is the result of an unwillingness to see below her own pleasing surface; Hetty's consciousness works like a mirror, bouncing any rays of sympathetic impulse back toward the reader. Though Dinah Morris serves as a model of affinitive sympathy, her vision of Hetty's interiority is spiritual and mysterious; it eschews the visible world and cannot offer the reader a similar path toward Hetty. Though the novel famously pauses a little to establish sympathy with Hetty's seducer, a sympathetic sense of the fallen woman's psychic interiority remains as unavailable to the reader as to Hetty herself.

Adam Bede centers on the titular character's one-sided affections for Hetty. Adam's hopes of marrying her and living a life of integrity and hard work are dashed by the combination of Hetty's frivolity and her resulting affair with Arthur Donnithorne, scion of the local gentry. In the aftermath of Adam's chance discovery of this relationship, though not its sexual component, he becomes engaged to Hetty, who is motivated by the need for a port in storm after Arthur's abandonment. But a marriage between Adam and Hetty never comes to pass because Hetty—eight months pregnant, though she seems only dimly aware of it, and those around her are completely unaware—runs away from fiancé and family. After giving birth, Hetty is put on trial for the murder of the infant she has abandoned to the elements. While in prison, Hetty's soul is reclaimed by the saintly Dinah, a Methodist preacher and the woman whom Adam finally marries. It is only at Dinah's prompting that Hetty ever articulates her maternity.

Prior to Adam's partial discovery of the relationship between Hetty and Arthur, he and Hetty both attend a dance given in honor of Arthur's coming of age. At the dance, Adam helps Hetty to recover a locket that—unbeknownst to him—was given to her by Arthur:

> While Hetty was in the act of placing [a small child, Totty] in Adam's arms, and had not yet withdrawn her own, Totty opened her eyes, and forthwith fought out with her left fist at Adam's arms, and with her right caught at the string of brown beads round Hetty's neck. The locket leaped out from her frock, and the next moment the string was broke, and Hetty, helpless, saw beads and locket scattered wide on the floor. . . . [The locket] had attracted [Adam's] glance as it leaped from her frock. . . . As Adam picked it up, he

saw the glass with the dark and light locks of hair under it. It had fallen that side upwards, so the glass was not broken. He turned it over on his hand, and saw the enameled gold back. (242)

In this scene we find the tragedy of Hetty's unmarried pregnancy writ small. The locket, like the mirror its description twice evokes ("glass"), reflects and enacts the themes and dynamics that circle Hetty in the novel. Like her virtue, the locket falls away from Hetty. Like her transgression, the locket must be concealed beneath brown beads, a covering of clothing or text that can delay exposure but not prevent it—indeed, a covering that can be "caught at" and pulled away. Like her pregnancy, the locket is given to Hetty by Arthur. Like her changing body, the locket is something Hetty seeks to conceal but that is dramatically exposed. Like her illegitimate child, the locket contains the bodily trace of two contrasting parents: dark and light locks of hair, privileged and working classes of people. Like Hetty herself, the locket is eye-catchingly beautiful and frivolous. Much as he tries to bolster Hetty after the discovery of what he believes to be a flirtation between herself and Arthur, Adam tries to retrieve Hetty's unbroken locket/virtue in the passage above. Perhaps most importantly, this passage employs a vocabulary of visibility, with "eyes," "attracted . . . notice," and three occurrences of "saw." The language of visibility works disproportionately hard throughout *Adam Bede* and in the narration of Hetty in particular. A dense vocabulary of eyes and seeing combines with bodily description to contribute to our readerly awareness of Hetty's sexuality and pregnancy despite her "native powers of concealment" (274).

Hetty's immodest visibility in *Adam Bede* functions more clearly because of the stark contrast of Dinah's modest, unassuming presence. At the start of the novel, the two women mirror each other: Each is in an unstable class standing as orphaned nieces of the Poysner household. Dinah is being courted by Seth Bede, Hetty by Adam. Indeed, for all of the emphasis placed on Hetty's love of being seen, the first chapter of the novel centers around Dinah's display of herself on the village green. These seeming similarities serve to highlight the differences between Dinah and Hetty.[9] For Adam early in the novel, thinking of Hetty and seeing Dinah "was like dreaming of the sunshine, and awakening in the moonlight"—both women are described in terms of light, but in terms of wildly different qualities of light (97). At one point after Dinah's departure from the Poysners' home, Hetty dresses up in her Methodist gown and cap. The contrast is stark enough to amuse the men in the room and to

---

9. For more on feminine binaries in the Victorian novel, see much of the foundational 1970s feminist scholarship on the nineteenth-century novel, such as S. Gilbert and Gubar; Auerbach.

disturb Mrs. Poysner. Though Dinah is pale where Hetty is dark, the impact of Hetty's game of dress-up has more to do with a difference in character than with a difference in appearance. Dinah is a paragon of sympathetic connection, where Hetty is insensible to the needs and wishes of others. Dinah is unconcerned with managing others' impressions of herself, where Hetty's senses of self and value function almost exclusively in markets of admiration.

The contrasts between the women are emphasized in the "Two Bedchambers" chapter, in which Dinah and Hetty are followed into adjoining bedrooms by a narrator probing each woman's consciousness. Hetty evinces almost no interiority but spends her time alone looking at her reflection in the mirror. Dinah, on the other hand, looks out at the world, toward the troubles of others, into her own soul, and finally, toward Hetty, to whom she is drawn in sympathetic concern. Indeed, Dinah's concern for others always outweighs thoughts of herself. When asked by the local clergyman, Mr. Irwine, whether, when preaching, she ever feels "any embarrassment from the sense of [her] youth—that [she is] a lovely young woman on whom men's eyes are fixed?" Dinah replies, "'No, I've no room for such feeling and I don't believe the people ever take notice about that'" (75). Hetty, on the other hand, is "quite used to the thought that people like to look at her," though such looking prompts no sympathetic response in her (80). Hetty experiences her visibility as proof of her own value and the inferior values of others: She "felt nothing when [Adam's] eyes rested on her, but the cold triumph of knowing that he loved her, and would not care to look at Mary Burge" (82). In contrast with the muted colors of Dinah's person and clothing, Hetty is "a bright patch of color, like a tropical bird among the boughs" and "a bright-cheeked apple hanging over the orchard wall, within sight of everybody" (108, 175). Hetty is doubly bright, visible, and evocative of the original fall even in her pre-fallen state.

Despite her hypervisibility, Hetty is a mistress of concealment. Her shallow, frivolous, thoughtless, and ungenerous nature is hidden from almost everyone who knows her. This concealment is made possible by Hetty's particular brand of infantile beauty. Both her childlike appeal and its failure to correspond with the innate femininity others imagine are emphasized in Hetty's lack of interest in nurturing. The narrator informs us that men who see Hetty share an assumption that "she will dote on her children [because] she is almost a child herself" (128). But not only does Hetty dislike children, she dislikes all young things:

> Those tiresome children, Marty and Tommy and Totty, they had been the very nuisance of her life—as bad as buzzing insects that will come teasing you on a hot day when you want to be quiet. . . . They were worse than the

nasty little lambs that the shepherd was always bringing in to be taken special care of in lambing time; for the lambs were got rid of sooner or later. As for the young chicken and turkeys, Hetty would have hated the very word "hatching," if her aunt had not bribed her to attend to the young poultry by promising her the proceeds of one out of every brood. The round downy chicks peeping out from under their mother's wing never touched Hetty with any pleasure. (129–30)

In short, the positive reaction that others have to seeing Hetty's beauty as "like that of kittens, or very small downy ducks . . . or babies," a beauty that "seems made to turn the heads not only of men, but of all intelligent mammals, even of women," is not matched, much less heightened, in Hetty by her possession of such beauty (68). Rather, such capacity for response in Hetty is negated. Like a child, she can think of nothing but herself; like an animal, she cannot even know that self. Not only does Hetty dislike infants of all stripes, but she wishes they could all be "got rid of," which is, of course, what she will do with her own. Hetty likes to be looked at, not to look after.

Hetty ought not to court and revel in her visibility; the novel teaches this by cataloging the wages of that particular sin. Furthermore, Hetty, visible in a way particularly evocative of a sympathetic response in her viewers, ought not to withhold a sympathetic return of feeling from others; it is that lack of sympathetic connection to small things that tug on the heartstrings of mothers in particular that leads to Hetty's crime. The immodesty of Hetty's mode of receiving the gaze of others contrasts directly with Dinah's brand of unconcerned public display; Dinah's determination to see past visible surfaces to spiritual interiorities transforms her public displays into acts of modesty and morality. Hetty's love of display and admiration are not only immodest but also lead her into immorality.

The romance between Hetty and Arthur Donnithorne is likewise marked by a vocabulary of visibility. The visibility of Hetty's body is that which necessitates her concealment of it. Hetty becomes interested in Arthur first through the medium of her own visibility:

Hetty had become aware that Mr. Arthur Donnithorne would take a good deal of trouble for the chance of seeing her, that he always placed himself at church so as to have the fullest view of her both sitting and standing. . . . [His] bright, soft glances had penetrated her, and suffused her life with strange, happy languor. . . . They had found a medium in Hetty's little silly imagination. (82–83)

It is Hetty's visibility that prompts Arthur's "penetration" of her, her own visibility that plants a seed of love for Arthur in her mind. Throughout, theirs is a courtship of the eyes; Arthur's glances seduce Hetty and Hetty's tears break down his resolve to give her up.[10] But there is a sense in which, much as Hetty becomes interested in Arthur because she notices that Arthur likes to look at her, Hetty's love for Arthur is a love for her own beauty, her own visibility. "The vainest woman," the narrator informs us, "is never thoroughly conscious of her own beauty till she is loved by the man who sets her own passion vibrating in return" (126). If the "poison" of Heathcliff's classlessness seems to infect those around him in *Wuthering Heights,* the "poison" of Hetty's working-class beauty in *Adam Bede* circulates similarly. Though Adam accuses Arthur of "mayhap poison[ing] her life," there is an implication that the root of the poison lies in Hetty herself (254). Though Mrs. Irwine declares that "nature never makes a ferret in the shape of a mastiff" and "You'll never persuade me that I can't tell what men are by their outsides," much of the novel that follows persuades the reader of the opposite (53). Hetty's "outsides" bespeak purity and soulful connection. Her interiority is at best selfish and thoughtless, and at worst empty. The narrator compares Hetty to water-nixies: "lovely things without souls" (211). Eyes may be the windows to the soul, but Hetty seems to use her own windows and those of others merely for their reflective attributes. Although Adam declares that "things don't lie level between Hetty and [Arthur]" because Arthur is "acting with [his] eyes open," these very open eyes are what make Arthur susceptible to the deception of Hetty's outside (261).

It is the contrast between this emptiness and a growing "fullness" that creates the central dilemma in the novel: Hetty cannot know her own pregnancy and, thus, cannot act in any way other than one that leads her to the inevitable decision that her infant must be "got rid of." Hetty's very unknowing, however, is one of the major points of access for the reader's knowledge of her pregnancy. The narrative emphasis on Hetty's formless internal dread as well as the emphatic employment of euphemism throughout the novel, but particularly during the lead-up to and course of Hetty's pregnancy, reveal her immodest and immoral body to the reader more clearly than to those around her or to herself.

---

10. See "Arthur ... was stooping towards Hetty with a look of coaxing entreaty. Hetty lifted her long dewy lashes, and met the eyes that were bent toward her with a sweet, timid, beseeching look. What a space of time those three moments were, while their eyes met and his arms touched her! Love is such a simple thing when we have only one-and-twenty summers and a sweet girl of seventeen trembles under our glance, as if she were a bud first opening.... While Arthur gazed into Hetty's dark beseeching eyes ..." (110).

There is dissonance between our knowledge that Hetty—living and working on a farm with Mrs. Poysner, the mother of three young children—must be aware of the "facts of life" and their markers on the body and our perception that Hetty seems to have very little conscious sense of her own pregnancy until its eighth month. Narrative sympathy doesn't reach Hetty in this lack of self-knowledge, but I think many readers will find the somatic plot familiar: An unprepared teenager does not allow herself to realize the full scale of her situation, hides her body from even herself in the baggiest clothing she can find, and moves inexorably toward a foreseeable bodily event that she refuses to foresee. A relationship between this plot and infanticide is sketched not only onto the Victorian novel but also onto contemporary American culture, where women who commit neonaticide tend to be young, unmarried, unsupported by their child's father, isolated from family and friends, and "exceedingly passive . . . [responding] to pregnancy with a combination of denial, wishful fantasy, and terror" (Oberman 710). Hetty's unknowing expresses both this familiar plot and the limitations of Victorian novelistic plotting: The novel works in a social context in which Hetty's knowledge of animal and human reproduction cannot be communicated by the text, and the text is, necessarily, the medium through which Hetty's consciousness—emptied out—is communicated.

Hetty's lack of self-knowledge and reproductive knowledge seems to stem partly, like Ruth's, from her lack of a mother.[11] Hetty's sense of her pregnancy is unmoored from a reproductive community in the novel. Though there are many mothers who figure prominently in *Adam Bede*, Hetty is the only reproductively active woman. The only textual community for Hetty is Vixen, the woman-hating Bartle Massey's dog, whose conscience, he says, has "all run to milk" (223).[12] Vixen, of course, has no conscience, and this is the point. Vixen has animal maternal instinct, and as Jill Matus demonstrates in *Unstable Bodies: Victorian Representations of Sexuality and Maternity* (1995), Hetty's social and moral instability are marked by her frequent association with the animal world. Unlike Vixen, however, Hetty cannot resort to instinct alone, and unlike the admirable humans of the novel (Dinah, Adam, Seth), she cannot replace the loss of an instinctually driven existence with the insight (literally,

---

11. Of course, absent mothers are hardly the exclusive territory of the fallen-woman plot in Victorian literature, as hidden mothers in early photographic portraiture attest (see Bathurst) and as, for example, Marianne Hirsch has explored at greater length in *The Mother/Daughter Plot*.

12. As Jules Law notes, "Alicia Carroll has persuasively argued that the act of infanticide at the center of *Adam Bede* (1859) is insinuated by the novel to be the result of excessive and disordering bodily energies associated with human lactation" (86). See Carroll.

here, "in-sight") that "within the body . . . there is an other" (Kristeva 237 qtd. in Matus 3).

Hetty's dual lack of instinct and insight propel her through eight months of seeming denial about her pregnancy. Hetty is about four months pregnant when Adam proposes. Hetty and Arthur likely consummate their relationship sometime in the month following his coming-of-age ball, a month that the narrative of the novel skips over. We know that Adam proposes three months after discovering Hetty and Arthur together (he thinks back to "the shock of three months ago") (304). Adam proposes in November; the narrative skips over December and January and picks up again in late February. Adam and Hetty intend to be married in March, when she would be almost or fully nine months pregnant.

Hetty never comes to any distinct awareness of her pregnancy. By the time she runs away from the Poysners' home and from her impending marriage to Adam, she is consumed by fear and the sense of a secret that cannot continue to be hidden. But even an awareness of the untenable nature of her situation is figured in an imprecise vocabulary of invisibility:

> After the first oncoming of her great dread, some weeks after her betrothal to Adam, she had waited and waited, in the blind vague hope that something would happen to set her free from her terror, but she could wait no longer. All the force of her nature had been concentrated on the one effort of concealment. (310)

Hetty's "great dread" and "terror" are obviously at least partially embodied—not "vague" at all, but specific and physical facts. Yet Hetty is "blind" to these facts and exerts her energy on keeping those around her blind as well; this is a strategy that extends to the text. The narrator, in exploring Hetty's consciousness, cannot tell what Hetty will not know, and the reader struggles to sympathize with what is not told.

Reading somatically, Hetty's "great dread" suggests fetal quickening to me. By this point, the reader may have diagnosed, consciously, what Hetty can only experience unconsciously or vaguely as the "dread" and "terror" of repressed bodily knowledge. Indeed, the very lack of specificity emphasizes the unspeakability of Hetty's situation. Hetty's "great dread" is certainly an embodied one. Occurring "some weeks after her betrothal," Hetty comes to this dread in the fourth month of her pregnancy or early in the fifth. But Hetty does not announce this quickening and the pregnancy remains unspoken and unseen. Because her only way of knowing herself is through the gaze of others, Hetty herself cannot know this pregnancy as pregnancy.

But because most twenty-first-century adult readers understand these embodied likelihoods (that a woman who is five months pregnant and experiencing fetal movement will most likely give birth to a child—the chance of miscarriage diminishes after the first trimester has passed), we understand also that in the months that follow the "oncoming of her great dread," more is happening than mere terror and hope. Marked changes in Hetty's body are occurring. Her belly and breasts are almost certainly growing in ways that make the "concealment" on which she focuses all of her energy a physical one, though it is a mental one too. Hetty must conceal both her growing body and her growing dread from those around her. The text must likewise conceal Hetty's swollen body.

Hetty's dread and terror, in their physical, specific embodiment, are potentially visible. This furthers the vocabulary of seeing and the gaze. Hetty knows that she must run away, "she must hide herself where no familiar eyes could detect her." Hetty knows, in other words, that she must escape the diagnosing view of those she knows (310). She cannot escape the reader, however, and it is on her journey from Hayslope to Windsor that the fact of her pregnant body becomes inescapable for both Hetty and for our understanding.

That the almost-full-term Hetty would find her journey on foot from Hayslope to Windsor more fatiguing than she had expected is unsurprising. If we pause for a moment to consider what we know about the bodies of women who are almost nine months pregnant and consider Hetty's journey and experiences in that context, we are likely to realize that walking is difficult for her. Whether the "men stared at her as she went along the street" because she was an unaccompanied young woman or because she was visibly struggling to move her weight forward (a feeling I remember distinctly), the narration here seems to run just above the image of a hypervisible pregnant body being diagnosed by those Hetty encounters (318). This recalls a similar shift in the visibility of Ruth's pregnancy when she moves from one setting in which there are no words for her condition to another in which those who meet her have an available framework for understanding her pregnancy. Certainly, as the narrator informs us, "the stranger's eye detects what the familiar unsuspecting eye leaves unnoticed," but if Hetty's "figure" makes it "plain enough what sort of business hers is" to all who see her body, it is difficult to imagine how her own dread could have been so very vague and how the sharp eyes of Mrs. Poysner could have overlooked the evidence that Hetty is "pretty well knocked-up" in multiple senses of the colloquialism (319, 320).

Certainly, many readers of *Adam Bede* will have been aware of Hetty's pregnancy long before the "eyes of strangers" detect it. Hints about Hetty's reproductive fate reach us even before she and Arthur consummate their affair. Before Hetty or anyone else could possibly know that she is pregnant, Arthur mistakenly promises Adam that he won't cause her "trouble." When he is about to send her the letter calling things off, Arthur has a "dread lest [Hetty] should do something violent in her grief; and close upon that dread came another, which deepened the shadow" (268). This unnamed dread, of course, is most likely to refer to an appropriate fear that he has impregnated Hetty. "Shadow" is an apt description; Hetty's pregnancy operates in a dark room in which all things lack specificity:

> There was a dim undefined fear that the future might shape itself in some way quite unlike her dream. . . . But the uncertainty of the future, the possibilities to which she could give no shape, began to press upon her like the invisible weight of air; she was alone on her little island of dreams, and all around her was the dark unknown water where Arthur was gone. (271)

The language here is of limited visibility ("dim" and "dark"), lack of specificity ("undefined" and "uncertainty"), and the menacing threat of growing embodiment ("shape" twice and "weight"). Though Hetty's mind shares these qualities—"she had no conception"—the very emphasis on her limited knowledge is ironic (what she has is exactly a "conception") and draws emphasis to that which it refuses to know and name (270). The narrator knows what the text does not directly say and invites the reader into a diagnosis of that knowledge while Hetty remains excluded, "alone" in a pregnancy she cannot fully know. We come closer to joining her in the unknowing by reading somatically, alive to the possibilities of pregnant bodies—the possibilities of Hetty's interiority—without access to any certainty about Hetty's pregnancy in particular. Not only is access to certainty about Hetty's pregnant body largely impossible, but access to certainty about pregnant bodies in general is a receding horizon. Bodies can experience twinges and aches, swellings and expansions whether or not they are pregnant. They exist beyond the language we use to try to pin them down, which is part of what makes it possible for scared and isolated teenage girls to avoid confrontation with the fact of pregnancy. But for pregnant people who desire facts and live in a historical moment where they can sometimes access them, they nonetheless remain elusive: the "two-week wait" between ovulation and the point at which a pregnancy test can register very early pregnancy, the dating of gestational age and related questions about whether a heartbeat has yet to appear or has failed to appear, the uncertainty of early kicks or a gassy stomach, the uncertainty of terrible stillness where there were kicks, the difference between false and true labor, the inability to plan for when a baby will arrive or what will happen when she does. Having lived in all of these uncertainties, I resist reading Hetty's somatic unknowing as only or primarily a marker of the limitations of her character.

Hetty's changing pregnant body is described in terms of frustrated mental process, the "press" of her fears on the mind charting the increase in her body, the change in her shape. That the language of reproductive euphemism peppers these chapters with "pregnant hint[s]," mentions of "actual condition[s]," and "vessel[s]" fuels our growing awareness of Hetty's pregnancy while her inability to understand herself limits our ability to establish an affinitive sympathy with her (287, 289). Moreover, Adam's affinitive sympathy proves incapable of apprehending the truth of her. Though he notices that "there was a change . . . something different in her eyes, in the expression of her face, in all her movements" and a "more luxuriant womanliness about Hetty of late," he fails to notice the significance of these changes (300, 305). Sympathy that relies on a positive affective relationship with Hetty fails to reach her in this novel. While diagnostic access makes it possible to read her pregnancy (and the infanticide she commits, though that falls beyond the scope of my analysis in this chapter), it fails to offer generous access to that condition as a deeply uncertain and unwanted experience of the body during which Hetty has no support and few options.

Fostering space for uncertainty over authority is particularly important in scholarship on texts that demand we read alongside classism, sexism, and racism, for example, in order to access meaning. Fostering space for uncertainty is also particularly important to the twenty-first-century reproductive imagination because access to "strong" data (rapid pregnancy tests, ultrasounds, genetic screenings, etc.) seems to offer "real" authority that remains a receding horizon. Pregnancy is always an encounter with the unknown and unknowable. In chapter 3, I think more about diagnosis as a narrative mode for managing uncertainty, and chapter 3, chapter 4, and the conclusion to this book work more carefully through narrative plays at authority over ambivalent and unwanted pregnancies in mid- to late Victorian fiction and twenty-first-century American culture. But first, I offer a short interlude that considers sensation as a kind of amendment—though hardly a corrective—to the ethical limitations of sympathy in reading pregnancy. This interlude opens onto questions about the ethical obligation to consider the role sensation plays in positioning pregnancy narratives—even pregnancy narratives in which race remains invisible—as expressions of racialized feminine danger and violence.

AN INTERLUDE

Sensation

The intersection of visuality, sympathy, and revelation calls up no Victorian genre more directly than the Sensation fiction associated with the 1860s. This famously visual genre plays with the relationship between gender, concealment, and revelation that is baked into the sympathetic settings of many Victorian novels and of Victorian depictions of pregnancy in particular. And thinking about the readerly body and Victorian fiction demands a grappling with Sensation and sensation. The genre was seen as a notably feminine one, immodestly willing to articulate or almost articulate things about the body and sexuality best left unsaid. It fixates on miscarried maternity as a central theme and what Audrey Jaffe has called "bodily sympathy" (96 *Scenes*). That bodily sympathy is a face of somatic sensation, the feelings registered by the body in response not only to the physical senses but also to the images, ideas, and stories we encounter. The significance of the texts we read inheres partly in the responses of our bodies to those texts, and the responses of our bodies are shaped by the embodied lives we lead in our own place and time.

Cultural theorists of "afterlives," notably Saidiya Hartman, whose work explores the afterlife of slavery, have demonstrated the knotty ways histories—particularly histories of violence—endure in bodies and cultural texts. In the recent "Black Feminist Theories of Motherhood and Generation: Histories of Black Infant and Child Loss in the United States," LaKisha Michelle Simmons contributes to the scholarly conversation on maternal bodies as sites on which these afterlives are written. Simmons reaches beyond the "statistics [that] reveal . . . Black infants in the United States have at least twice as high a rate of infant mortality as white infants" toward "narratives [of infant loss and miscarriage] that help contextualize the numbers and make Black maternal pain visible" (311, 312). The afterlives of the Victorian maternal moralization I have explored thus far in this book are not explicitly marked by the distinct, systemic violence of the transatlantic slave trade and slavery in the Americas. But Victorian maternal moralization itself was shaped by that violence; the nineteenth-century shift toward an emphasis on women's roles as primarily spiritual and domestic, best expressed by the mother in the home raising good Christians to go out into the world as civilizing forces, reflects the needs of a global empire fueled by the slave trade, slavery, and the subjugation of Black and Brown people beyond the scope of the slave trade to and practice of slavery in the Americas. Furthermore, the afterlives of Victorian maternal moralization intersect with the afterlives of slavery in twentieth- and twenty-first-century narratives about and policies affecting Black mothers and families. These narratives and policies often "make Black maternal pain visible" in culture not as pain but as guilt.

This project began as a dissertation I wrote before I had myself been pregnant. During the years I revised that dissertation into this book, I was pregnant five times: One pregnancy ended in a third-trimester stillbirth, one in a first-trimester miscarriage, one in a live birth complicated by postpartum preeclampsia, one in another first-trimester miscarriage, and one in a relatively uncomplicated live birth following a closely monitored and medically mediated pregnancy. These experiences often felt to me like the echoes of my scholarship. In trying to navigate the line between "bad luck" and guilt, my research—always informed by contemporary cultures of and data on pregnancy and childbirth—became more entwined in National Institutes of Health reports on race and infant and maternal mortality, media coverage of miscarriage and stillbirth, and studies on gestational hypertension and generational trauma, for example. All of these research nodes pointed toward the ways racism fuels and mediates the data and narratives of maternal loss in which I caught reflections of my own experience, albeit as a white and economically privileged woman. The afterlives of slavery and Victorian maternal moralization both have shaped my readerly sensations by making clear how present anti–Black and Brown racism is in Victorian novelistic narratives of pregnancy that exclusively depict white women. Prior to the fin de siècle, representations of pregnancy in the Victorian novel do not articulate race or explicitly racialized contexts. In trying to catch a glimpse of these contexts and to do so without employing Black experience in the service of white women's stories, this interlude moves further away from the direct representations of pregnancy to which I limit my focus in the rest of this book and takes wilder, more gestural leaps across space and time.

In thinking through *East Lynne*—one of the three novels most responsible for kicking off the Sensation craze of the 1860s and, of those novels, the most concerned with pregnancy—I "unfasten the buttons" of literary scholarship to incorporate the somatic sensations of reading and the somatic sensations beyond reading that we draw into the practice of criticism (Dabashi 951). Arousal, pain, loss, and guilt plot a network of somatic suggestion, representation, and response: The throbbing, implicit sexual desire Lady Isabel feels for Levison, for example, connects to the explicit representation of her physical experiences of guilt; both these nodes connect to what a reader might know and feel about the body's ability to desire something from which the mind recoils and about the ache, the actual ache, of regret. This network plots its points from text to reader on the same plane, connecting present to past and to imaginary. "We have always been presentist" (to borrow a phrase from Emily Steinlight), and reading, even—perhaps especially—critical reading, is one of the sites at which our presentism functions palpably, alive in the body that responds, say, to both the office chair (perhaps produced in twenty-first-century America by prison labor) in which we sit and to *East Lynne*'s narrative command to "fall down upon [our] knees," while our knees bump up against a desk (Steinlight; Wood 283).[1] If the present is always with us in our reading bodies, then we should explicitly bring our bodies into our critical modes and questions. On the plane of bodily knowledge and bodily uncertainty, the story *East Lynne* tells about maternal loss and guilt is connected to my own experience by pregnancy loss. My own experiences of pregnancy loss are contemporary American experiences, connected to questions of race by damning statistics regarding Black infant and maternal mortality, which are connected to the stories the tabloids tell about, for example, Chrissy Teigen and Meghan Markle. These are pointedly weak rather than strong connections.

EAST LYNNE

Writing on *East Lynne,* Jaffe argues that rather than serving as an "erasure of representation," the bodily sympathy the reader of Sensation fiction feels is a "response to representation, affirming . . . the role of cultural representa-

---

1. "We have always been presentist" is taken from the title and "basic claim" of Emily Steinlight's piece for the 2016 V21 Forum on presentism in *Victorian Studies*.

tions . . . as mediators of sensation and its meaning" (*Scenes* 96). This interlude asks about the role of twenty-first-century cultural representations in the mediation of our somatic responses to Victorian literary representations and vice versa. I am not arguing that reading or sensation is or could ever be an "unmediated bodily response" but rather that the ways our bodily responses are mediated by culture should prompt us to read our own cultural contexts alongside Victorian novels (97). We should read somatically not because reading somatically offers access to authenticity or transcendence beyond text or judgment but because the ways somatic reading can speak to lived experience and the role of culture in mediating that experience help us to better understand not only that which is articulated differently but also that which is not articulated at all.

Sensation was a Victorian fiction of contemporary life in which the buttons of literary formality were unfastened. Sensation novels treat somatic topics like sexual attraction in comparatively frank terms in ways the Victorians understood as "reaching out to touch the reader's body" (P. Gilbert, *Disease* 4). Such transgressions of the private space of reading participated in a larger thematic of public/private transgression centered on feminine, domestic spaces. Lyn Pykett's foundational *The Nineteenth-Century Sensation Novel* frames the genre as a response to anxiety about punctured domestic sanctity in the wake of the Matrimonial Causes Act of 1857, which allowed many more people to access a divorce by pulling the "private affairs" of marriage "into [the] public spectacle" of civil proceedings (2).[2] When marriage is made public in a court of law, pregnancy is one of the private affairs that can be exposed.

Though it predates the Matrimonial Causes Act of 1857 by three decades, the Gardner Peerage Cause of 1825–26 (following the 1804–05 divorce proceedings of Captain—subsequently Lord—Alan Gardner and Maria Elizabeth Gardner, subsequently Jadis) reads like a Sensation novel. Records of the Cause offer a fascinating look at the ways courts of law concerned with the arbitration of marital fidelity approach the specificities of pregnant bodies and the significance of those specificities, particularly the specificities of chronology. The case dealt with the question of whether a child born within a marriage but assumed to be the result of adultery could inherit peerage and properties. In assessing the potential legitimacy of Henry Fenton Jadis/Gardner, the court heard detailed evidence from witnesses and medical experts regarding possible timelines for Jadis's conception and the conceivable duration of pregnancy

---

2. Prior to the Matrimonial Causes Act, divorce could be granted only by Parliament and was an incredibly expensive undertaking.

in general. As Isabel Davis notes in "The Experimental Conception Hospital: Dating Pregnancy and the Gothic Imagination," "nineteen medical witnesses [and six laywomen] were called to give evidence" on the medical and experiential facts of pregnancy as an embodied condition (778). Again and again, these witnesses were asked some version of the questions posed to Charles Mansfield Clark, an accoucheur:

> According to your Experience . . . what is the full Period of a Woman's Gestation, under Ordinary Circumstances? . . . In your Judgement, is it possible, that a Child born on the 8th of December, and which has lived, could have been the Result of any Sexual Intercourse subsequent to the 11th of July? . . . In your Judgement, could a Child, born on the 8th of December, and which lives, have been the Result of Sexual Intercourse anterior to the 30th of January? . . . Could it have been the Result of an Intercourse anterior to the 7th of February, being 43 Weeks and Four Days? . . . Supposing a Woman's Labour to be protracted, could that have made such a Difference as to have enabled the Child to be the Result of an Intercourse at the Dates given? . . . How long could a Labour be protracted without proving fatal to the Mother, or the Child, or both of them? (Gardner 2–3)

Questions at this level of detail proliferate in the questioning of Clark and the other witnesses called to give testimony on the bodily possibilities and impossibilities of pregnancy. These questions remind me of nothing so much as the sound of my own anxious mind looking for certainties during pregnancy. What is a due date, after all? Of course, medical science has now gathered data that gestures toward answers in the aggregate, but individual variation resists certainty.

This testimony proved less relevant to the verdict against Jadis than evidence—like that used against Effie Deans in *The Heart of Midlothian* (1818)—of Mrs. Gardner having concealed facts about the pregnancy. Again and again, nineteenth-century narratives of pregnancy rely on familiar structures of concealment and revelation. But part of the reason the medical evidence was insufficient for a verdict was because it, too, seemed, if not to conceal, then to confuse the facts of the case. Robert Lyall's 1826 commentary on the medical evidence bemoans its inconsistencies ("Medical Evidence"). Davis places the "science fiction fantasy" of a site for the study of conception in conversation with Bentham's panopticon and other period visions of access to scientific, objective clarity about the murky unknowns of people and their bodies (773). If only we could better see these bodies and the mysteries they contain, we could better know them scientifically, better judge them legally and publicly. And if we could only make these bodies spectacles, they could better offer us sensation, the tactile tickle of objectification.

Like the Gardner case, the plots of adultery, bigamy, madness, and murder so strongly associated with Sensation fiction predate the rise of a coherent market for (and concomitant public outcry regarding) the genre. The 1860s was a decade that saw not only rising divorce rates following the Matrimonial Causes Act but also a furor regarding infanticide, though the record doesn't seem to indicate any historical shifts in infanticide rates. Following the Matrimonial Causes Act, men could petition for comparatively affordable civil divorce on the grounds of a wife's infidelity alone, but women had to demonstrate not only that their husbands had been unfaithful but also that the adultery was "aggravated" by violence or additional crimes against morality like bigamy or incest. Women's adultery, then, became more publicly visible and more spectacular than men's just as a hue and cry about infanticide highlighted women's parental failures. Spectacular stories of misbehavior, especially the misbehavior of those in whom decorum is most valued, are pleasurable in the way conflict makes narrative pleasurable. When these stories of misbehavior incorporate an innocent victim, that pleasure meets horror at a sublime, sensational intersection.

East Lynne narrates the fall of Lady Isabel Vane. After Isabel is left penniless by the death of her libertine father, she marries the upwardly mobile lawyer, Archibald Carlyle, though not before she has fallen in love with the villainous Francis Levison, and Barbara Hare, the daughter of a domineering local justice, has fallen in love with Carlyle. Though Barbara resigns herself— with some difficulty—to Mr. Carlyle's marriage, she does not resign herself to her brother's responsibility for a murder he is generally assumed to have committed. For much of the novel, Richard Hare lives in hiding by assuming a working-class persona in the confusion of London. His fight to clear his name embroils Mr. Carlyle in secret assignations with Barbara that lead Isabel, particularly in moments of postpartum recovery, to assume an affair where there is none. She, in turn, runs off with the manipulative Captain Levison, is divorced by Carlyle and cut off from her three children from that marriage, bears Levison's child out of wedlock, almost dies in a train accident that kills the baby, and eventually decides to return to the Carlyle home—where Barbara has since been installed as mistress—as a governess, concealed by her disfigurement from the accident and an elaborate disguise. Isabel is driven to return by her longing for her children, but once she's back at East Lynne, she watches those children call another woman Mama while one, William, sinks toward death. After nursing her son through his final days, Isabel herself succumbs to an illness that kills her, though not before the dramatic revelation of her identity.

The novel insistently engages the reader in moral judgment of Isabel that is prompted by encouragement to imagine the emotions and physical sensations of guilt, shame, and regret that one would experience if one made the mistakes Isabel does. This is particularly marked in a direct address to the reader following Isabel's flight from her husband:

> Oh, reader, believe me! Lady—wife—mother! Should *you* ever be tempted to abandon *your* home, so will *you* awake. Whatever trials may be the lot of *your* married life, though they may magnify themselves to *your* crushed spirit as beyond the endurance of woman to bear, resolve to bear them; fall down upon *your* knees and pray to be enabled to bear them: pray for patience; pray for strength to resist the demon that would urge *you* so to good conscience; for be assured that the alternative, if *you* rush on to it, will be found far worse than death. (283; emphasis added)

The text here "reach[es] out" to the reader, reaches out "to touch the reader's body" (P. Gilbert, *Disease* 4). Not only does the text speak directly to the (assumed female) reader, the "lady—wife—mother" in the opening line, but it speaks directly to "you" (or "your") eight times in a four-sentence passage. This "you" is you, reader; it is me. And the knees we "fall down upon" are at least evocative of our actual knees. The "crush[ing]," "rush[ing]" language works on the idea of our own bodies; the repetition of "bear" emphasizes the weight we sit with as we read and the weight of what we soon realize to be Isabel's heavily pregnant body in this particular scene.

In *Violent Women and Sensation Fiction*, Andrew Mangham is centrally concerned with "the period's conflicting ideas on progress and degeneration" and "how the author used representations of female violence as a vehicle for expressing undecided or ambivalent views" about self-advancement (129). But I want to home in not on Mangham's explorations of social class and mobility but on the specter of infanticide that he reads in the novel. As he notes, "Isabel's progress through the narrative leaves a trail of dead children" (131).

East Lynne is a novel about child loss and maternal guilt. Scholarship on the novel has emphasized the sublimation of maternity and sexuality into suffering in the novel, though there is less work on the particular role of reproductive anxiety and child death.[3] Though the deaths of babies and children

---

3. For more on the sublimation of maternity and sexuality into suffering, see "Isabel's Spectacles" in Jaffe, *Scenes*.

occur in the novel at a remove from the reproductive body, the threats of pregnancy loss and infant or maternal death during childbirth recur, and the theme of lost children exceeds loss through death; Mrs. Hare's loss of access to her son Richard drives the first half of the novel toward its climax, and Isabel Carlyle's loss of access to her children drives the novel's second half. As these twin plots near their close, Barbara Carlyle—still in postpartum recovery—asks Isabel (as Madame Vine, the governess) to hold Barbara's newborn so that she can get up:

> "I might have half smothered it, had I attempted before," continued Barbara, still laughing. "I have been here long enough, and am quite rested. Talking about smothering children, what accounts we have in the registrar-general's weekly returns of health. So many children 'overlaid in bed;' so many and often there are as many as eight and ten. Mr. Carlyle says he knows they are smothered on purpose." (Wood 595)

Here, Barbara places her own maternal choices (not to attempt to stand up while holding her baby because to do so would risk "smother[ing]" it) in direct contact with "so many" accounts of children "overlaid in bed," a term that covers accidental deaths we might now call Sudden Infant Death Syndrome (SIDS) and "purpose[ful]" deaths. In handing her baby to Isabel—a convenience available because Barbara lives in a home with domestic staff—she is taking care not to become a murderer by negotiating the relationship of her body to the body of her child.

Certainly, dangerous women and the particular threat of dangerous wives and mothers is standard fare in both Sensation fiction and scholarship on the genre. Mangham, for example, reads this same "overlaid in bed" passage (137). And a perceived relationship between infant death and maternal misbehavior is well-worn territory. So is a perceived relationship between fetal death and maternal misbehavior. Consider the "mis-" ("wrongly") in "miscarriage." An assumption that fetal or infant death often results from maternal action or inaction is not a Victorian perspective we've set aside in twenty-first-century America, as the 2015 conclusions on a US survey of ideas about miscarriage demonstrate:

> Respondents to [the] survey erroneously believed that miscarriage is a rare complication of pregnancy, with the majority believing that it occurred in 5% or less of all pregnancies. There were also widespread misconceptions about causes of miscarriage. Those who had experienced a miscarriage frequently felt guilty, isolated, and alone. (Bardos et al. 1313)

A contemporary misunderstanding of miscarriage as "rare" (rather than affecting "5% or less of all pregnancies," as the survey respondents believed, "about 10 to 20 percent of known pregnancies end in miscarriage [though] the actual number is likely higher" ["Miscarriage"]) combined with "widespread misconceptions about the causes of miscarriage" (Bardos et al. 1313) that place outsized responsibility for miscarriage on "lifting heavy objects," "having had a sexually transmitted disease in the past," or "past abortion," for example, almost certainly contribute to 47 percent of women who experienced miscarriage reporting that their miscarriage made them feel guilty (1316, 1317 fig. 1., 1317). Most miscarriages are the result of chromosomal abnormalities over which pregnant people have no control ("Miscarriage").

As historians of American miscarriage Shannon Withycombe and Lara Freidenfelds remind us, miscarriage has not always been and does not necessarily now need to be an occasion for guilt, even in the case of a wanted pregnancy.[4] In Withycombe's research for her important *Lost: Miscarriage in Nineteenth-Century America*, she "found individual women who described the experience [of miscarriage] openly, without reference to shame or failure, and some who even expressed outright joy at the event" (4). And in Withycombe's interview with Lara Freidenfelds on the publication of her 2020 *The Myth of the Perfect Pregnancy: A History of Miscarriage in America*, Freidenfelds expresses an interest in historical attitudes toward miscarriage that leave more room for something like her own emotional experience: "Wait a minute, maybe I don't have to mourn this pregnancy, maybe I shouldn't have been encouraged to get so attached to it in the first place" (Withycombe, "How"). Both historians' work helps us to think through the varied emotional responses to pregnancy loss, particularly losses that occur very early in pregnancy. Perhaps a wide range of affective responses to pregnancy loss is easier to glimpse in historical contexts in which reproductive planning was uncommon and difficult; early miscarriage was often indistinguishable from a late, heavy period; fetal, infant, and maternal mortality was much more common; in short, death was more easily integrated into the ways people thought about giving life. Freidenfelds explores "how a diverse array of social, medical, and technological innovations came together to reshape pregnancy and thereby create a new experience of miscarriage" as a failure rather than as one of many pieces of evidence that life is uncertain (6).

Though we have—at present—no answering book-length history of Victorian miscarriage, recent articles such as Felicity Jensz's "Miscarriage and Coping

---

4. Withycombe also cites the 2015 study on perceptions of miscarriage in "Happy Miscarriages."

in the Mid-Nineteenth Century: Private Notes from Distant Places" indicate an answering interest in the topic, motivated, as were Withycombe's and Freidenfelds's books, by the author's "own history of . . . miscarriage" (270).[5] Indeed, a lot of contemporary scholarship on embodied aspects of maternity is explicitly motivated by personal experience because personal experience shapes how and what we know and ask about the body. I suspect that my own difficult pregnancies and pregnancy losses make me more sensitive than I might otherwise be to the ambient anxiety about the welfare of pregnant characters in *East Lynne*, for example—and more aware of the way this anxiety is more marked in *East Lynne* than in most Victorian fiction. *East Lynne* is a novel about child loss in which the possibility of pregnancy loss thrums.

Victorian literary logic for the revelation of the pregnant body responds to maternal misbehavior, but Isabel is always already exposed. *East Lynne* reads like the British great-grandmother of punishing expectations for contemporary young female celebrities that Sarah Banet-Wieser calls an "economy of visibility" (ix). The hypervisuality of the narration of Isabel anticipates her fall almost as directly as the explicit warnings to the reader about what she will become while narrating her youthful innocence and purity. Her first pregnancy is articulated directly in a conversation regarding her ill health and the advisability of carriage rides ("I shall be better when baby is born") (170). But "when baby is born," Isabel "l[ies] between life and death" and Mr. Wainwright, who's attending her, suggests that Mr. Carlyle should send for the clergyman, which causes Carlyle to fear for his wife's life (171). Wainwright clarifies that it's "for the child. Should it not live, it may be satisfactory to you and Lady Isabel to know that it was baptised" (173). It is during her slow postpartum recovery that the jealousy of Barbara Hare that eventually prompts Isabel to leave her husband—the cause of her guilt—takes root. This jealousy, which rears its head again after the birth of her third child, takes on the texture of what the Victorians called puerperal insanity ("diverse forms of mental illness associated with childbirth") and that we might now term postpartum depression, anxiety, or even psychosis (Marland 3). In both Victorian and contemporary contexts, these conditions are considered dangerous to the well-being of mother and child alike. So, Isabel's reproductive body is attended by the threat of death and the germs of her guilt for the loss of her children.

After the birth of this first child, two more children are born in her marriage to Carlyle. Isabel is twelve months postpartum with the youngest when she is sent away to recover from "an illness" with which she had been

---

5. There is work on miscarriage in the British context, though it doesn't tend to focus on the Victorian period. See R. Woods; Evans and Read; Oren-Magidor; Donaghy.

"attacked" a "month or two" before (196). During this time abroad, she is reintroduced to Levison. He plays on the circumstances of Barbara's conferences with Carlyle regarding her brother to intensify Isabel's jealousy, which by this point is figured in the sensational language of bodily compulsion.

Isabel's fourth pregnancy is also attended by narrative visibility, danger, and bodily compulsion. The novel draws on the reader's sense of the inescapability of pregnant chronologies (like those the Gardner Peerage case worked to pin down) to communicate Isabel's urgency regarding a divorce from Carlyle that will allow her to marry Levison in time for her child to be born legitimate. This chapter, "Charming Results," emphasizes chronology and plays on the vocabulary of time throughout, opening "nearly a year went by," repeating "nearly a year went by; save some six or eight weeks," and hinging on the arrival of divorce news "before the birth of her child" in the arrival of the *Times* (282, 284, 285). Indeed, "time" appears in this chapter eighteen times, with particular insistence when its role as a euphemism for pregnancy is most marked:

> "Were you to go to England, you might not be back in *time*."
> "In *time* for what?"
> "Oh, how can you ask?" she rejoined, in a sharp tone of reproach; "you know too well. In *time* to make me your wife when the divorce shall appear."
> (287; emphasis added)

Though Levison plays dumb ("In time for what?"), he knows only "too well" that "in time" means in time for the birth of the child; it would be hard not to. The broad outlines of this chronology are sketched for the reader by that repetition of "nearly a year went by" with the addition of "save some six or eight weeks," and the specifics of this chronology are finally pinned down by Levison himself: "There's a month yet," he tells Isabel (288). But the "broad" outlines of the embodied necessity Isabel insists upon in this chapter wouldn't be likely to demand articulation. Levison sits across from a woman who is seven or eight months pregnant with her fourth child. *East Lynne* encourages a visual, sensory engagement with its events; it is hard to imagine a visual representation of this scene that doesn't include the notable presence of a large belly, at the very least. When I was pregnant, my hands often moved to my belly when I spoke about it; I imagine each repetition of "time" accompanied by such a movement as I read.

If the repetition of "time" works in *East Lynne* to summon a sense of the embodied chronology of pregnancy, the repetition of "bear" to describe Isabel's state summons an embodied sense of the loss of her children. Looking again at the address to reader in "Charming Results," we see dense reference to "bear" as an emotional state always about to slip into a somatic one:

> Whatever trials may be the lot of your married life, though they may magnify themselves to your crushed spirit as beyond the nature, the endurance of woman to *bear*, resolve to *bear* them; fall down upon your knees, and pray to be enabled to *bear* them—pray for patience—pray for strength to resist the demon that would tempt you to escape; *bear* unto death, rather than forfeit your fair name and your good conscience; for be assured that the alternative, if you do rush on to it, will be found worse than death. (283; emphasis added)

Though this passage speaks to the reader's "spirit," "fair name," and "good conscience," it does so in the "crush[ing]" physical language not only of "falling down upon your knees" but of "endurance," ability ("enabled"), "strength," and "death." Better to "bear [trials] unto death" than to bear the wages of sin. Though, of course, women often bear both, as well as literally bearing death in miscarriages and stillbirths.

Isabel bears the wages of sin not only as Eve, who "[brought] forth children [in sorrow]," but also beyond the bringing forth of children (Genesis 3:16). Isabel bears the wages of sin in traumatic repetitions and intensifications of what she must "bear." *East Lynne* employs this term at least forty-seven times.[6] Though thirty-two of those instances occur *after* the conclusion of Isabel's reproductive career, they often retain an embodied maternal valence. This is particularly marked as Isabel decides to return to East Lynne in disguise:

> How should she *bear* to see Mr. Carlyle the husband of another—to live in the same house with them, to witness his attentions, possibly his caresses? It might be difficult; but she could force and school her heart to endurance. Had she not resolved, in her first bitter repentance, to take up her cross daily, and *bear* it? No, her own feelings, let them be wrung as they would, should not prove the obstacle.
>
> Evening came, and she had not decided. She passed another night of pain, of restlessness, of longing for her children; this intense longing appeared to be overmastering all her powers of mind and body. The tempta-

---

6. This figure does not include the past-tense "bore," which is more often used in *East Lynne* to describe male characters than female, as though the physical immediacy of "bear" is heightened for Isabel. Of course, it is not only Isabel who "bears" in East Lynne, but it is disproportionately so. It's worth noting that another character around whom this vocabulary clusters is Afy Hallijohn, also a "fallen" woman.

tion at length proved too strong; the project having been placed before her covetous eyes could not be relinquished, and she finally consented to go. . . .
"I could *bear* that as I must *bear* the rest and I can shrink under the hedge and lay myself down to die. Humiliation for me? No; I will not put that in comparison with seeing and being with my children." (398; emphasis added)

The text's questions about what Isabel can bear first center on her ability to be in physical proximity not only to her former husband but also to the marital "caresses" she might witness between him and his new wife (she does end up witnessing such a scene, which replays a similar scene of love and distance with her role in the triad shifted). In considering her "endurance," the narrator imagines her "feelings" as sensations that can be "wrung," a physical act of squeezing and twisting. The physicality of the first paragraph intensifies as attention shifts from the former husband to the children in the second paragraph. Isabel passes a "night of pain," with "intense longing" that "overmaster[s] . . . mind and body." Certainly, the use of physical language to describe ideas and feelings is common and doesn't necessarily signal some significant play on the somatic, not to mention the reproductive. But *East Lynne* identifies the slippage between mind and body directly, and it identifies this slippage as happening at the site of a maternity defined by loss, guilt ("bitter repentance"), and the ever-present threat of death ("I can shrink under the hedge and lay myself down to die").

"SPECTACULARLY AND DANGEROUSLY VISIBLE"

Scholarship on *East Lynne* has often seen maternity as a key site of the novel's play with theatricality, its emphasis on literal and figurative spectacle and performance.[7] My interest here in maternity as a site of the novel's thematics of guilt and loss and the particular significance that holds for cultures of pregnancy in the Victorian novel and beyond builds—albeit loosely—on the scholarship of the theatrical in *East Lynne* by pulling the Victorian legacy of guilt, loss, and pregnancy into conversation with twenty-first-century cultures of celebrity. The pregnant body is an accessory to contemporary celebrity, and like so many of the visible, embodied accessories to celebrity associated with women, it is both demanded and also a source of judgment in the court of public opinion. These tendencies are heightened in cases of pregnancy loss and particularly pointed with maternal bodies of color.

---

7. See Jaffe, *Scenes*; Kucich; Litvak.

Pregnancy loss has shifted into public discourse in the last decade in ways that some hope can ease the feelings of guilt Bardos et al. found to be so strongly associated with the experience. However, the cultural visibility of pregnancy loss, especially early miscarriage, intersects with anti-choice priorities in ways that encourage the criminalization of women who miscarry or experience stillbirth. Women of color are particularly vulnerable to the loss of abortion rights and were already particularly vulnerable to legal punishment for pregnancy loss. For example, in the fall of 2021, the *New York Times* covered the conviction of Britany Poolaw for manslaughter following an accidental miscarriage at seventeen weeks (Goldberg). In 2019 Marshae Jones was charged with manslaughter after her five-month fetus died from a shot to Jones's stomach fired by another person (Mervosh). Such cases occur with disturbing regularity in America, and Black women are disproportionately represented (Paltrow and Flavin 310). We inherit and perpetuate cultures of pregnancy and maternity in which loss is implicit evidence of guilt, and the stakes of this tendency are heightened in post-Roe contexts. The association between loss and guilt was writ with particular clarity in Victorian Sensation fiction because of the genre's employment of spectacle; as Jennifer C. Nash argues in *Birthing Black Mothers,* "Black mothers in the United States have become spectacularly and dangerously visible through the frame of crisis" (4). In contemporary America, the association of guilt with pregnancy and maternal loss is writ with particular clarity on the spectacularized bodies of Black women and women of color more generally.

One way to read these patterns is in the explicit spectacle of celebrity. In 2020 both Chrissy Teigen and Meghan Markle, Duchess of Sussex—whose earlier "baby bumps" had been compulsively tracked by fans and paparazzi—faced social media backlash for sharing about their pregnancy losses. In September, Teigen delivered a stillborn son, Jack, at twenty weeks' gestation. She posted to Instagram and Twitter about the loss alongside intimate photos from the delivery room. The comments sections on these platforms became opportunities not only to offer condolences but also to shame Teigen generally ("What goes around comes around!" and "Gotta love when bad things happen to bad people"), to castigate Teigen for her support of abortion rights ("The woman supporting abortions to the fullest and shaming those who don't"), and to censure her decision to post the images, in particular ("Who takes a pic like this? I'm so sorry for your loss, but this is inappropriate") (Teigen, Photo). Teigen was judged guilty because of who she already was when she lost her son, because her support for abortion rights was understood as negating her pain upon the loss of a wanted pregnancy, and because—in the most recurring refrain—her decision to share images from the delivery room was an "inappropriate" grab at attention. More than that, many commenters expressed conviction or shared evidence to corroborate the theory that Teigen's stillbirth was fake and these photos were performance rather than true suffering ("I read this is [sic] a staged photo shoot for your fake miscarriage that was a result of your fake pregnancy to garner sympathy?"). Teigen is guilty from multiple angles, then: guilty for the stillbirth because she is a bad woman who deserves to have bad things happen to her, guilty for expressing grief about the stillbirth because that expression showed too much, and guilty of plotting a fake stillbirth to create a sympathetic spectacle (and, as she noted in a widely reported talk at a September 2022 Propper Daley summit after the Supreme Court ruling that nullified *Roe v. Wade* and *Dobbs*, guilty also of abortion, which is the medical procedure she underwent). Another example of conspiracy theories regarding a "fake" celebrity pregnancy is the 2011 uproar about Beyoncé's "deflating bump," covered by relatively reputable news outlets ("Beyonce's"). The guilt assigned to celebrities for performing the reproductive body is notably assigned to celebrities of color.

In an October 2020 post to *Medium* about her stillbirth and the social media reaction, Teigen wrote about refusing to feel guilty for the negative sensations experienced by some of those who saw the posts ("I cannot express how little I care that you hate the photos"), but she wrote also about feeling guilty, not for the stillbirth, necessarily, but for the publicity of her joy and grief:

> I feel bad our grief was so public because I made the joy so public. I was excited to share our news with the world. Stories leading up to this had been chronicled for all. It's hard to look at them now. I was so positive it would be okay. I feel bad that I made you all feel bad. I always will. ("Hi")

"Public" appears twice in Teigen's opening sentence and "I feel bad" appears twice in the paragraph. For Teigen, the sensation of guilt is a "bad" feeling of visibility that elicited bad feelings in her audience, the same audience eager for photos of women's bodies that make them feel good or that prompt pleasurable judgments with no demand for sympathy.

Sympathy is the explicit topic of an op-ed Meghan Markle published in the *New York Times* that November. In "The Losses We Share," Markle—whose royal role bridges a British-past/American-present divide similar to the one I'm imagining in this interlude—writes about a miscarriage she experienced the previous year. In Markle's piece, this experience and the experience of being asked whether she was okay are gateways into thinking more generously about the suffering of others. For example, Markle thinks about the suffering of those who lost family members to COVID and the suffering of Breonna Taylor and George Floyd, who lost their lives to police violence. Markle doesn't articulate explicitly that she is writing about her miscarriage as a Black or mixed-race woman, but she places that miscarriage in direct conversation with the vulnerability of Black bodies to racism. Black women in America are significantly more likely to experience miscarriage, stillbirth, and maternal death than their white counterparts (Pruitt; Petersen et al.). This data as well as the role of the Black mother, to whom George Floyd called out during his murder, contribute to Nash's sense of Black mothers having "become spectacularly and dangerously visible." And that visibility is the cudgel used in comments on the op-ed to suggest that Markle is somehow guilty for her loss:

> It is the exhibitionism of this piece that bugs me endlessly, and I have a very hard time conciliating it with what genuine empathy is. As if the pain of suffering a miscarriage, known by many couples, had been deviated to the benefit of the writer's popularity. Sometimes less is more. (Comment on Markle)

The "exhibitionism" of saying that she had a miscarriage and learned to frame sympathy through her experience of that miscarriage shifts, for this commenter (and, one can assume, the 570 commenters who "recommended" the comment and the many others who posted similar comments on the op-ed and to Twitter), the "pain of suffering a miscarriage" into a play for "benefit" and "popularity." As though the feeling were made into nothing more than performance by the publicity, Markle is guilty for her visibility.

Somatic reading can demand that we think more actively about the connections between contemporary racism and aspects of our fields of study that have not usually or always been associated with racialized bodies. In looking for embodied representations of pregnancy in the Victorian novel, explicit reflections to race are few and far between. But in reading for what is represented about bodies with an explicit focus on how those representations plot somatic narratives that connect the text to a reader's sense of body, I engage in a presentism that makes the felt connection between Sensation fiction and Meghan Markle a possible—if messy and partial—topic of critique.

CHAPTER 3

Diagnosis

Direct novelistic articulation of pregnant bodies often relies upon narrative employment of a doctor's diagnosis. In the nineteenth century, medical education and practice was extended, formalized, and gentrified.[1] This historical shift drove an increasing medicalization of women's reproductive bodies and—in a (post-)Enlightenment scientific mode—shifted the primacy of knowledge about pregnancy from a subjective, internal knowledge of bodily sensation to an objective, external knowledge of seeing and a corresponding profession of saying.[2] Growing up alongside the modern doctor, the nineteenth-century novel is a gentrifying literary form balancing interior experience, external visibility, and formal articulation. In his exploration of bodies, books, and visibility, Peter Brooks calls attention to "bodies emblazoned with meaning," bodies that we desire to read because we "desire to know," bodies that are the "site of signification—the place for the inscription of stories—and . . . prime agent[s] in narrative plot and meaning" (5–6). In reading George Eliot's *Middlemarch* (1872), I call attention to the ways moral meaning emblazoned onto visibly pregnant bodies in Victorian novels becomes a source of medical signification, a narrative metaphor for masculine processes of professionalization founded

---

1. See Peterson *Medical*.
2. See Duden.

on the authority to see, know, and say, and a site of resistance to medical and narrative discourse.[3]

This chapter reads the Victorian novel's familiar tendency to conceal pregnancy in cases of maternal immodesty and immorality in the historical context of an increasing medicalization of women's reproductive bodies. As I have already demonstrated, the concealment and revelation of pregnant bodies according to their adherence to or transgression of feminine codes of behavior often maps onto vocabularies and plots of illness; this mapping has the effect of positioning textual pregnancies as moral ailments. When a pregnant body acts in space and time, moral and medical judgment intertwine.[4] Though morally pure characters are often struck down by illness in Victorian fiction (morally succeeding though medically failing—indeed, as Miriam Bailin has argued in *The Sickroom in Victorian Fiction,* perhaps morally succeeding *because* medically failing), characters struck down by narratively visible pregnancies are almost always morally unstable.[5] In the context of that instability, pregnancy seems to invite authoritative attention to both body and mind. The Victorian period saw the normalization of such attention to pregnant bodies from medical professionals but also a normalization of narrative attendance upon medical characters.[6] In reading the convergence of these phenomena, I consider the discursive attitudes toward pregnancy in Victorian novels and contemporary criticism to reach toward ways of encountering the narration of pregnancy as the representation of embodied experience as much as symptom and metaphor.

The first section of this chapter theorizes what it means to read Victorian novelistic observations and articulations of pregnancy in two primary contexts. The first of these is a critical context shaped by the work of Michel Foucault and ongoing investigations of discursive cooperations between creative literature and medicine; the second is a historical context of codifying medical practice. In nineteenth-century novels, the doctor who treats pregnancy

---

3. In *Unstable Bodies,* Jill Matus also discusses ways in which the doctor can function as the moral arbiter of a realist novelistic gaze. For example, Matus states that "even a brief look at the titles of medical treatises of the period shows that morality, ethics, and hygiene were legitimate areas of professional concern" (2).

4. As opposed to the passing mention of pregnancy that remains either offstage or highly euphemistic, as is the case—and as I explore more fully in my introduction—in Dickens, for example.

5. For more on the ways in which moral and medical judgment can diverge and converge in the literary representation of a particular condition, see Byrne.

6. For more on the rise of obstetrical medicine, see Moscucci; Cody; Ehrenreich and English; Hanson; Lewis; Oakley; Peterson, *Medical*; Wilson, *Medicalization*. For more on the treatment of doctors in the Victorian novel, see Sparks. See also Erika Wright's *Reading for Health* (2016) for "health [as] an epistemological problem" in the nineteenth-century novel (4).

is a narratively visible figure mediating mostly invisible bodies, but the very relationship between the doctor and those bodies expresses a historical sea change in the ways women experience reproduction. Though pregnancy has not always been managed by licensed medical practitioners, from the eighteenth century onward, doctors came to predominate in the attendance of reproductive women's bodies in ways that shifted—and reflected shifts in—the ways women's bodies were seen, spoken, and known. I draw on these critical and historical contexts in order to articulate an ethical dilemma in which the reader of pregnancy in the Victorian novel finds herself: Like the doctor, we are primed to diagnose, suspicious of the meanings hidden beneath reticent narrations of women's bodies. As critics, we are trained in metaphor; insofar as we are able to read women's pregnant bodies at all, we often read their presence on the textual surface as symbol rather than somatic experience.[7]

The second section of this chapter explores pregnancy in *Middlemarch*, in particular the pregnancy and miscarriage of Rosamond Lydgate, married to the doctor Tertius Lydgate. I retrace textual modes for pregnancy concealment and revelation to consider the relationship between these tendencies and a protagonist who is also a medical professional pointedly charged with the diagnosis and critical observation of women's reproductive bodies. Though Rosamond hints at specific somatic experiences of her pregnancy and miscarriage, both her doctor-husband and the novel's narrative seem to push toward a reading of her miscarriage as symptomatic of her moral failings and as a metaphor for her husband's social and professional troubles.[8] This symptomatic reading of Rosamond's pregnancy shapes my analysis of the metaphorical uses of pregnancy in this novel, in the Victorian novel, and in a broader cultural discourse of pregnancy that idealizes a private communion of mother and child yet pathologizes conditions that challenge tidily bordered conceptions of the individual body.

SEEING, KNOWING, SAYING: DISCURSIVE MEDICAL PRACTICE, OR FREE INDIRECT DIAGNOSIS

Ornella Moscucci argues that "since the beginning of the nineteenth century, the science of gynecology has legitimated" stereotypes that "sex and repro-

---

7. I build here on the work of disability studies, particularly David T. Mitchell's *Narrative Prosthesis: Disability and the Dependencies of Discourse* (2001), in critiquing the tendency to read somatic situations as signs rather than embodied experiences.

8. In her 2000 article, "Near Confinement," Cynthia Northcutt Malone employs this terminology of "doctor-husband" (368).

duction are more fundamental to women's than the man's nature" (2). Moscucci claims that this belief shapes and is shaped by the "medical treatment of women" and that that medical treatment is based on an understanding of essential difference based on the ability to become pregnant and bear children, which in turn "is used to prescribe very different roles for [public] men and [private] women"—what Moscucci calls "a pervasive ideology which proposed a model of femininity in our society" (2, 5, 4). Moscucci's articulation of the intertwining work of reproduction, medicine, and gender in cultural discourses offers a helpful encapsulation of my central concerns in reading *Middlemarch*.

The last quarter-century has seen a surging interdisciplinary interest in literature and medicine.[9] The application of literary critical methodologies to medical texts and of medical expertise to literature has made the discursive cooperations of text-based art and scientific training increasingly legible. My work builds in particular on *A Cultural History of Pregnancy*, in which Clare Hanson reads pregnancy across European modernity using close analysis of a combination of literary, popular, and medical texts and contexts.[10] Though this project's interest in the significance of pregnancy to the novel limits my focus on medical texts, women's pamphlets, or periodicals, these are all rich sources of information on pregnancy discourses. My investigation of pregnancy discourses in Victorian novels works in useful conversation with critical and theoretical scholarship examining nonliterary texts in greater depth. This vein of scholarly inquiry is, in turn, almost always in necessary conversation with Michel Foucault's work on the discursive practices that seek and may seem to make "visible that which lies below the human surface" but are also always already shaping the ways we see and do not see these depths (Flint 13).

---

9. See, for example, the publication of texts such as—beyond what I cite more extensively in this chapter—Caldwell; Carpenter; Charon; Epstein; Kennedy, *Revising*; Tougaw; Rothfield; and the 1982 foundation of the journal *Literature and Medicine*, the purpose of which its first editor, Kathryn Allen Rabuzzi, explained as being "to explain, probe, and illustrate the nature of the strange marriage between literature and medicine" (Belling vii).

10. Hanson's book—though broader in scope than my own project—also explores the interrelation of medical and cultural discourses in the shaping of our ways of conceiving pregnancy:

> The premise with which [the] book begins [is] that the pregnant body (itself arguably a form of double embodiment) is doubly mutable. It is mutable in the obvious sense that it undergoes continuous physiological (and sometimes pathological) change, and mutable culturally, in that it is viewed through constantly shifting interpretive frameworks. These interpretive frameworks are constructed through the interrelation of medicine and culture. (3)

In *The Birth of the Clinic,* Foucault treats shifts in ways of seeing and saying that follow the codification of medical education in the eighteenth century.[11] Foucault argues that "a new alliance was forged between words and things, enabling one *to see* and *to say*" (xii). The ability of a specialized few to see and to say enabled, in turn, the development of a medical gaze that codified a separation of mind and body. Though we should not think through medical attendance on the bodies of middle- and upper-class ladies in Victorian novels in the same way Foucault thinks through the teaching clinics treating primarily working-class patients, his interest in changing modes of seeing and saying does provide a useful structure for theorizing how pregnancy is narrated in the Victorian novel (particularly insofar as immodesty can "class" the bodies of ladies with the bodies treated in the clinic by exposing their pregnancies to the medical and readerly gaze). Barbara Duden has argued that through much of the eighteenth century, pregnancy was generally said and seen only after a woman's own announcement of quickening (43–44).[12] It is interesting to think about this model, one in which women speak their pregnancies into being on the basis of subjective, internal bodily sensation, in contradistinction to the Victorian model, one in which pregnancies remain publicly unspoken by men and women alike, even past the point at which they are being undeniably seen. In this case, it is the doctor's "objective" assessment rather than the woman's "subjective" announcement that makes pregnancy "exist." The exception to this silence about and invisibility of the pregnant Victorian body lies, of course, with the doctor. Established medical authority positions the doctor as seer, sayer, and knower of bodies. As such, he pivots between the otherwise unseen, unsayable, and secret and the visible, articulable, and social. The doctor is a visible, masculine figure that mediates largely invisible, feminized bodies based on his opinions regarding observable surfaces: the surface of the belly and breasts, or perhaps the vaginal canal and cervical opening, depending on the methodologies of his practice and the position of his patients.

Victorian novels avoid asserting themselves as seers, sayers, or knowers of pregnant bodies. However, Victorian novels often do assert a moral authority based on the ability to see, say, and know, an ability that filters through both

---

11. In thinking about seeing and saying pregnancy through a Foucauldian lens, I hope both to engage with the most ubiquitous vein of medical criticism in the humanities and to avoid what some have called Foucault's "stranglehold" on thinking about medicine and culture. For challenges to Foucault's approach not explored more closely in this section, see, for example, Otter; Willis.

12. Duden seems to base an implication that this was a widespread practice throughout Western Europe on limited continental evidence that I find anecdotally compelling rather than comprehensively convincing.

direct narrative intervention and the use of free indirect discourse. This latter is a technique that enables narrative to represent and articulate not only a visible surface of experience but also internal experience, to pivot between objective and subjective ways of knowing. I suggest that when the moral authority of the nineteenth-century novel aligns itself—as it does with increasing frequency over the course of the Victorian period—with the emerging medical authority of the doctor, we might usefully rethink free indirect discourse as free indirect diagnosis, particularly as it relates to the representation of women's reproductive bodies. Similar to the ways that the medical humanities help to clarify the value of thinking humanistically about medical contexts, understanding free indirect diagnosis as such helps to clarify the value of responses to pregnancy narratives that don't only center diagnosis.

Free indirect diagnosis fosters in the reader an alignment with a diagnosing perspective, most often that of a doctor or narrator. Narrative moments that employ free indirect diagnosis often prompt the reader to think about bodies—particularly "nonnormative" bodies—from a perspective of distance and authority. The judgments we as readers make about bodies represented with the use of free indirect diagnosis can feel like our own, but they are seldom just that. So, for example, when we walk away from *Middlemarch* with strong pathological impressions about Rosamond—about whose actual interiority we know very, very little—we do so in part because our perception of character and plot is aligned both with the perceptions of her doctor-husband and with the perspective of a narrator who excludes Rosamond, like Hetty, from the sympathetic networks of the novel and uses pregnancy to do so.

In *Revising the Clinic* (2010), Meegan Kennedy connects Foucault's theories of medical seeing and saying to an explicitly literary context and a vibrant scholarly interest in the relationship between that literary context and visual cultures.[13] In answer to a question about "how and why . . . physicians and novelists share" the discursive practices of scientists and poets, Kennedy posits that "changes in seeing made new forms of representation necessary, while new theories of representation codified and valorized particular kinds of seeing" (2, 3). The "clinical realism" Kennedy explores is one that extends far beyond the free indirect diagnosis of explicitly medical narratives or characters. Nonetheless, Kennedy's clinical realism serves as a useful frame for thinking about the ways reading the medicalization of pregnancy in the Victorian novel can help us to read much larger formal, thematic, historical, and

---

13. Evidence for this vibrant scholarly interest can be demonstrated by the texts Kennedy cites as influential to her own project. Among them are I. Armstrong; N. Armstrong; Beer "Tidings"; Flint; Brooks, *Vision*; Anderson, *Powers*; Levine; Crary; and Cartwright.

scientific concerns about the permeability of the individual, concerns that become central to later-nineteenth-century narrations of pregnancy.

Feminist theorists (particularly of the American second wave) and natural birth advocates have articulated pregnancy's potential as a source of self-knowledge and emphasized the loss of women's ways of knowing their own pregnant embodiment that accompanied the medicalization of childbirth.[14] I resist an uncomplicated acceptance of this formulation; pregnant people with access to quality medical care in the twenty-first century are much, much less likely to die or to experience infant loss than has ever before been the case. But these advances have limited the scope of subjective knowledge about pregnancy, a condition most people experience in primarily subjective ways. As medical men gained power relative to pregnant women and midwives over the course of the nineteenth century, the authority over pregnant subjectivity shifted. Furthermore, the increasing medicalization of pregnancy and childbirth speaks to an increasing organization and specialization of the medical professions. What had been an unregulated practice of questionable gentility in the eighteenth century was, during the nineteenth, increasingly regulated, trained, and compatible with middle- and upper-middle-class social standing. An Enlightenment impulse toward the exploration of categories of knowledge and the establishment of formal institutions for that exploration had prompted the creation and expansion of medical programs to train professionals as well as increasing regulation of medical practice.[15] For example, readers of *Middlemarch* will be familiar with the distinctions the novel draws between apothecaries, surgeons, doctors, and physicians in Lydgate's early 1830s professional world. The shifting medical norms of the period both reflect and spur an increasing tendency toward the kind of medical specialization that prompts the establishment of obstetrical schools and the growth of medical knowledge about and practices for treating reproductive women's bodies.

Public controversy about shifting medical practice during the nineteenth century twice focused on reproductive (royal) bodies: The labors of both Princess Charlotte and Queen Victoria reflected and drove shifts in popular ideas about the role of medicine in pregnancy and childbirth. In 1817 Princess Charlotte of Wales—heir to the British throne—died after the stillbirth of her first child. She had been attended prenatally and during labor by a male midwife, not a doctor. Although an obstetrician had been summoned after her labor became complicated, he was not given access to the princess. There was widespread speculation after her death that the obstetrical use of forceps could have

---

14. See, for example, Rich; Ehrenreich and English; Young. From the French context, see Irigaray; Kristeva.

15. See Peterson, *Medical*.

saved her life or the life of her child. Increasingly, medical interventions—such as the use of forceps and, by mid-century, anesthesia—came to be seen as a reason for middle- and upper-class women to hire a doctor rather than midwife, male or female, as a prenatal and birthing attendant. Meanwhile, the number of (male) obstetrical students and practitioners grew rapidly, and medical research—including James Marion Sims's influential invention of the speculum and treatments for vaginal fistula developed by experimenting on the bodies of enslaved Black women—on pregnancy proliferated.

Thirty-six years after Princess Charlotte's death, medical attendance during pregnancy and childbirth had been largely adopted among the upper and middle classes, though the scope of that practice was hotly debated. In 1853 Queen Victoria gave birth under anesthesia. Following five years of public controversy about the desirability of pain management during labor, this event conferred upon the practice a royal stamp of approval; the use of anesthesia during childbirth quickly became common practice among the upper and middle classes of Britain.

The social and professional authority of the rising medical professional, then, was clearly articulated in the context of specialized training—with tools like the forceps and the administration of drugs like ether—and the specialized ability to see and say that which cannot be seen or said by the layperson. Pregnancy, though certainly seeable in "real" life by laypeople, is difficult to "see" in text and difficult to say in Victorian "realities" and texts alike. In this way, a gendered Victorian culture of pregnancy concealment participates in broad shifts in medical practice, assisting in the creation of a secret space fully visible, knowable, and articulable only by the medical professional. Insofar as the specificities of women's reproductive bodies are articulable in the period, they are articulable as invitations to medical attention.

Victorian novels frequently express anxieties about the shifting and ambiguous social role of doctors. Anxieties about shifting and ambiguous social roles, in turn, are often expressed in Victorian novels via the complications of the marriage plot.[16] Tabitha Sparks's 2009 *The Doctor in the Victorian Novel* argues that doctor characters tend to have difficulty prioritizing their professional drive in marriage-plot novels and that marriage plots have difficulty maintaining their conventions in novels that feature driven medical professionals; Sparks charges the narrative rise of the doctor with the fall of the marriage plot over the course of the nineteenth century. In this chapter and the

---

16. I take the marriage plot to be not one single form, but a network of narrative structures that tend to frame and or play with the idea of a frame in which marriage is the culmination of personal striving and, sometimes, the beginning and, sometimes, the conclusion of effective (masculine) professional striving.

next, I posit that the narrative rise of the doctor cooperates with an increasing visibility of the pregnancy plot. As doctors gained increasing authority as the sayers of women's pregnant bodies, novelistic narratives were able to draw on both literary conventions (free indirect discourse) and medical forms (the case study) in ways that made the representation of pregnant bodies in particular and bodies in general differently accessible.

The rise of the doctor, then, informs a literary discourse of pregnancy in which we participate when reading reproductive bodies. Access to characters vested with the medical authority to diagnose can imbue the reader with similar authority. That authority in both announcing and thereby creating a "fact" that then seems to have always already existed inscribes pregnancy as discourse in the Victorian novel. Discourse seems to organize information about a preexisting phenomenon while that organization also produces the very phenomenon it describes, stranding critical discourse in the grammar of that which we seek to analyze. In avoiding a medical diagnosis of pregnant bodies in Victorian fiction, it is easy to practice literary diagnosis instead, to read the "real" meanings of pregnancy as the textual metaphors employed in pregnancy's concealment: Bessie Keith's pregnancy is not an embodied experience but a punishment; Ruth Hilton's pregnancy is not a somatic state but a spiritual calling; Rosamond Lydgate's pregnancy is not—as she suggests—a period of recurring bodily trouble followed by a surprising, specific, painful, fruitless labor but a reflection of her doctor-husband's social and professional miscarriage.

Let us return to Malone's argument that novelistic representations of pregnancy go from casual, unabashed mention of women "big with child" in the eighteenth century to being articulated primarily euphemistically in the Victorian period. In this formulation, a veil is thrown over pregnancy during the very period in which male medical professions are formalizing women's reproductive bodies as a category of professional knowledge. This invites the creation of a discourse of pregnancy because it establishes a literary space in which pregnancy seems to require organizing articulations, in which it seems unseen, unsaid, unknown, and in need of authoritative investigation. But pregnancy was certainly not any less a part of women's embodied experience during a historical period in which middle- and upper-class norms elevated and emphasized maternity and in which birth rates were high.[17] A novelistic discourse of pregnancy that assesses women's reproductive bodies as markers of modesty/morality and test cases for masculine diagnostic acuity while

---

17. Nineteenth-century birth rates for the middle and upper classes start declining from the 1870s onward. See Peterson, *Family*.

avoiding the representation of those bodies as *bodies* encourages metaphorical readings of pregnancy. It is very difficult—often impossible—to push toward readings that acknowledge the diagnostic and metaphorizing push and pull of narrative reticence and device. It is difficult to read these bodies as bodies we can imagine experiencing physical sensation and taking physical space. In the section that follows, I approach the narration of Rosamond's pregnancy loss to navigate a critical space for somatic reading.

LOSS

The prelude to *Middlemarch*—a novel associated with the nuanced portrayal of community—anticipates a tale primarily concerned with the fate of latter-day women of genius, consigned to the still doom of alternating ineffectually "between a vague ideal and the common yearning of womanhood" (3). We might ask of the narrator after only these first three paragraphs the same question that narrator asks of themselves twenty-four chapters later: "Why always Dorothea?" (175). Why would the novel that will introduce me to Tertius Lydgate, to the Vincys and Garths, to Misters Bulstrode, Casaubon, Featherstone, to Will Ladislaw, to Camden Farebrother, why would this novel instruct me to pay particular attention only to "cygnet[s] reared uneasily among the ducklings" (3)? Why would the narrator take such pains to represent to me the nuance and development of subjectivities across lines of class, gender, age, and talent if I am ultimately to prioritize the nuance and development of one subjectivity in particular?

Though I join not only the narrator of *Middlemarch* but also 150 years of critics in questioning the prelude's seeming elevation of Dorothea to the role of heroine in a novel that makes heroes and heroines of even the low-minded and unexceptional, I offer a singular (if singularly overblown) option for reading the novel's seeming focus on "later-born Theresas" as suggested by the prelude (3). The "born" of "later-*born* Theresas" is only one usage of the word among three in as many paragraphs. These paragraphs investigate the "natures of women," their "common yearnings," the "shape" or "dim . . . formlessness" of their "offspring." Certainly, the prelude employs a vocabulary of reproductive female bodies to express an anxiety about the situation of women—so often understood in the context of their reproductive capacity—in the social body; a vocabulary of women's reproductive bodies is employed metaphorically to suggest their challenges as individuals in society. Saint Theresa is never pregnant, but the womanhood and potential for internal growth that she represents is manifest or miscarried in the external world in ways that seem to invite metaphorical deployments of reproductive vocabulary. I suggest that this reproductive vocabulary is most usefully read not only in conversation with *women's* biological capabilities—and certainly not only in conversation with exceptional women's—but as an expression of a more general anxiety about the role of individuals, both female and male, biologically reproductive and not, in the social body, about their abilities to develop and express an inner life in coherent conversation with outward "realities." The prelude to *Middlemarch* can be usefully read not as an articulation of Dorothea's singularity but as applying her singular position to the common yearnings of humanity; this is achieved, in part, through the metaphorical deployment of language often associated with pregnancy.

Reading this metaphorical deployment of pregnant vocabulary in the novel's opening section anticipates my reading of the deployment of Rosamond's pregnancy loss in the misdevelopment of her husband's professional identity. Rosamond's pregnancy is narrated in hindsight and diagnosed in the context of medical care. The narrating hindsight and medical care in Rosamond's case, however, are those of her husband, the "doctor [who] must have opinions." Not only does the revelation of Rosamond's pregnant body and pregnancy loss function as narrative punishment (particularly in comparison with the extreme reticence that marks the narration of Celia Chettam's pregnancy), but it serves, too, as narrative metaphor for her husband's professional miscarriage in particular and as an expression of anxieties about the shifting personal, public, and social position of the medical profession in general. As my reading of the prelude demonstrates, *Middlemarch* employs a vocabulary of women's reproductive bodies to express anxieties about the potential for and limitations on individual development in a complex web of shifting social contexts.

The narrative deployment of pregnancy as a metaphor for individual (often masculine, often artistic) development is more familiar territory than thinking about literary pregnancy as an exploration of embodiment. Pregnancy as a period of development and a site of creation offers a useful transhistorical filter through which to understand artistic production: Classical notions of art as born, Athena-like, from an artist's mind; medieval ideals of art as planted, á la divine annunciation, in the soul of the artist; Enlightenment emphases on stages of development and progress; Romantic visions of art as an expression of the artist's feeling and soul. It can be very difficult, however, to sustain focus on actual pregnant bodies marked by internality, mutability, privacy, and, often, a reluctance to be fully seen, said, or known. I trouble the easy slide from analysis of explicit representation of pregnant bodies into the implicit, metaphorical use of those bodies as a symbol for something *else*. In the context of my ongoing questions about how it works and what it means to read pregnant bodies that resist legibility, my reading of *Middlemarch* performs—and analyzes its performance of—the skidding motion of the critical gaze on representations of "actual" pregnancy to a critical investigation into the symbolic significances of pregnancy.

We have already seen how the direct representation of pregnant bodies as bodies in Victorian literature serves to fuel moralizing attitudes. In *Middlemarch* too, the pregnant body revealed in most detail belongs to the novel's least modest, faithful, and obedient woman. The misdevelopment of Rosamond's interiority miscarries as surely as does her fetus. It is Lydgate's interiority that develops in the space of Rosamond's stunted growth, allowing him to better understand the conflict of personal and professional investments that will trigger the miscarriage of his own career as a doctor in Middlemarch. Though Rosamond suggests that she knows her pregnancy and its loss through her own particular, embodied experience, Lydgate and the narrative both disregard the significance of such experience in favor of his moral and medical opinion.

•

Middlemarch narrates the life of a provincial community in the 1830s with a particular focus on two protagonists: Dorothea Brooke, a pious, intellectual heiress who makes a spectacularly underwhelming marriage, and Tertius Lydgate, a gentle-blooded country doctor with high scientific aspirations who makes a similarly unwise matrimonial choice. Though both marriages are childless for the majority of the novel, a vocabulary of "conceiving" and "conception" pervades the narration of Dorothea and Lydgate's consciousnesses.[18] These conceptions are not, of course, physical but mental processes, as in the instance of Lydgate's "enkindled conceptions of . . . genius" (366). There seems, however, to be a cooperation between mental conception and reproductive conception necessary for successful pregnancy in *Middlemarch*. Dorothea, capable for much of the novel only of mental conception, remains childless. Rosamond, capable of physical conception (and capable before her marriage of a "preconceived romance" [106]) but unable or unwilling to "conceive" of her husband's professional aspirations and personal investments, miscarries. Celia, Dorothea's practical sister, able to see the worth of things and people clearly—able, in other words, to conceive of the world as it is—is the only character who becomes a mother in the scope of the novel, though both Dor-

---

18. In the novel's closing chapters, a future is sketched out for Rosamond and Lydgate in which they have four children before his early death.

othea and Rosamond are narrated as having children after the close of the novel's primary events (360).

In becoming a mother, Celia is fulfilling a Victorian feminine ideal. Once her son is born, Celia, "all in white and lavender like a bunch of violets," watches "the remarkable acts of her baby" with maternal adoration, unable to imagine that another child could be "such a dear as Arthur" (331–32). And Celia's pregnancy—the physical process through which she achieves her spotless maternity—remains almost completely invisible and unsaid for the reader of *Middlemarch*. The only articulation of Celia's condition is filtered at great remove, through—and in the service of—the protecting mind of her husband:

> Sir James Chettam's mind was not *fruitful* in devices, but his *growing* anxiety to "act on Brooke" [regarding his tenants and the hiring of Garth] once brought close to his constant belief in Dorothea's capacity for influence, became *formative*, and *issued* in a little plan; namely, to plead Celia's *indisposition* as a reason for fetching Dorothea by herself to the Hall. (241; emphasis added)

As I will demonstrate is the case with the more direct representation of Rosamond's pregnancy, Celia's pregnancy here serves the narrative development of her husband's interiority and aspiration. Sir Chettam's thoughts about the maintenance of the lives and land dependent upon his uncle-in-law are sketched in the language of his wife's "fruitful," "growing" "form[ing]," and soon-to-"issue"-forth body. This gentle, euphemistic reference to Celia's "indisposition" is the only textually legible hint at her pregnancy; her near-total protection from any representation during the months of her visible pregnancy, however, also hints—though only to the trained reader of the "pregnancy-less plot" in the Victorian novel—at the potential visibility of her sexual body. That "indisposed" pregnant body is confirmed only after the fact, and only in passing, when Dorothea can "not have the carriage to go to Celia, who had lately had a baby" (295). As with Sir Chettam's little plot for getting Dorothea to the Hall, Celia's implicitly immobile postpartum body is expressed through Dorothea's limited or facilitated mobility.

Our ignorance about Celia's sexual body heightens our awareness of knowledge about Rosamond's; Celia's pregnancy is a whitewashed wall against which Rosamond's pregnancy appears more vivid. The narrative invisibility of Celia's pregnancy heightens the significance of the narrative visibility of Rosamond's as the novel's avoidance of explicit "pregnant" language in the narrative of reproductive bodies heightens the significance of that word's deployment in contexts that seem to have nothing to do with reproductive bodies.

That Celia's pregnancy makes such a slight impression on the surface of the plot demonstrates the textual protections granted to normative, modest, feminine bodies; Celia's pregnancy offers no moral lesson for characters or readers. Rosamond's pregnancy and pregnancy loss, however, demonstrate the connection between feminine immodesty and immorality and the narrative visibility of the sexual female body; the visibility of her pregnant body can be read as punishment for her pursuit of sexualized visibility and power. The connection between feminine transgression and the punishment of legible pregnancy is heightened by the preterm birth of Rosamond's child; as we have seen, preterm birth carries the suggestion of female misbehavior. A generally insensible Rosamond is punished for her misbehavior with a "miscarriage" that we are meant to understand she brings upon herself and from which, we are meant to understand, she fails to learn a lesson. It is her husband and the reader who learn a lesson from Rosamond's loss. It is only from Lydgate's perspective that Rosamond's pregnancy is narratively visible, only through Malone's "narrative zone of the doctor-husband" that it is articulated. Our perception of the pregnancy thwarts rather than invites better knowledge of Rosamond herself and deepens our access only to the interiority of Lydgate, an interiority primarily marked by professional aspirations (368).

Lydgate—embroiled after his marriage to Rosamond in the beginnings of a professional crisis that limits his income—is disturbed by financial obligations. It is in the context of these obligations that Rosamond's pregnancy is revealed: "A letter insisting on the payment of a bill for furniture [arrived]. But Rosamond was expecting to have a baby, and Lydgate wished to save her from any perturbation," so he doesn't tell her of it (290). Though Lydgate conceals these struggles from his wife, the narrative simultaneously reveals both these struggles and Rosamond's pregnancy to the reader. Not only are the two revelations made side by side; the revelation of Lydgate's financial difficulties prompts the revelation of Rosamond's pregnancy. As Celia's pregnancy was hinted at by the managerial aspirations of her husband, Rosamond's pregnancy is exposed in the context of Lydgate's professional condition.

Though Rosamond's pregnancy is detailed most explicitly in narrative hindsight, it is also hinted at as it occurs. Lydgate and Rosamond marry in the summer of 1831 and have returned from their honeymoon by early fall. In "mild autumn" (268)—during what must be her first trimester—Rosamond's growing reproductive body seems likely to be working beneath the narrative representation of her growing sexual knowledge:

> Rosamond *felt* herself *beginning to know* a great deal of the world, especially in discovering—what when she was in her unmarried girlhood had

been *inconceivable* to her except as a *dim* tragedy in bygone costumes—that women, even after marriage, might make conquests and enslave men. At that time young ladies in the country . . . read little French literature later than Racine, and public prints had not cast their present magnificent *illumination* over the scandals of life. (271; emphasis added)

This passage seems to depict Rosamond's mental process in language that could also be used to describe somatic sensation ("felt"). And when read with an awareness that Rosamond is "beginning to know" both that sexual energies do not move only in marital channels *and* that sexual consummations move in particular ways in the body, the embodied possibilities of language take on added weight.[19] A newly pregnant Rosamond would likely be experiencing the cessation of her menstrual cycle and perhaps the nausea of morning sickness, tender or swollen breasts and nipples, unusual fatigue, or emotional swings. Insofar as such things would not have been spoken about in front of Rosamond as a middle-class Victorian maiden prior to her legitimate marriage, they would likely have been "inconceivable." Rosamond's newfound ability to conceive is rendered in a visual language ("dim" and "illumination") of enlightenment: She is now able to see and know that which she had not before been able to see and know. These nascent abilities, however, do not extend to any ability to say. Rosamond could no more publicly announce that she now knows that she can flirt with men other than Lydgate than she can announce that she and Lydgate are having sex or that she is no longer bleeding every month. The free indirect narration (the tone of "might make conquests and enslave men" is Rosamond's) of this early stage of an as yet invisible pregnancy affirms her necessary silence. Her character must be assumed to have an experiencing body, but those experiences are not incorporated into narrative discourse.

We can date Lydgate's first articulation of Rosamond's pregnancy—seen above—to September or October of 1831 by the reference to the debate over John Russell's bill in the House of Commons that frames the narration of the Middlemarch debate over Lydgate's new fever hospital. It is in the context of this provincial controversy—in the context of Lydgate's professional struggles—that the narrative diagnoses Rosamond's pregnancy during what is likely the end of her first trimester, when the symptoms of pregnancy would be legible to her doctor-husband.

---

19. Thierauf and Matus also consider this section of the novel, arguing that "we can trace 'the subjective state of the woman approaching . . . motherhood'" (Matus 3 qtd. in Thierauf 482).

It is summer (probably June) of 1832 when Mrs. Vincy refers to Rosamond having lost her baby. By this time, Rosamond has "got over it nicely" and "regain[ed her] brilliant health" over a "few months" (364). So, we can assume that the miscarriage, stillbirth, or premature birth followed by infant death occurs in early spring, perhaps March, of 1832. If this is the case, then the loss is likely better ascribed to stillbirth or premature birth followed by infant death than miscarriage as it would almost certainly take place in the late second or early third trimester of her pregnancy, most likely around the eight month if we assume that she conceives around August of 1831 and loses the baby around March of 1832.[20] It is possible, however, that Rosamond is only in the first or second month of her pregnancy when Lydgate diagnoses it and that the "few months" of her recovery refer, perhaps, to four or five rather than the three I have taken into account in my most likely chronology of her pregnancy. At the least, then, Rosamond could have conceived in September of 1831 and lost the fetus in February when she would be about five months along; if this were the case, then a more appropriate twenty-first-century diagnosis for the second trimester disappointment might be miscarriage, though a later than usual miscarriage. The novel, however, refers to the event as a premature birth; I will explore possible significances of this in the coming pages.

Mrs. Vincy declares to her husband that she "felt for [Rosamond] being disappointed of her baby; but she got over it nicely" (352). Mr. Vincy, however, dismisses the importance of this "disappointment" with the baby: "Baby, pooh! I can see Lydgate is making a mess of his practice, and getting into debt too, by what I hear. I shall have Rosamond coming to me with a pretty tale one of these days. But they'll get no money from me" (352–53). Rosamond's father equates the "mess" of the loss of her baby with the mess of her husband's professional life, as though the experience speaks most tellingly not to her own narrative but to her husband's.

---

20. Though the difference between miscarriage and stillbirth is articulated differently in different cultural and historical contexts, both describe the intrauterine death (or death in labor) of a fetus (or embryo in the case of some miscarriages), and they tend to be roughly distinguished by whether or not the fetus could have been viable had it been born alive. So, in twenty-first-century American contexts, for example, pregnancy loss after about week twenty—the point at which medicine can on very rare occasions preserve the life of a premature baby—is referred to as stillbirth, and pregnancy loss prior to that point is referred to as miscarriage. In nineteenth-century contexts—such as the reference to a stillborn son in the opening paragraphs of Jane Austen's 1817 *Persuasion*, for example—"stillbirth" likely refers to the birth of a dead baby further along in pregnancy. Premature labor followed by infant death is different from either miscarriage or stillbirth because it refers to a baby born alive.

Later, when we learn the details of Rosamond's "being disappointed of her baby," the passive narrative voice of the telling suggests the distance of a clinical assessment:

> [Rosamond's] baby had been born prematurely, and all the embroidered robes and caps had to be laid by in darkness. This misfortune was attributed entirely to her having persisted in going out on horseback one day when her husband had desired her not to do so. (359)

Though we are not told by whom the misfortune of her loss "was attributed" to her horseback riding, the implication in what follows is that it is an opinion that originates with her husband, the diagnosing doctor who had desired her not to ride on grounds both personal and professional. The narrative marriage of the coolly distant "was attributed" to the emotionally weighted "having persisted" and "desired" suggests a play of free indirect diagnosis in this passage. Our narrator has thrown their hat in Lydgate's ring, harnessed the tone of Lydgate's moral and medical authority, and invited the reader to read the primary significance of Rosamond's pregnancy as its influence on Lydgate's personal and professional development. Much as Rosamond's pregnancy is revealed in the context of a financial situation prompted by the first stirrings of Lydgate's twinned personal and professional failures, so is that pregnancy's end narrated in the context of Lydgate's beginning to recognize the inevitable external limitation those failures must have on his interior universe.

Rosamond, however, seems to be either unable or unwilling to recognize (or unnoticed in the recognition of) the necessary limitation posed by the outside world on the interior life she tries to will into being. The lesson of limitation Lydgate begins to learn over the course of her pregnancy and the confirming message of the loss of her pregnancy don't seem to dent the impenetrable surface of Rosamond's conviction that her internal and external worlds can align. The dreams she harbors during pregnancy of forging an elevating connection with a more genteel branch of the Lydgate family, a connection through which she will be maintained and appreciated in the manner to which she has always intended to become accustomed, are not dampened by her loss but reenforced and intensified. Rosamond's pregnancy loss seems both to result from and demonstrate her moral misdevelopment. Though Rosamond will not, Lydgate, the narrator, and the reader likely perceive a harvest of hubris in Rosamond's loss; this is a harvest that we are primed to perceive because it is one reaped by almost every character in the novel, at one point or another. *Middlemarch* suggests not only that Rosamond's pregnancy signifies most meaningfully in the moral development of her husband—a development that requires his recognition of professional misdevelopment—but that pregnancy in general signifies most meaningfully overall as a metaphor for moral development, not as a particular embodied condition.

As the Lydgates set aside the particular "robes and caps"—each a distinct physical result of female labor—intended for their child, the novel sets aside the distinct physical details of Rosamond's pregnancy and labor. The details set aside—distinct physical experiences of, for example, nausea or discomfort, spotting or abnormal contractions that result in one particular ill-fated labor—are those which communicate women's embodied experiences of pregnancy rather than its scientific observation and diagnosis. Though her pregnancy loss is ascribed to her having gone horseback riding against her husband's advice, Rosamond mentions an alternative, embodied interpretation of its cause. The potential validity of this interpretation is implicitly dismissed in the "entirely" of the doctor's opinion, which he must have and which we, it seems, must accept. Should we resist accepting this opinion, an opinion that relies, in part, on a metaphorical reading of miscarriage as punishment for misbehavior—should we, sans medical expertise, wish to read the pregnant body itself rather than its moral—then we, like the hubristic Rosamond, "persist" in our attachment to surface rather than depth. To resist reading pregnancy as primarily a metaphor in the Victorian novel troubles the increasingly medical discourse through which we are able to read pregnancy at all.

That Lydgate's medical opinion should govern our access to both Rosamond's bodily and moral condition speaks to the complicated overlap of public and private in the rising medical profession of the nineteenth century. Though Lydgate hardly shouts his wife's pregnancy from the rooftops, there is a difference between his direct thoughts of "Rosamond . . . expecting to have a baby" and Sir Chettam's euphemistic thoughts of Celia's "indisposition." Lydgate's profession goes a long way toward an explanation of this difference. Dealing as he must with the direct proffering of professional opinion in private settings, if Lydgate's thoughts were to narrate any other character's pregnancy, it would be in his capacity as a professional authority. Married as he is to Rosamond, if Lydgate—employed in any other profession—were to think his wife's pregnancy, it would be in his private moral capacity as her husband. The articulation of Rosamond's pregnancy via the "narrative-zone of [her] doctor-husband" offers a particularly legible example of medicine's complicated overlap between private and professional and, in so doing, demonstrates a fusion of moral convention and medicine (Malone 368). In its articulation, Lydgate's medical opinion (that Rosamond's loss can be attributed solely to her disobedient decision to go "riding" repeatedly with his military cousin) diagnoses a moral condition. That Rosamond carries on an extended "flirtation" with both Will Ladislaw and Captain Lydgate reflects her discovery "that women, even after marriage, might make conquests and enslave men" (271). Though Rosamond never *quite* crosses a strict moral line with her flirtations, she exposes herself to the wonder of pious Dorothea by spending time with Will while her husband is out, and she exposes herself to all of Middlemarch by riding with Captain Lydgate unaccompanied.

Though Rosamond's transgressions are more moral than medical, Lydgate's responses to those transgressions seem to prioritize professional opinion over personal feeling. As Rosamond urges him to play a better host to Captain Lydgate, Lydgate declares, "My dear Rosy, you don't expect me to talk much to such a conceited ass as that, I hope. . . . If he got his head broken, I might look at it with interest, not before" (360). In refusing to talk to the "conceited ass" who is his houseguest, Lydgate refuses personal responsibility, but in acknowledging that the captain would interest him "if he got his head broken," Lydgate shifts his vantage point to an ostensibly professional one. This mirrors the function of pregnancy as a metaphor for Lydgate's professional misdevelopment in the novel more generally and as a metaphor for moral (mis)development in Victorian novels most generally.

We can again observe a rhetorical elevation of professional opinion over personal consideration in Lydgate's reaction to Rosamond's moral transgressions when he articulates his direct prohibition—following a gentle request, which he had assumed would be honored—of horseback riding while pregnant: "Lydgate was more than hurt [that Rosamond had been out riding with Captain Lydgate]—he was utterly confounded that she had risked herself on a strange horse without referring the matter to his wish" (361). In first considering his wife's disobedience, Lydgate is "hurt" and "confounded" at her failure to heed his "wish"—these lines employ the vocabulary of personal emotion and desire. However, Lydgate soon shifts toward a professional vocabulary, employing a "decisive tone" to inform Rosamond with authority that she "will not go again" and to declare that "surely I am the person to judge for you. I think it is enough that I say you are not to go again" (361). That Lydgate is surely the person to judge for Rosamond is a reflection of his authority as doctor-husband "who must have opinions," arbiter and articulator of bodies and behaviors. His disappointment that "his superior knowledge and mental force, instead of being, as he had imagined, a shrine to consult on all occasions, was simply set aside on every practical question" reflects Rosamond's resistance to both arms of his authority: Lydgate bemoans her refusal to worship at the sacred "shrine" of her husband and to "consult" the professional expertise of her doctor (362).

Rosamond resists the terms of Lydgate's professional and personal authority by responding to his speech of remonstrance speechlessly. Rather than offer a direct reply to Lydgate's edict, Rosamond deploys her body, a body Lydgate continuously misreads:

> Rosamond was arranging her hair before dinner, and the reflection of her head in the glass showed no change in its loveliness except a little turning aside of the long neck. Lydgate had been moving about with his hands in his pockets, and now paused near her, as if he awaited some assurance. (361)

Rosamond's "little turning aside of the long neck" seems to be communicating somatically with as much precise intention as Lydgate's words. The exact meaning of Lydgate's spoken judgment seems (almost) incontestable: He means that she should accept his authority and stop going for horseback rides with Captain Lydgate. The exact meaning of Rosamond's little turning of the neck, however, is subsumed in its surface, a surface like that of the mirror before which she sits. The narrator describes the visible surface of Rosamond's body acting in space. As readers of a realist tradition that narrates saliences, we assume that for this action to be worthy of narration, it signifies some interior purpose, much as we, as livers in a world with bodies, assume the visible surface of an enlarged belly signifies a purposeful interior. But as the Lydgates could never have known whether the pregnant Rosamond was carrying a viable child or an unviable fetus, a boy or a girl, neither Lydgate, the narrator, nor the reader knows what exact meaning this movement of Rosamond's body carries. A critical approach that hews as closely as possible to Rosamond's body can read the surface of this action, but in speculating about its significance, we are likely to commit errors similar to those Lydgate commits in attempting to diagnose his wife's interiority on the basis of her surface.

In her speechless response to Lydgate's authority, Rosamond establishes an embodied authority of her own that leaves Lydgate "waiting" and pacing awkwardly with "his hands in his pockets," a stark contrast to the single controlled movement of his wife. Indeed, when Rosamond does deign to speak, she does so in order to initiate a bodily ritual over which she exercises authority:

> "I wish you would fasten up my plaits, dear," said Rosamond, letting her arms fall with a little sigh, so as to make a husband ashamed of standing there like a brute. Lydgate had often fastened the plaits before, being among the deftest of men with his large finely formed fingers. He swept up the soft festoons of plaits and fastened in the tall comb (to such uses do men come!); and what could he do then but kiss the exquisite nape which was shown in all its delicate curves? (361)

In requesting that Lydgate pin up her hair, Rosamond asks that he do as he has "often [done] before." That this act is not limited to the fastening of plaits but clearly extends to a sensuous sweeping up of the "soft" hair and a kissing of the "delicate curves" of the neck positions Rosamond's request as foreplay, a move with particular responses from the "deftest" of fingers, a move established by the couple over time. Furthermore, the emphasis on Rosamond's "long neck" and its "nape" is suggestive of the Latin word for neck, "cervix," first attested as "pertaining to the neck of the womb" in 1832 (Harper).[21] Though Rosamond's particular bodily experiences of pregnancy go unnarrated, here a pregnant Rosamond—perhaps a visibly pregnant Rosamond as she is likely in her second trimester—asserts authority through her sexual body and the power it wields over her husband and over the text itself. As before, the narration of this section employs a telling use of free indirect discourse, though with a difference: The "so as to make a husband ashamed of himself" expresses the emotion that prompts Lydgate's obedient engagement with Rosamond's foreplay. However, I think that what we are reading here can be best understood as the narrative thinking Lydgate thinking Rosamond. Rosamond, still seated in front of the mirror, having turned her head just a little and not enough to face her husband, speaks to Lydgate through that mirror, and Lydgate's "ashamed" ascription of her "little sigh" to his own brutishness reflects his desire to read the meaning of her speech—I would like you to do me this little favor and you are a brute if you refuse me when I am asking you so calmly, dear—and the meaning of her body's observable surfaces as aligned. With her polite request, Rosamond translates somatic implication into plain expression; she is "verbally subdued, yet bodily loquacious" (Thierauf 484).

However, because the section that narrates Rosamond's pregnancy is filtered through Lydgate's memory and begins with a diagnosis of the cause of her pregnancy loss, we are able to intuit potential disconnects between her "plain" meaning and somatic possibility. Lydgate himself senses a dangerous potential for misunderstanding. Even after considering himself a brute in the reflection of her reflection, fastening her plaits, and kissing her neck, Lydgate pushes Rosamond to speak more explicitly to his intended purpose:

Lydgate was still angry, and had not forgotten his point.

"I shall tell the Captain that he ought to have known better than offer you his horse," he said, as he moved away [from pinning Rosamond's hair].

"I beg you will not do anything of the kind, Tertius," said Rosamond, looking at him with something more marked than usual in her speech. "It

---

21. I am indebted to Miciah Hussey for reminding me of the cervix/neck connection.

will be treating me as if I were a child. Promise that you will leave the subject to me."

There did seem to be some truth in her objection. Lydgate said, "Very well," with a surly obedience, and thus the discussion ended with his promising Rosamond, and not with her promising him. (361)

The "something more marked than usual" with which Rosamond looks at Tertius communicates an inarticulate, bodily depth of meaning additional—perhaps even contrary—to the meaning of her speech. In asking that he promise to "leave the subject" of her riding with Captain Lydgate while pregnant to her, Rosamond's tacit obedience to Lydgate's authority might be read into that "marked" look of hers. Certainly, it seems that Lydgate reads the mark thusly—is, in fact, himself "obedient" to that interpretation of her body's meaning. But again, the problem of Rosamond's body language—for Lydgate and for the narrator—remains the difficulty of translating it into plain English and the novel's discursive logic. Rosamond's persistence in riding after this conversation signals that her meaning look does not indicate any willingness to bow to her doctor-husband's authority. In fact, the look indicates a practice of misleading signification—she avoids offering verbal clarity and communicates somatically instead. "She had been determined not to promise" all along because "Rosamond had that victorious obstinacy which never wastes its energy in impetuous resistance" (361).

•

What the marked meaning of Rosamond's look may have been, we, like Lydgate, will never fully know. We will know only the effect: Because of this look and the inarticulate meaning it seems to contain, the scene of Lydgate's attempt to assert his moral and medical authority on Rosamond ends with that attempt's failure. Instead, Rosamond asserts her own somatic authority. That the victory of Rosamond's body—Lydgate's loss of "illusion at the blank unreflecting surface of her mind"—increases "his ardour for the more impersonal ends of his professional and his scientific study" suggests a broader pattern in which the unknowability of women's reproductive bodies fuels medical discourse (363). *Middlemarch* seems to endorse that medical discourse: Though Lydgate himself never achieves a personal assertion of moral/medical authority over Rosamond, the reader's preexisting knowledge of her disobedient persistence and "the misfortune [that] was attributed entirely" to that disobedient persistence (her "obstinacy") achieves narrative legitimacy. Though Rosamond refuses to acknowledge that Lydgate is right, the reader is encouraged to.

When, against the dictates of Lydgate's "superior knowledge," Rosamond again goes riding, misfortune of the very vaguest sort occurs: "The gentle grey, unprepared for the crash of a tree that was being felled on the edge of Halsell Wood, took fright, and caused a worse fright to Rosamond, leading finally to the loss of her baby" (362). It is odd that the narration should set up a scene in which a bodily trauma resulting from Rosamond's illegitimate assertions of autonomy and authority *could* offer the entire explanation for her loss and yet stops short of declaring such a cause. Though a tree falls in this scene, Rosamond—it seems—does not. Though she could easily have been jarred, jostled, or shaken by the fright her horse takes, she is only "caused a worse fright" herself; the trauma seems to be emotional rather than physical, much as, in the diagnosis of her loss that opens this chapter, its cause seems to be her persistence in riding rather than the riding itself. Again, it seems that the exact significance in plain English of Rosamond's somatic expression and experience is unnarratable. Furthermore, these indirect causes of Rosamond's trauma while riding and, "finally," the loss of the baby (How much time has passed, exactly? An hour? A day? A week? The chronological indeterminacy of that "finally" adds to the imprecision of the narrative diagnosis) suggest that the transgression for which the narrative must punish Rosamond is the unapologetic inaccessibility of her body to narrative language and the authority of the doctor-husband.

How much more fully convinced would we be by the authoritative free indirect diagnosis of the premature birth of Rosamond's child if she were to have fallen from her horse? If cramping, labor, and/or birth were to have occurred, explicitly, within a few hours of the incident? The narrative indirection and imprecision of Rosamond's pregnancy loss suggests the possibility that Lydgate mistakes the meanings of her body in this instance as we have seen him do not only in the passages I have read closely but throughout his courtship and early marriage. Lydgate's mistaking of Rosamond's surface for her substance is thematized as his fatal flaw, that but for which all might have been well. That this mistake is one that amounts to a medical man's misreading of somatic meanings, however, is the point I drive home here and one the Shakespearian epigraph to the chapter narrating these events also emphasizes:

> For there can live no hatred in thine eye,
> Therefor in that I cannot know thy change:
> In many's looks the false hearts' history
> Is writ in moods and frowns and wrinkles strange;
> But Heaven in thy creation did decree
> That in thy face sweet love should ever dwell;

Whate'er thy thoughts or thy hearts workings be,
Thy looks should nothing thence but sweetness tell. (359)

The speaker of these lines—mystified by the opacity of his lover's body—anticipates the confusion Lydgate will finally come to feel in the face of his wife's illegible surfaces. The speaker's interpretative limitations also reflect those of the narrator, however. Though the surface of Rosamond's body—like the surface of Hetty's—receives much attention from characters and narrator alike, the only serious attention her "heart's history" receives is filtered through the crisis of her conflict with Dorothea, as Hetty's heart's history filters through her confession to Dinah. Not only do "mood and frowns and wrinkles strange" refuse to offer keys to Rosamond's "hearts workings," but they seem also to refuse keys to the workings of her body below its surface.

The narrative authority framing Rosamond's pregnancy and its end with these lines on bodily inscrutability is one that does not narrate her body's meanings and certainly does not narrate her somatic possibilities with anything approaching the nuance granted the narration of her husband's psyche. Indeed, this same narrative authority aligns its past-tense narration of Rosamond's pregnancy and loss very closely with the memory of "our Tertius" (399). We think these scenes primarily through Lydgate, but Rosamond's resistance to authority has also already been framed by the chapter's thematic epigraph and opening paragraph. Therefore, though "Lydgate could not" and the narrator does not "show . . . anger toward" Rosamond after the loss of the baby, the reader can. That "this misfortune *was attributed* entirely to her having persisted in going out on horseback one day when her husband had desired her not to do so" seems, then, to prophesy and shape our own diagnosis, the vague referent of the attribution as much the reader's own as the narrator's or any particular character's. This convergence of an implicit agreement between narrator, authoritative character, and reader demonstrates the workings of a discourse of pregnancy in *Middlemarch*: It is as though the attribution of Rosamond's pregnancy loss to her transgressions of femininity has always already existed and yet also as though that attribution is being created through each act of reading.

But the chapter that narrates Rosamond's pregnancy and its end within a moralistic discourse of pregnancy also hints at the limits of that discourse and offers the possibility that Rosamond's pregnant body itself may function in ways not fully tethered to discourse. Though I have shown that the direct representation of the pregnant body often constructs a moralizing discourse of pregnancy in which its visibility marks feminine transgression, I have also explored the ways in which the representation of pregnant surfaces avoids the narration of the embodied experiences of the pregnant characters themselves. Though Hetty's pregnant body—cut loose from the protections of community and family—communicates her immorality to innkeepers and readers alike, *Adam Bede*'s narrative avoidance of her experience occupying that pregnant body seems to exclude internal experience in the textual discourse of pregnancy. Though reading the surface of pregnant bodies in Victorian novels often engages us in the practices of a moralizing discourse, attending to the possible stirrings of morning sickness, quickening, and contraction, for example, offers the possibility of a critical space in which we might try to consider bodies without necessarily sympathizing with or diagnosing them. Heather Love's question about what it would mean for humanist scholars to "talk *about* rather than *for*" our subjects prompts me to wonder what it would mean to talk about Rosamond's pregnancy and loss themselves, rather than to talk about what we take their moral and narrative significance to be ("Ecologies"). Caught up with a narrator who aligns their representation of Rosamond with Lydgate's moral and medical authority, we can attempt to do this by imagining the unnarratable significances of Rosamond's body; though Thierauf's helpful attention to the possibility of abortion as such an unnarratable significance signals the ways that Rosamond's pregnant body opens critical space for resistance to normative plots, I think it is also important to read the pregnancy loss as a loss—whether abortion, late-term miscarriage, or stillbirth—that evokes certain uncertain but distinct and painful somatic experiences.

However, in seeking to attend to an embodied, experiential space of pregnancy not entirely circumscribed by the terms of narrative discourse, we must also notice Rosamond's own assessment of the end of her pregnancy. Perhaps, as Lydgate's understanding of the significations of his wife's body is shown to be, our diagnosis of the meaning of Rosamond's pregnancy and loss—in which we take miscarriage as a moral metaphor for her sympathetic failings and inaccessibility—is flawed. Rosamond, we are told in passing, "in all future conversation on the subject [of her loss] . . . was mildly certain that the ride had made no difference, and that if she had stayed at home the same symptoms would have come on and would have ended in the same way, because she had felt something like them before" (362). Rosamond's "mild[ ] . . . certain[ty]" regarding the unimportance of the ride can be read in multiple ways. Thierauf reads in it "an indication of Rosamond's previous attempts to induce an abortion" (481). Readers seem primed by the narrative perspective on her character to interpret Rosamond's mildness as an indication that the subject of her pregnancy loss doesn't particularly interest her—because, the implication seems to be, she is the kind of woman, wife, and mother to whom the loss means very little. But perhaps Rosamond's expressions of certainty are "mild" because Lydgate attaches little legitimacy to their substance. She may be "certain," but that certainty carries no real narrative importance. Or, perhaps Rosamond is herself only a little "certain" of her own opinion, experiencing an alternative narrative of causation as vaguely as the vague "symptoms" she cites as that alternative cause's evidence.

Similarly, it is unclear whether we would do best to ascribe the imprecision of these "same symptoms" and the "something like them" that mark both the end of the pregnancy and some mysterious period of time preceding it to a reserve that is narrative, husbandly, ladylike, or—possibly—a silent affirmation of the body's ability to function outside of discourse. This announcement that Rosamond "had felt something like [the symptoms of the loss] before" is the only hint that Rosamond's pregnancy might be anything other than a marker of Lydgate's escalating personal and professional crisis, that it might also be an internal condition, experienced by a particular woman's body in particular ways that function outside of the boundaries of narration, marriage, medical opinion, or pregnancy discourse. Readers likely struggle to sympathize with these inarticulate symptoms as we can sympathize with even the pregnant symptoms of Cathy in *Wuthering Heights*, narrated as they are in the language of illness and pain that invites that mode of readerly engagement. Yet it must be that the premature birth of Rosamond's child represents a physically painful experience even if Rosamond were not particularly excited about the prospect of becoming a mother. Readers also likely struggle to diagnose these symptoms, the complete blank of "something" resisting the will to seek out detail. Yet it must be the case that this is Some Thing in particular: Perhaps Rosamond experienced the fetal quickening that would, a century before, have authorized her to articulate her own pregnancy, to become the authoritative knower and sayer of her reproductive body. Or perhaps Rosamond had bouts of early contractions. A second-trimester or—more likely the case for Rosamond—third-trimester pregnancy loss is much less common than first-trimester miscarriage, and because we later learn that Rosamond carries four children to term, a diagnostic approach to the Some Thing that she feels during pregnancy rules out certain chronic conditions of the womb and cervix that would have hindered her ability to carry any fetus to term. Though we cannot rule out sexually transmitted disease—which can also cause late-term miscarriage, stillbirth, and/or premature birth and which would deepen the specter of Rosamond's immorality—with the same certainty, I do not believe that there is a strong reading to be made of Rosamond as a syphilitic antiheroine. In short, though the impulse to diagnose Rosamond's experience of pregnancy loss can prompt us to consider the embodied possibilities of internal reproductive experiences, the extreme narrative imprecision of Rosamond's oppositional opinion serves best to make our lack of sympathetic or diagnostic access to her pregnant body legible in its very deployment of her illegible body.

And the very prematureness of the birth carries the suggestion of immodesty and immorality. The immodesty of Rosamond's prematureness, however, is narrated not only implicitly in chapter 58 but also explicitly before she marries:

> Do you imagine that [Rosamond's] rapid forecast and rumination concerning house-furniture and society were ever discernible in her conversation, even with her mamma? On the contrary, she would have expressed the prettiest surprise and disapprobation if she had heard that another young lady had been detected in that *immodest prematureness*. (169; emphasis added)

Before Lydgate has declared his love for Rosamond, she has planned the details of their married life together, a sexual-domestic space in which they will share "house-furniture" and through which she will be elevated in "society." Rosamond clearly understands that such planning oversteps the bounds of normative femininity: She is committing herself before and beyond the invitation of her lover. Her understanding of this is obvious in the censure with which she would treat "another young lady who had been detected" in such anticipations. In other words, Rosamond's immodesty is made visible and magnified by her own awareness of it and her own attempts to conceal it. Likewise, in her decision to horseback ride with Captain Lydgate against the advice and request of her doctor-husband, it is Rosamond's attempt to deceive Lydgate and conceal her actions from him that seem to heighten rather than lessen her transgression. In representing Rosamond as trying to shield her questionable behavior from sight, the narrative brings it into greater focus for the reader, paving the way for our participation in a moral discourse that ascribes the revelation of Rosamond's pregnancy and its premature end to her misbehavior. This ascription aligns our reading of Rosamond's actions with Lydgate's diagnosis of her body.

However, just as Lydgate's masculine medical authority over Rosamond ultimately miscarries, my reading of the ways in which her body seems capable of signifying outside of discourse and resisting precise interpretation demonstrates the ways our own critical authority over Rosamond may miscarry. If we do not quite feel that "surely [we are] the person[s] to judge *for* her," we are more likely to feel that we are the persons to judge her. But Rosamond's interiority is almost always narrated as a surface, as an awareness—as in the scene of her premarital prematurity above—of how she might or must appear to others. Though the revelation of Rosamond's pregnancy would seem to offer the reader privileged access to her interior life, that access functions to highlight our lack of knowledge, our ignorance regarding the "something" she suggests she feels and has felt before.

Another tantalizing suggestion of Rosamond's interiority, of her affective and somatic engagement with her pregnancy loss, occurs later in the novel, following the scene in which Dorothea happens upon her excessive intimacy with Ladislaw:

> After he was gone, Rosamond tried to get up from her seat, but fell back fainting. When she came to herself again, she felt too ill to make the exertion of rising to ring the bell, and she remained helpless until the girl, surprised at her long absence, thought for the first time of looking for her in all the down-stairs rooms. Rosamond said that she had felt suddenly sick and faint, and wanted to be helped up-stairs. When there she threw herself on the bed with her clothes on, and lay in apparent torpor, as she had done once before on a memorable day of grief. (481)

Rosamond's struggle here is painted in the language of the body ("sick and faint") and framed at a kind of remove that suggests dishonesty, that this is a performance rather than sincere sensation (she "*said* that she had felt suddenly sick and faint" rather than "she was suddenly sick and faint"; she lays "in apparent" rather than real "torpor"). But this does not seem like a performance, and that narrative suggestion works against the connection that's drawn between these feelings of guilt and disappointment and the way she felt "once before on a memorable day of grief." It's hard to locate the possibility of any similar day of grief in the novel because, of course, nowhere else has *Middlemarch* suggested that Rosamond experienced any emotion at all regarding her pregnancy loss. But what else could this memorable day of grief have been? It's living here, peeping its head up from beneath the narrated surface of the novel.

"THIS PREGNANT LITTLE FACT"

Though Rosamond's pregnancy is explicitly revealed to the reader, Rosamond is described not as "pregnant" but as "expecting a child." There are only three uses of "pregnant" in *Middlemarch,* and none of these refer to reproductive bodies.[22] Of course, this reflects a historical context in which the terms "preg-

---

22. As compared with fifty-one uses of "expectation" and twenty-three uses of "conception" in the novel, for example.

nant" and "pregnancy" were less frequently employed; NGram Viewer graphs suggest that we don't start to see a significant rise in the use of those words until the 1970s ("pregnant,pregnancy"). Where *Middlemarch* does employ the word "pregnant," it is to convey a coming to knowledge that can be shared by the character, narrator, and a reader. This pregnant knowing is linked to both seeing and saying, to diagnosis of the visible/revealed world. The novel's first deployment of "pregnant," for example, plays with the tension between surface and "fact" in a language of vision and visibility:

> An eminent philosopher among my friends, who can dignify even your ugly furniture by lifting it into the serene light of science, has shown me this *pregnant* little fact. Your pier-glass or extensive surface of polished steel made to be rubbed by a housemaid, will be minutely and multitudinously scratched in all directions; but place now against it a lighted candle as a centre of illumination, and lo! the scratches will seem to arrange themselves in a fine series of concentric circles round that little sun. It is demonstrable that the scratches are going everywhere impartially and it is only your candle which produces the flattering illusion of a concentric arrangement, its light falling with an exclusive optical selection. These things are a parable. The scratches are events, and the candle is the egoism of any person now absent—of Miss Vincy, for example. (166–67; emphasis added)

It is possible to read "pregnant" here as a synonym for either "telling" or "revealing" (e.g., "a telling little fact" or "a revealing little fact")—and though I will demonstrate the ways in which this passage uses "pregnant" in more ways than just that, even this dimension of the usage is significant to the interests of this chapter and the book more broadly. Reading "pregnant" as a possible synonym for "telling" and "revealing" demonstrates the ways in which the form and function of the term move in similar conceptual grooves in the Victorian novel. As I have argued, embodied pregnancy in the Victorian novel is told only insofar as it is "telling" of a moral lesson, which is to say that pregnancy acts not primarily as a mirror held up to nature (nature being something like those "multitudinous[ ] scratches in all directions") but, rather, as a mirror held up to the secrets of nature. That which is "pregnant" in this sense is that which reveals—as pregnant characters are revealed from behind the veil of modesty—or shows us a hidden, secret, internal truth. (And we might think here of our own modern usage of "showing" to describe the state at which a woman's pregnancy begins to be easily visible on the surface of her body). In being used as a kind of synonym for "telling" or "revealing," then, "pregnant" is also being used to connote those "internal structures" of body and mind that so captivate and mystify Lydgate. The "fine series of concentric circles round [a] little sun" suggests something of the shape a pregnant belly takes around a fetus, "sun" and "son" holding a hackneyed but relevant relationship. But that suggestion of meaning, as any suggestion of meaning found in the light of individual interpretation, may be only a flattering illusion. In the end, the desire to see a recognizable shape around a knowable center is only a reflection we catch and cast of ourselves—imagining coherent and comprehensible interiorities that we can incorporate into "a suffusive sense of its connections with all the rest of our existence"—in the pier glass. A "pregnant little fact" like the one above may seem to hold out the key to all mythologies, but pregnancy in *Middlemarch*, both literal and "parable," finally offers only an opportunity to glimpse our unknowingness in the reflective surfaces of bodies that seem to offer meaning. In the case of Celia, our unknowingness is the pregnancy altogether, hidden from us despite what we know must be the blatant inescapability of her pregnant body. In the case of Rosamond, our unknowingness is what we share with Lydgate, that which cannot imagine what the depths beneath her smooth blonde surface might be. In the case of the "pregnant little fact" about the mirror, our unknowingness is depth and surface together; not only is there no way to understand what lies beyond the pier glass, but even the surface of the pier glass itself is inscrutable.

Thinking through Eliot's use of "pregnant" in the context of her representation (or lack thereof) of pregnant bodies makes legible the discursive practices of pregnancy in the novel in ways that speak to the discursive practices of pregnancy in the Victorian period more generally. The way Eliot employs the term "pregnant" in the passage above, as a showing fact that requires and reveals the deceptions of surfaces, reflects the way in which we read pregnancy itself—as an unavoidable fact that manifests avoidably beneath the surfaces of articulability. A discourse of pregnancy in Victorian novels both articulates embodied reproduction as a description of something that has always already existed and also brings embodied reproduction into existence as a marker of immodesty and immorality.

As reading Rosamond's reproductive body in *Middlemarch* demonstrates, searching for a "deeper" truth behind discursive narrations of bodies is an endeavor likely to miscarry. There is no hidden reality behind the textual curtain of Rosamond's representation in the novel. That representation both diagnoses and creates her. In seeking to attend to Rosamond's surface, we—like Lydgate—are thwarted by her body's resistance to interpretation. Interestingly, we come perhaps closest to an understanding of the surface of Rosamond's embodied experience in her own passing reference to interior sensation. This nexus of complications in thinking through surface and depth demonstrates the particular value of literary representations of pregnancy to ongoing critical conversations about reading practices.

My suggestion that reading pregnancy—an interior state that complicates the very notion of singular interiority and is eventually marked by surface signs legible to all—might give us access to the complications of knowing what is individual and what is other, of knowing where, between surface and depth, the "truth" of experience lies, is hardly innovative. *Middlemarch* itself teases these matters out of the term "pregnant" even more directly in the second instance of its use in the novel. In seeking to calm a group of working men resistant to the imminent arrival of a railroad, Caleb Garth asks, "'Why, my lads, how's this?' . . . taking as usual to brief phrases, which seemed *pregnant* to himself, because he had many thoughts lying under them, like the abundant roots of a plant that just manages to peep above the water" (346; emphasis added). The free indirect play of the narrative with Caleb's mind here defines "pregnant" as that which grows primarily beneath the surface of shared knowability but which may be possible to intuit insofar as it "peep[s] above the water." Or it may not. Caleb's hope that his "brief phrases" will carry their intended meaning to the men he addresses proves tenuous at best. Once "Why, my lads, how's this?" hits the surface of shared experience, its meaning can be interpreted differently by anyone who encounters it.

The "strictly scientific view of woman" that Lydgate takes in his dealings with Rosamond—as learned by his mishap with the murderess Laure—would seek to read shared meaning where it may never be (99). Lydgate fails to account for Rosamond's hidden depths, and the novel refuses to correct this mistake except insofar as Rosamond's depths are shown to be consumed by an immodest concern for surface and an immoral desire for the admiration of her own surfaces. Like Hetty, Rosamond seems to be largely excluded from the sympathetic gaze of her narrator and seems to remain almost completely incapable of internal growth. Her ability to become a self who recognizes the existence of other selves is represented as being at best stunted and at worst miscarried. Rosamond's hyperinclusion in Lydgate's medical gaze does nothing to treat this problem but rather seems to extend the reach of her loss of child and sympathetic self to the realm of her husband's professional aspirations, aspirations that eventually falter under the weight of his domestic demands. The way in which Rosamond's pregnancy can be read as a kind of metaphor for Lydgate's professional misdevelopment speaks to the ways in which representations of pregnancy in the Victorian novel more generally resist being read as embodied female experience and push toward metaphorical uses.

We see the metaphorical significance of pregnancy also in Dorothea's marriage to Casaubon. The marriage is a sterile one, likely almost completely sexless, but in the place where a pregnancy could be conceived—in the period during and immediately following their honeymoon, the period during which both Celia and Rosamond do conceive and Dorothea, possessed of "powerful, feminine, maternal hands," might also have done—she conceives her sympathetic self instead (25). Dorothea learns to read beneath the surfaces of those around her to depths that equal her own in nuance and significance. She develops, in other words, an ability to recognize other interiorities—"dubious eggs called possibilities"—within her own (53). This is "the mental act that was struggling forth" in Dorothea after her marriage more successfully than the physical body that struggles forth from Rosamond (123).

The third and final use of "pregnant" in *Middlemarch* occurs in the context of Dorothea's sterile marriage. The passage narrates Dorothea's nascent sympathetic (or "moral") rebirth in a vocabulary of reproduction, bodies, surface, depth, and visibility:

> There was the stifling oppression of that gentlewoman's world . . . where the sense of connection with a manifold *pregnant* existence had to be kept up painfully as an *inward vision,* instead of coming from without in claims that would have *shaped* her energies. . . . Marriage, which was to bring guidance into worthy and imperative occupation, had not yet freed her from the gentlewoman's oppressive liberty: it had not even filled her leisure with the ruminant joy of unchecked tenderness. Her *blooming full-pulsed* youth stood there in a *moral* imprisonment which made itself one with the chill, colorless, narrowed landscape, with the shrunken furniture, the never-read books, and the ghostly stage in a pale fantastic world that seemed to be *vanishing* from the *daylight.* (173; emphasis added)

Why always Dorothea, indeed? Why has a reading of *Middlemarch* concerned with the literal representation of pregnant bodies in the novel begun and ended with Dorothea, who is only pregnant after the conclusion of the novel's central plots? Why might I seem to be suggesting that the only fully envisioned pregnancy in the novel is that of a character who never becomes pregnant? The answer to these questions lies in the gap between the actual pregnant bodies that the novel conceals and reveals in the discursive patterns of pregnancy representation in Victorian fiction and these three "pregnant" moments in which no pregnant body figures. The narration of *Middlemarch* encourages a metaphorical readerly engagement with the idea of pregnancy and a moralistic engagement with its embodied facts. Reading Lydgate's role in the narration of Rosamond's pregnancy and the role of Rosamond's pregnancy in the plot of Lydgate's professional miscarriage demonstrates the ways in which medical discourse participates in a moralistic authority over pregnancy in Victorian literature. The workings of free indirect diagnosis that I have traced in *Middlemarch* invite the reader into such authority, while reading pregnant bodies like Rosamond's somatically suggests a mode that fosters more resistance to the siren song of such knowing. This chapter has sketched a relationship to bodies that allows room for "pregnant" uncertainty as a critical mode. Such a mode is necessary, I argue in the next and final chapter of this book, if we are to conceptualize the shift that occurs in the mid- to late Victorian literary medicalizations of pregnancy that rely increasingly upon notions of interiority as such notions develop into a specialized theory of psychology. Only by thinking through this shift are we able to untangle some of the relevance of Victorian literary representations to our own radically altered and troubled relationships to reproductive bodies and questions of knowledge.

CHAPTER 4

Impression

As the Victorian period draws to a close, pregnancy is represented with increasing candor and the anxieties evoked by textual representations of pregnancy shift in emphasis from the expression of fear about women's unruly bodies and behaviors to broader fears about unruly minds. Scholarship on disability often asks that we question the cultural, literary, and critical conflation of embodied states with metaphorical meanings. Jennifer Esmail, for example, signals Victorian "attempts to use signing deaf people as a site for exploring larger concerns about the relationship between the human body, ability, and language" (9). This is a useful structure for thinking through representations of pregnancy at the fin de siècle: Though pregnancy is represented more directly in the novels this chapter treats than it was in earlier Victorian fiction, this shift does not tend to increase our ability to read pregnancy as an embodied state. Rather, we see a shift toward symbolic deployments of pregnancy not as a physical marker for maternal misbehavior but as an impressionistic gesture toward larger concerns about the relationships among body, mind, and social future. In this chapter, I map out this tendency and continue to push toward reading pregnant bodies somatically, as bodies and not only as metaphors.

The 1890s saw major shifts in the normative ideologies we tend to associate with the Victorian period, including the ideologies of gender, sexuality, bodies, and mind so central to shaping the ways in which pregnancy is represented. That these shifts would change how pregnancy is represented in novels of the period is unsurprising. Not only in the novelistic pregnancies I'll examine in this chapter but also in notable pregnancies in short stories like George Egerton's 1893 "A Cross Line" or Thomas Hardy's 1894 "An Imaginative Woman," reading pregnancy in the 1890s requires that we read the ways in which immodesty and immorality have moved out of women's bodies, now manifesting as social disease, paternal legacy, psychological state, and racialized threat.

The novelistic representation of pregnancy at the fin de siècle shifts from emphasizing fears about gendered transgressions of normative morality to emphasizing fears about the impressive, decadent power of the (unconscious) mind. Certainly, the pregnant unconscious remains deeply gendered, shaped by ideologies that position the potential powers of women's minds and bodies as particularly dangerous. But anxieties about a pregnant unconscious also hinge on the possibility that masculine minds and bodies might be unstable and dangerous in ways that can be impressed upon futurity through women's reproductive bodies.

This shift toward concern with the dangers of the unconscious reflects the emergence of and an increasing cultural investment in the "new psychology" dating to the 1860s but converging markedly with medical practice, narrative form, and theories of gender and sexuality in the fin de siècle. As is the case, for example, in Freud's 1895 *Studies on Hysteria,* women's minds and bodies—often understood as such through their "ultimate" and "exceptional" ability to reproduce—serve medical and psychological fields as backdrops against which to explore "the [blurred] line between body and mind" beyond the bodies and minds of women only (Mazzoni 24). Indeed, recent scholarship has explored the ways Victorians came, particularly at the close of the nineteenth century, to understand thinking in general as not necessarily conscious or brain-centric.[1] My contention is that reading fin de siècle pregnancy can help us to read the ways in which the period expressed anxiety about the impressions the unconscious might make on increasingly embattled expectations for

---

1. The revelation that Vanessa L. Ryan plagiarized sections of her influential 2012 *Thinking without Thinking in the Victorian Novel* troubles the debt this chapter owes to her work on what she calls the "not wholly agential or wholly conscious" thinking that occurs in Victorian fiction, thinking Ryan's book demonstrates "is not confined solely to the brain" (13). That the plagiarism in the book seems to have been in sections dealing with the details of Victorian scientific theory supports Ryan's claims, I think, that the argumentative thrust of her book is original—and this argumentative thrust is certainly one with which this chapter is in conversation. This is a conversation, however, that need hardly rely wholly upon Ryan's work, as Elisha Cohn's *Still Life: Suspended Development in the Victorian Novel* and Elaine Auyoung's *When Fiction Feels Real* attest.

explicitly classist and racist "civilized" and "civilizing" progress. Some of the best arguments for the continued march of progress in the 1890s—a decade that saw real unravelings of popular faith in imperial projects, in the gendered, middle-class mores and norms that had undergirded those projects, and in the definitions of civilization upon which their rhetoric and practice relied—were the huge strides in medical knowledge the nineteenth century had seen and that late Victorians were beginning to see reflected more often in their daily lives.[2] However, strides in medical knowledge were themselves untethering the knowable body of the patient from the knowing mind of the doctor and hinting at the inaccessible powers of the unconscious minds of patients and doctors alike. As the Victorian period draws to a close, familiar anxieties evoked by textual representation of pregnancy increasingly come to encompass fears about the disruptive social and physical agency of a pregnant unconscious that is not necessarily tethered to pregnant bodies themselves but deeply somatic nonetheless, written on the body as disease, disability, and race.

The goal of this chapter is to demonstrate the shift from the representation of pregnancy as an expression of a female character's immodest or immoral relationship with her body in the world toward the representation of pregnancy as an expression of the overflow of disordered minds and societies onto and into the bodies that shape the future. I position this shift within a medicalization of mind that, while occurring over the course of the mid- to late nineteenth century, gains particular momentum at the fin de siècle. In all of the novels I read here, the danger of pregnancy has shifted from being a physical expression of transgressive sexuality to being a mental expression of decadent power. In Sarah Grand's 1893 new woman novel, *The Heavenly Twins,* the transgression mapped onto the bodies of pregnant characters is not the pregnant woman's own but rather that of an immoral, masculine society to which she has been sacrificed. Pregnancy is punishment for social wrongs practiced by men; the dangers these social ills pose to posterity are made visible on the canvas of pregnant bodies and minds. In Thomas Hardy's writing, pregnancy is an almost invisible site of danger in which the workings of inheritance are unknowable and/or illogical. In both *Heavenly Twins* and Hardy's 1895 *Jude the Obscure,* the decadence of paternal impressions is emphasized in children who are "unnaturally" old. In Lucas Malet's underread, generically complex 1901 magnum opus, *The History of Sir Richard Calmady,* pregnancy is the site at which an old, outdated theory of mind and an old, ancestral curse rise to shape a body suggestive of a dangerously disabled future. It is in Victoria Cross's 1901 *Anna Lombard,* however, that the presentist stakes of this project's

---

2. See Carpenter for more on these shifts.

investigations into pregnancy are most legible; the novel figures the heroine's decadent psychology as racialized passion, the risks of paternal impression as the risk of racial confusion, and the solution to such dangers as the death and murder of people of color.

In the first section of this chapter, I explore the theories and histories of impression at work in the literary readings that follow. The second section moves through the fin de siècle to read the ways that novels of the period frame paternal impression as a dangerous blurring of the boundaries between mind and body in *The Heavenly Twins,* the work of Thomas Hardy and *Jude the Obscure* in particular, *The History of Sir Richard Calmady,* and *Anna Lombard.* I explore the convergence of the Victorian novelistic tendency to represent only the pregnant bodies of women who misbehave, which I explored in chapters 1 and 2, with the narrative encouragement toward metaphorical readings of pregnancy I examined in chapter 3; I trace the mapping of fin de siècle fears about the dangerous power of minds onto increasingly frank representations of pregnant bodies in order to suggest that the modes of reading posited and debated in contemporary literary criticism can be usefully understood in the context of the pregnant paternal impressions that haunt the final decade of Victorian literature. By reading with an attention to the body that resists certainty and hard fact, can we intuit something like the shape of pregnancy at the end of the nineteenth century and the shadow that legacy casts on our own cultures of body?

UNSTABLE MINDS

In *Unstable Bodies,* Matus makes a case not only for the instability of representations of transgressive female sexuality and maternity—these representations tend to elide seemingly distinct categories of human and animal, "civilized" and "uncivilized"—but for the instability of these representations themselves. There is no one way in which dangerous female sexuality and maternity is or can be represented. In her conclusion, Matus sketches connections between this instability in a seemingly ideologically coherent period and the broader shifts of modernity leading into a twentieth century in which a sense of ideological coherence proves increasingly elusive. Matus argues that the subversion of ideology is baked into ideological structures:

> The [Victorian] notion of sexuality as culturally and environmentally responsive offered ways of defining differences among women of different classes, nationalities, and races. And given the instability of representations

and their capacity to be used in oppositional or subversive contexts, ideas about unstable sexual difference were available to be mobilized to undermine the very ideologies with which they have been associated. (249)

The close readings in *Unstable Bodies* stop at *Middlemarch*, but Matus's emphasis—as in the passage above—on the potential for the unstable representations of those bodies to "undermine" the stability of ideologies of gender, class, nation, and race gestures toward the workings of pregnancy in fin de siècle novels.

Matus helpfully sums up late nineteenth-century notions of the collusion between morality and medicine in citing Elizabeth Blackwell's 1884 *Human Element in Sex*. Blackwell argues that "medicine and morality being related to function and use, are therefore inseparable in a Christian state" (2). Though twenty-first-century criticism tends to look with suspicion on such equations, I have traced the ways Victorian narrative judgments participate in contemporary modes of reading. These are not simply historical ideologies we have set aside; we can't read the Victorian novelistic pregnancies that resist somatic legibility without reading the habits of our own deducing minds and their unstable tendencies to impress themselves upon text. The afterlives of Victorian medicalizing and moralizing perspectives live in us.

Though the slim critical tradition on pregnancy in nineteenth-century fiction has not been centrally concerned with modes of reading, Cristina Mazzoni has demonstrated the importance of mental process to the representation and critical reading of pregnancy, particularly at the fin de siècle. Mazzoni's reading of pregnancy and childbirth in turn-of-the-century Italian literature hinges on notions of impressions: "the impressions of a mother . . . the impressions others have of mothers, the impressions mothers have of others—and of themselves" (ix). "Impression," says Mazzoni, "is a dual word," and this chapter demonstrates the ways that attempting to think through how pregnancy works in Victorian novels brings me to a reading of fin de siècle novels that represent pregnancy as a bodily condition through which unconscious minds think and impress. These thinking, impressing minds belong not only to the mothers in these novels but also and importantly to paternal figures. Reading not only the workings of maternal impression theory in the novels of the fin de siècle but also the workings of paternal impression makes legible the myriad ways in which late-Victorian novels position pregnancy as a condition through which the mind thinks itself and shapes bodies and futures.

•

The administration of anesthesia during childbirth offers a possibility of separation between mind and body. In the context of childbirth, space is opened in which the maternal mind is separated from the functions of and actions upon her body and the fetal body she carries. The opening of this space in the mid-Victorian period shifts ways of knowing pregnancy. Similarly, the increasing medicalization of women's reproductive lives over the course of the nineteenth century (a process spurred, in part, by medical training in forceps use and other labor interventions) offers a possibility of separation. Obstetrical practice opens between the maternal body and fetal body a space in which action relies upon the doctor rather than the laboring woman. Both forceps use and anesthesia administration suggest an impulse to organize reproduction by erecting boundaries between maternal bodies and minds. This is an impulse to classify maternal bodies, medical bodies, and medical minds as essential to reproduction and maternal minds as inessential. But what if maternal minds transgress that organization? And what if minds, more generally, are capable of transgressing the boundaries of body?

We can read familiar fin de siècle concerns about such transgression of mind/body anew by reading pregnancy as an embodied condition with particular relevance that intersects with but is not identical to work on permeable borders and female sexuality or maternity at the close of the nineteenth century. A vocabulary of impression—particularly what I call paternal impression—is helpful for this project. I build this vocabulary of paternal impression out from maternal impression theory (also called maternal imagination theory), a theory no longer in medical favor in the nineteenth century, which posits that what a pregnant woman sees or experiences can be directly reflected in the fetus she carries.[3] Ann Oakley calls maternal impression a "key theory about pregnancy commonly held prior to the modern obstetric era stat[ing] that the condition and viability of the fetus was profoundly influenced by the mother's mental and emotional state" (23).[4] Mazzoni calls maternal impression "the belief that the fetus can be affected by its mother's desires, fears, [and] experiences" (ix). Philip Wilson calls it "an age-old belief, which persists in many cultures, [that] alleges that a pregnant woman's imagination, frights, or longings can be transferred to her unborn child, thereby imprinting the child with characteristic marks or deformities" (2). Wilson offers the

---

3. Clare Hanson notes, "Erasmus Darwin was characteristically wayward in supporting [at the close of the eighteenth century] a notion of impressions—but in his case, it was paternal impressions. In *Zoonomia* he argued that the world had 'long been mistaken in ascribing great power to the imagination of the female' and that 'the real power of imagination, in the act of gestation, belongs solely to the male'" (27).

4. Mazzoni also employs this passage from Oakley.

literary and cultural instances of, for example, a "strawberry-shaped birthmark" understood to result from a pregnant craving for strawberries, a leech marking on the child of a woman who was bled with a particularly large leech during pregnancy, and "a child's resemblance to either parent." This is to say that maternal impression is associated with pregnancy cravings, with strong fears and emotions experienced during pregnancy, and with a mother's looking with strong feeling at herself or her partner during pregnancy.

Though Marie-Helene Huet traces maternal impression theories from the classical age though the modern one, Mazzoni cautions that such a lineage conflates maternal impression with a "different, ancient theory" that what a couple or woman saw during conception marked the fetus (16). In any event, maternal impression theories regarding the connection of body and mind during pregnancy specifically were particularly prevalent during the Renaissance and sustained themselves through the medical and scientific revolutions of the Enlightenment. Though there was some "lively intellectual debate" during the eighteenth century as to whether or not the kinds of markings and "monstrosities" that had hitherto been ascribed to maternal imagination were indeed a result of cravings and scares in pregnancy, creative literature of that period frequently and uncritically engages with notions of maternal impression (Mazzoni 16). Philip Wilson notes the deployment of maternal impression, for example, in the novels of Henry Fielding, Lawrence Sterne, and Tobias Smollett.[5]

Literary and serious scientific treatments of maternal impression theory largely recede from view for much of the nineteenth century along with frank representations of sexuality and pregnancy more generally. Like Mangham, I find it notable that maternal impression "survived at a time when one would

---

5. Wilson writes about the influence of notions of maternal impression on Fielding, Sterne, and Smollett:

> The maternally derived birthmark in Fielding's *Joseph Andrews* ultimately reveals the true identity of a main character. Jonathan Wild, Fielding's protagonist in his 1745 novel of the same name, has his whole criminal future impressed upon him by his mother's "violent desires to acquire all sorts of property" during her pregnancy. Sterne's novel, *Tristram Shandy*, also concerns an individual whose life is marked via in utero influence, a point that readers learn from the opening pages of the work.
>
> Tobias Smollett, a trained surgeon and physician, presents a more elaborate account of the action of maternal impression upon the character development of his protagonist, Peregrine Pickle. Smollett's attention to maternal matters in this work is understandable given that, while composing *Peregrine Pickle*, he was concurrently editing and annotating a Treatise on the Theory and Practice of Midwifery for the Edinburgh physician and male midwife, William Smellie, to whom he had served as an apprentice. (10)

assume it to have been outdated," and this chapter focuses on analyzing what ongoing beliefs in maternal impression are *doing* in the period (Mangham 32). As women's reproductive lives fell under increasing medical controls, ascriptions of pregnant agency often shifted from female minds and bodies to masculine expertise. But at the fin de siècle, when pregnancy reemerges as a condition that it might be possible to narrate with physical and psychological nuance, impression theories make notable appearances in literature. It is the deployment of a scientifically outdated theory in these narratives that suggests that impression is *doing something* in late-Victorian fiction. That *something* is an articulation of rising concerns about impressions more broadly, an articulation of concern about the disruptive social and physical agency of the unconscious mind and decadent breakdowns of clear boundaries. These rising concerns dovetail with a moment at which, when pregnancy is being thought, that thinking is unlikely to remain confined to the borders of the maternal mind alone.

A concern about impression as a psycho-physical phenomenon is named directly in only one of four novels I read in this chapter, Malet's *Calmady*. Though Grand, Hardy, and Cross don't use the term to describe reproductive processes, *The Heavenly Twins, Jude the Obscure,* and *Anna Lombard* also work on the cluster of anxieties associated with impression. All of these novels demonstrate rising anxieties about maternal impression at the fin de siècle and the ways that these anxieties slip toward less coherent but equally threatening fears about paternal impression. These themes are hardly confined to these novels—which, in their chronological and generic range suggest a broader tendency and pattern of concern—but appear throughout the final decade of the nineteenth century.

I argue that we can best see what impression theories are doing by broadening outward from established understandings of maternal impression—understandings that recur across cultures and history and with which we are also familiar in the guise of, for example, attitudes surrounding maternal alcohol and drug consumption—toward an interest in impression as a force on pregnancy not necessarily tethered to the maternal mind and body. Just as strong a force as maternal impression in late-Victorian representations of pregnancy is a notion of paternal impression that speaks tellingly to fears about decadent breakdowns of boundaries. There is a cultural and historical shift from Victorian ideologies built upon, concerned with, and threatened by unstable bodies to a fin de siècle moment in which the site of ideological articulation, concern, and threat lay increasingly with unstable minds.

A simplistic Enlightenment model of the impressive powers of the mind would tend to suggest that increasingly cultivated minds lead toward increasingly cultivated societies, that education tends toward "civilization," and that civilization marches toward progress. The widening tolls of industrialization and threats to "civilizing" imperial projects at end of the British nineteenth century, however, threatened faith in progress. Additionally, though the Enlightenment had prompted a modern medical revolution and the creation of a new professional cadre of body experts impressing their mental powers upon disorderly bodies, that discipline, by the late-Victorian period, had begun to verge increasingly upon a different order. Where mid-Victorian bodily symptoms were often understood as moral markers, late-Victorian bodies increasingly come to be understood by emerging psychological professionals and society at large as markers of disorderly minds. If the mind has the power to shape the body, then the cultivation of the mind might not lead only toward progress and improvement but perhaps—according to an illegible calculus—also toward degeneration and decadence. Futurity might not be shaped by the things we can see and say but by the things we cannot.

That pregnancy should be spoken of with increasing frequency and specificity in the fiction of this period speaks to a rising sense of the power of and threat to futurity posed by the invisible and inarticulate.[6] The increasing narrative visibility of pregnancy also demonstrates the impossibilities of such control: We can see the pregnant body and we can say what happens to it and we still cannot understand, much less control, its outcomes in any stable way. "*Jude*," argues Irving Howe, "is a novel dominated by psychology" (403). This psychological domination is most directly expressed in the strange degenerate child who seems to spring from nothing we could have foreseen or diagnosed rationally but rather from the impressions of Jude's decadent mind. Indeed, the impressive powers of the unconscious were of general interest in the fin de siècle. The ways maternal impression theory is mobilized in *The Heavenly Twins, Jude the Obscure, The History of Sir Richard Calmady,* and *Anna Lombard* is perhaps most legible in all four of these novels when we read the workings of paternal impression. Such readings require attention to narrative and medical diagnosis, certainly, but also to the unknown in our somatic imagination of women's bodies.

IMPRESSIONS

The Heavenly Twins is the didactic tale of young women damaged by a society that requires their complete sexual innocence while encouraging male indis-

---

6. For other late-century examples, see, for example, Olive Schreiner's *Story of an African Farm* and George Moore's *Esther Waters*.

cretion. The ethereal Edith Beale is destroyed by her parents' naive decision to allow her to marry the villainous Sir Mosely Monteith. Soon enervated by her marriage to a man who cannot contain his open interest in prostitutes even while walking with his brand-new wife, Edith's syphilitic decline first maddens, then kills her. Though Evadne Frayling survives the novel, her fine abilities are squandered when she is deceived about the character of her husband, Colonel Colquhoun. After learning of his moral turpitude on her wedding day, Evadne refuses to consummate her marriage and, over time, falls into a hysteria of sexual and mental repression. When Colquhoun dies suddenly, Evadne is able to enter into a seemingly satisfactory marriage with her doctor, Dr. Galbraith. She is not, however, able to regain the full measure of mental or physical health she enjoyed before her sacrifice on the altar of decadent male sexuality. Evadne's hysteria returns with a vengeance during her first pregnancy when she tries to kill herself and the unborn child she is convinced will be impressed by Evadne's exposure to "vice." Evadne's fears echo the fate of her friend, Edith. In *The Heavenly Twins,* syphilis works—through women's pregnant bodies and unconsciousnesses—as a dangerous mechanism of paternal impression upon futurity.

Syphilis in *The Heavenly Twins* makes legible a transition from mid-Victorian notions of articulable pregnancy as a site of visible immorality toward fin de siècle notions of pregnancy as a site for the play of impression on vulnerable, permeable bodies. In the novel, the immorality evidenced on women's reproductive bodies is not primarily their own but that of the men expected to protect them. As most critics have noted, *The Heavenly Twins* treats masculine immorality as an infectious social illness practically synonymous with syphilis.[7] In order to combat the spread of this disease through their impressionable pregnant bodies, women must be able to see and say it. Women must, in short, "read and diagnose the bodies of men 'exhausted by vice'" (Kennedy, *Revising* 269).

As Meegan Kennedy notes, however, in her 2004 "Syphilis and the Hysterical Female: The Limits of Realism in Sarah Grand's *The Heavenly Twins,*" Grand maintains the very reticence regarding explicit depictions of male syphilitic bodies that her novel decries. The infectious immorality that makes Edith and Evadne mentally and physically ill is primarily evidenced on both women's reproductive bodies. Edith's syphilitic decline is at first indistinguishable from a delayed postpartum recovery. And Evadne's hysterical fear that there is "no past in the matter of vice, [that the] consequences become hereditary, and continue from generation to generation," surfaces most strongly during

---

7. In addition to the work of Meegan Kennedy that I cite in this chapter, see also, for example, Liggins; Senf.

her first pregnancy, even though neither she nor Dr. Galbraith is personally guilty of sexual vice nor infected with syphilis (Grand 80). Although male sexual license is figured as contagious disease, a degeneration that "moral . . . leper[s]" "help[ ] to spread" through the social body, the novel narrates the impression of that vice on women's pregnant bodies through physical disease and mental illness and the threat that impression poses to futurity manifest in the bodies of children (79). We cannot read syphilis in Grand without reading pregnancy. We read the significance of collaboration between the two better through a lens of impression.

The didactic narrator of *The Heavenly Twins* explains the damage and degeneration caused by unread and unchecked syphilis in a language of bodily expansion:

> There are injuries which set up a carcinoma of the mind . . . cancer spots confined to a small area at first, but gradually extending with infinite pain until all the surrounding healthy tissue is more or less involved, and the whole beautiful fabric is absorbed in the morbid growth. (678)

This description of the "cancer" of the mind that results from the injury of contact with vice reads like a gothic narration of a pregnancy "gradually extending" into full-grown evil that consumes the "healthy tissue" of the mother. Such a "morbid growth," though referred to in the passage above with reference to Evadne's hysteria during her first pregnancy, also latches onto Edith after her marriage to Monteith and her postpartum decline. Edith's marriage takes place despite Evadne's strenuous objections to a man she felt to be legibly marked by vice. Evadne considers Monteith "bad—thoroughly bad" and she declares herself to have "a consciousness which informs me of things my intellect cannot grasp. And I do know!" (232). Her inability to describe an uncanny sense of the evil Monteith will inevitably "set up" inside Edith speaks both to Grand's disinclination to represent the markers of syphilis on the bodies of men and also the impressive power of the illness and the male bodies that spread it on the minds and reproductive bodies of women.

Though Evadne can point to nothing concrete to which to object in the person of Monteith before his marriage to Edith, Edith's person is clearly—though imprecisely—marked by disease after it. A discussion between her parents names vague signs of syphilis on Edith's body only insofar as they name that body's postpartum condition:

> "That child is not right," the Bishop said when Edith had gone to bed. "Have you noticed her face? I don't like the look of it at all; not at all."

"Isn't that rather unkind, dear?" Mrs. Beale replied. "I always recovered in time."

"You never were as ill as the poor child evidently is," he answered. (283)

Edith's face, which we can assume bears the lesions or scarring common to syphilitic decline, is read by her parents as showing some indefinite sign of a failure to "recover" from childbirth in good "time." That the marks of illness are indeed definite is evidenced soon after when Angelica Hamilton-Wells—the novel's third heroine and the only one who, through an essential denial of sexuality, fully escapes the dangers of syphilis—calls Edith "disfigured" (287). Though no one will speak the precise details of this disfigurement, the *something* that is wrong with her face, there are clearly specific, identifiable changes in Edith's physical appearance.

What those changes are, exactly, is never articulated directly but rather gestured toward vaguely and repeatedly with an increasing insistence that emphasizes Edith's own ignorance, an ignorance the novel attacks as a mistakenly protected feminine state of mind. In speaking of her vague condition with her mother, Edith explains that diagnosis is intentionally withheld from her:

"The doctor again!" Edith groaned. "It has been nothing but the doctor and 'tonics' ever since I have been married."

"What does he say is the matter exactly?" Mrs. Beale asked.

"All his endeavor seems to be not to say what is the matter exactly." (285)

The very reticence of the doctor to "say what is the matter exactly" speaks to its illicit nature. That "all his endeavor" must be put to the effort of concealing Edith's condition from Edith herself demonstrates that the doctor is not unaware of its cause but hyperaware. The doctor will not speak of syphilis to Edith because syphilis must not be spoken of to a lady, despite that lady being in serious danger from it. In seeking to protect Edith's mind from the knowledge of syphilis, the doctor seeks to erect a barrier between mind and body that cannot hold, much as the narrative barrier between pregnant bodies and plot could not hold in mid-Victorian fiction: Even a pregnancy that skirts articulation nonetheless tends to result in the undeniable birth of a child. And Edith's case of syphilis, though it skirts direct articulation, nonetheless results in the undeniable degradation of two bodies.

The sociomedical ideal of a barrier between bodies and minds, particularly between privileged women's bodies and minds, maps onto matters of reproduction when Angelica's maidenly ignorance regarding babies emphasizes the unnameability of the problem with Edith's:

> Angelica had never been in the same house with a baby before, and she was all interest....
>
> "Have you seen the baby?" she asked Elizabeth, when the latter was brushing her hair for dinner....
>
> "Yes, Miss," Elizabeth answered.
>
> "Is he a pretty baby?" Angelica wanted to know.
>
> Elizabeth pursed her lips with an air of reserve.
>
> "You don't think so?" Angelica said—she had seen the maid's face in the mirror before her. (288)

Working-class Elizabeth clearly knows what Angelica does not, and—as a lady—ought not. As with the doctor, Elizabeth's hesitance to speak of the baby's appearance speaks suggestively to the specificity of her knowledge about its cause. If she found him simply not a very pretty baby, there would be little cause for marked "reserve," a reserve expressed in the "purs[ing of] her lips" around something she knows but will not say. Angelica is able to read this general something rather than its specific significance, but her deductive ability proves insufficient preparation for the reality of the child's condition, much as Edith's education proved insufficient to prepare her for the reality of the social illness to which she unknowingly exposed herself in marrying Monteith. When Angelica does finally meet Edith's child, her "astonishment and horror" at the sight of a baby vaguely described as "old, old already and exhausted with suffering" drives her from the room, though it still offers the reader no specific symptoms (289).

The specific symptoms from which Edith's child is likely suffering are only ever spoken at a remove, through the description of a different infant who turns out to be Monteith's impoverished, illegitimate child. This baby "was small and rickety, with bones that bent beneath its weight, slight as it was," and it is when Edith learns that he is her husband's son that she seems to begin to put together the details of what has happened to her (290). Though she never names the syphilis that infects her and her child, she brings together the men in her life—her father, doctor, and husband—"who represent the arrangement of society which has made it possible for [her] and [her] child to be sacrificed in this way" in order to articulate her knowledge of the disease they have spread (300).

The implied consummation of Edith's knowledge of syphilis does not, however, resolve all the elements of plot that are mysterious without this shared understanding of the unnamed workings of venereal disease in the novel. Though literary critics tend to speak of the disease as killing both Edith and her child over the course of the novel, there is actually an interesting lack of clarity about the fate of her baby. It is true that Evadne says of her disinclination to visit Morningquest that "Edith died there; and then that child" (590). This would make it seem that both Edith and the child are dead, or at least that Evadne thinks this is the case. However, not long after, Dr. Galbraith says that he "had seen how [Evadne] shrank from going to [Morningquest] because of the association with Edith's terrible death and the chance of seeing her poor, repulsive looking little boy there" (595). This would make it seem that the child is still living but that Evadne has a strong aversion to seeing him. Perhaps her thinking him dead is a sign of the hysteria for which Galbraith is treating her by this point in the novel, a hysteria that comes to fixate on the dangers of syphilis to children. A later appearance of "Mrs. Beale . . . with Edith's boy" confirms either that the error is Evadne's—not a possibly careless Grand's—and/or that her saying "and then that child" might better be read, "and then that child . . ." leaving his horrible condition unspoken (677). This child seems, in fact, to be still alive at the novel's close, evidence of the threat posed to the future by decadent paternal impressions that live on after the women sacrificed to them have died.

Unlike Edith, Evadne's marriage to a sexually impure man does not result in her contraction of syphilis. This may be due to her refusal to consummate her marriage to Colquhoun, a refusal based on the illicit medical education Evadne cobbled together for herself through adolescence, against the wishes of her parents. Though her body remains untainted by syphilis, Evadne's mind falls prey to the specter of the disease. Evadne fears that her "healthy tissue" has been irredeemably exposed to the carcinogen of Colquhoun's vice, a fear that peaks at a moment in which her own body, like that figurative cancer, is "gradually extending," "absorbed in the . . . growth" of generations (678).

Though Edith remains unaware of her husband's moral cancer until shortly before her own death and her pregnancy is skipped over entirely by the narrative, Evadne's first pregnancy is revealed to the reader by her doctor-husband as salient evidence in his case study of her hysterical symptoms. Dr. Galbraith's description of his treatment plan for his wife emphasizes Evadne's physical body and hints at her condition, explaining that "there was active exercise enough for her . . . so long as she was able to take it, and when it became necessary to curtail the amount she drove both morning and afternoon, and took short walks," Galbraith also explains that he "began to hope that a new interest in life was coming to cure her of all morbid moods forever" (659). Of course, the new interest that cures her and curtails Evadne's active exercise is her pregnancy, though this kind of delicate revelation—particularly at the close of the century—hardly constitutes a radical retraction of modest mid-Victorian textual conventions for the representation of pregnant bodies.

The more radical retraction of those conventions occurs only after Evadne attempts suicide, an act she is driven to by reading—against Galbraith's advice—medical texts on the "heredity of vice" (662). Evadne's suicide attempt is doubly suggestive: First, it is fueled by her desire to halt the heredity of vice she believes to be lodged and growing in her body after her exposure to her first husband's infectious immorality, an exposure that even her total chastity in her first marriage could not avoid. This signals her perception of the dangerous impressive powers of masculine decadence. Second, though this suicidal impulse is similarly framed by Dr. Galbraith as the result of masculine decadence, he views the suicide attempt as a manifestation of the hysterical mental illness Evadne has contracted from her exposure to her first husband's vice, or, rather, has developed as a result of her desire to limit her sexual exposure to her husband's cancerous immorality. This is to say that the medical/psychological reading of the suicide attempt locates the very direct threat to futurity in Evadne's literally pregnant unconscious.

In any reading, Evadne's pregnant body is the site at which her own potential for moral illness, her exposure to an illness of the social body, and her resulting tendency toward mental illness is evidenced. After the vice that haunts her psyche is fully revealed, so, too, is her pregnant body fully exposed to the medical gaze of her husband, the psychological specialist Sir Shadwell Rock, and the reader. Her pregnancy makes the sinister hold of syphilis on her mind legible. This, in turn, makes the embodied details of her pregnancy legible. This collaboration is psychologically and narratively motivated by the threat that a degenerate masculine illness will impress itself upon the body of Evadne's unborn child. Of course, because Evadne is suicidal, a threat to the life of the fetus is real enough. For the "forty-six days and nights" that remain of Evadne's first pregnancy after her suicide attempt, Dr. Galbraith explains, with chronological precision uncharacteristic in earlier Victorian narrations of reproduction, "[he] never left her an hour alone" (666). Dr. Galbraith's constant supervision of Evadne during these six weeks is made possible by their marital relationship; even the most dedicated doctor would not be able to commit so much constant care to only one patient. Dr. Galbraith's medical function in the novel slips smoothly into his function as Evadne's husband and narrator, though his success in all three roles is tenuous.

Our "success" in reading Evadne's pregnant body here is tenuous too. Certain physical and chronological information is more readily available than it was in mid-Victorian fiction, but that doesn't seem to help us to read the pregnancy as primarily an embodied state, just as the novel's descriptions of syphilis don't much help us to read the somatic specificities of illness. Both syphilis and pregnancy function primarily, rather, as metaphorical conditions of minds and dangerously permeable bodies. Our diagnosis of Evadne's pregnancy—as her own diagnosis of her infection with vice—is only ever partial and tends toward its own metaphoricization. This is a pattern of metaphoricization with which the reader of *The Heavenly Twins* is already familiar, having been instructed throughout the novel's pages in the reading of syphilis as a marker for diseased society. Evadne imagines Edith's child dead before his time, but the reader must imagine syphilis as alive (in Evadne and in a patriarchal structure that fosters its impressive powers over futurity) where it is not if we are to make sense of her hysteria. We do this through recognizing its impressing paternal power on the futurity promised and threatened by her pregnant body.

•

When Jude Fawley is an ambitious and idealistic young man, he pursues a course of study that he hopes will open the doors of scholarly life to him. His passionate desire for this life, or what he imagines it to be, anticipates his passionate desire—and that desire's ultimate unattainability—for his cousin, Sue. The unsustainability of their union will be explosively marked by the deaths of two of their children at the hands of Jude's son from a previous marriage, a child who seems to inherit nothing from his biological mother but, rather, seems to be the aged and concentrated essence of Jude, a concentration that personifies and displaces the fears Jude and Sue share about the danger of their reproducing. Though Sue mothers this child, called little Jude or Old Father Time, she is not his mother. Though Jude's first wife, Arabella, gives birth to this child, she never mothers him, and he renounces her: "You be the woman I thought were my mother for a bit, till I found you wasn't" (245). Old Father Time, then, with two potential mothers living, is conceived into a lack that echoes nothing so much as the lack that marks his father's blighted life. He is the fruit of his father's thwarted imagination and of an imaginary pregnancy. Old Father Time, in other words, seems to be the inconceivable result of paternal impression, sprung from the head of a father whose mind has the tendency to become "impregnated" with unrealizable ideas (29).[8]

In Hardy's 1891 *Tess of the D'Urbervilles: A Pure Woman Faithfully Presented*, Tess's rape and illegitimate pregnancy form the dark center of the novel, the unnarrated—perhaps unnarratable—trauma that works like a force of nature driving subsequent events. By the logic of pregnancy representation

---

8. Suzanne Keen's excellent *Thomas Hardy's Brains: Psychology, Neurology, and Hardy's Imagination* addresses the failure of Hardy criticism that has "understood [Hardy] neither as a student of psychology nor as a reader of neurology, Victorian brain science" (6).

in the mid- and high-Victorian novel, Tess's pregnant body should be up for narrative grabs, the visible marker of her fall. The novel's refusal to represent her pregnancy serves as a formal affirmation, a "Faithful[ ] Representation" of her status as a "Pure Woman." Although any discussion of pregnancy in Hardy demands that we consider *Tess of the D'Urbervilles,* what happens with Tess's reproductive body in that novel demonstrates a familiar dynamic inverted rather than a real shift in the ways pregnancy is represented in Victorian fiction.[9] It is in *Jude the Obscure* that a broader potential for the expression of anxiety about the dangers of a pregnant unconscious not necessarily tethered to the female body or feminine mind is sounded most significantly.

The seemingly supernatural powers of the pregnant unconscious in *Jude the Obscure* express the novel's naturalism. In literary naturalism, the forces that shape individual and social (un)consciousnesses are beyond our control and understanding, part of what Suzanne Keen has called "an indifferent universe in which the actions of humans shrink to meaninglessness against the backdrop of the cosmos" (7–8). Clearly, the role of medical "professionals" in such a universe is a fraught one. The possibility of rational knowledge about the body and mind can only ever struggle to encompass the unknowable, and even the best doctor's knowledge could only ever be partial, a psychoanalytic story rather than a reliable diagnosis. In *Jude,* the doctor that tenaciously haunts the borders of the novel is most certainly not the best doctor and holds less than partial authority. Dr. Vilbert is a "quack" who offers Jude the tantalizing and unrealizable possibility of authoritative knowledge—in the form of the Latin and Greek grammars he longs for and from which he is unable to glean the meaning he seeks—while dealing in treatments of and for the imagination (23). Dr. Vilbert, hawking "female pills" and quack advice for the staging of at least one particularly significant quack pregnancy, stalks the novel like a malignancy, the specter of medical authority that cannot hold (24). Whenever there is crisis, there is Dr. Vilbert, helping no one but Arabella, mistress of superficial deceptions signifying nothing. Indeed, Vilbert's final appearance on the novelistic stage suggests what is perhaps the most promising union possible in the universe of *Jude the Obscure.*

A marriage between Vilbert and Arabella, if we imagine that it might take place in their hazy afterlives, would be a fitting match for two characters who

---

9. Though Rosemarie Morgan argues convincingly in her 1988 *Women and Sexuality in the Novels of Thomas Hardy* that Hardy's treatment of female embodiment does mark a radical shift away from Victorian literary norms, this shift does not fully encompass his treatments of pregnancy. In part, I would argue that this is due to the metaphorical weight of pregnancy in Hardy's novels (as in Western culture). For more on Hardy's treatment of women and sexuality, see, for example, Boumelha.

intentionally use the body, particularly the reproductive female body, as a canvas for the imagination. Just as Arabella's dimple, conveying the impression of innocent joy and guileless sexual appeal, is in fact a carefully acquired and painstakingly practiced superficial accomplishment quite divorced from the spontaneity it seems to communicate, so, too, is the "pregnancy" without which Jude's life might have escaped disaster. When friendly advice about catching Jude with a real pregnancy leaves "Arabella . . . dissatisfied . . . always imagining, and waiting, and wondering," a conversation with Vilbert seems to "brighten" in her the idea of a false pregnancy with real power to shape the future (47).

"A few weeks" after the marriage, Arabella confides to a friend that she was "mistaken" about the reason for the marriage, but it is almost certain from the two months of "disappointment" that precede her conversation with Vilbert that Arabella—who would no doubt have educated herself on the signs and chronologies of pregnant bodies—was not mistaken but calculating (50). That this conversation with the friend should come "a few weeks" after the marriage heightens the possibility that Arabella is literally calculating the time from one menstrual cycle to the next:

> It was with a little uneasiness that Arabella approached the time when in the natural course of things she would have to reveal that the alarm she had raised had been without foundation. . . .
> "You'll soon have plenty to do now, dear, won't you?"
> "How do you mean?"
> "Why, of course—little things to make."
> "Oh."
> "When will it be? Can't you tell me exactly, instead of in such general terms as you have used?"
> "Tell you?"
> "Yes—the date."
> "There's nothing to tell. I made a mistake."
> "What?"
> "It was a mistake."
> He sat bolt upright in bed and looked at her. "How can that be?"
> "Women fancy wrong things sometimes." (51)

In "approach[ing] the time when in the natural course of things" Arabella will have to reveal to Jude that she is not pregnant, she is likely approaching her first menstrual "course" since her marriage, a thing difficult to conceal from a new husband. Arabella's attunement to the impending unsustainability of her deception further supports my reading of the nature of her two months of "disappointments" prior to the marriage as having been marked by the menstrual cycles she would have liked to be able to "imagine" away. However, that Jude seems relatively uninformed regarding the timing of Arabella's courses (and perhaps of the timing and significance of women's courses more generally)—"Can't you tell me exactly, instead of in such general terms as you have used?" he asks—suggests that Arabella *was* able to imagine her unwanted menstrual cycles into a "pregnancy" prior to her marriage, though she will not be able to do so after. The explanation that she gives Jude for the imaginary pregnancy, that "women fancy wrong things sometimes," asserts the mental location of this pregnancy. With a menstrual flow coming, Arabella could easily ascribe this misplaced pregnancy to miscarriage. She could call one kind of vaginal bleeding another and never have Jude any the wiser, but she doesn't. She—who knows well how to lie when she likes—ascribes it to a "mistake," a fancy of the mind, and, of course, the mind's fancy here has had the very real consequence of her marriage. And the bodily consequence of that marriage may already—unbeknownst to them both—be taking root.

Though Arabella's imaginary pregnancy has such very real and immediate consequences, her "real" pregnancy remains completely invisible to both Jude and the reader for half of the novel. Arabella knows that the imaginary pregnancy will reveal itself through blood; neither Jude nor the reader (nor Arabella herself, she later claims) knows that the physical pregnancy will conceal itself through blood. The spilling of the slaughtered pig's blood that prompts the argument that ends Arabella's living with Jude and motivates her emigration to Australia seems a strange shadow of the miscarriage or infanticide that Old Father Time later declares he wishes had taken place ("I think that whenever children be born that are not wanted," he says, "they should be killed directly, before their souls come to 'em, and not allowed to grow big and walk about"). But the spilling of the pig's blood is only an imaginary miscarriage that frees Arabella to move out of the novel's narration at the moment at which her pregnancy with Old Father Time threatens to become legible to herself (practiced in the arts of course counting) and to the reader (practiced in the arts of Arabella body reading). In this way, Old Father Time seems to remain in the imaginary realm of the conception that is not, always already a dark "fancy" somehow shaped in the mind of a father who does not know he is imagining him.

So dangerously imaginary is Old Father Time that Arabella, who doesn't usually feel overmuch need for detailed explanation, is moved to give some "proof" of his legitimacy. Like the "pregnancy" that brings about her marriage to Jude, Arabella's proof of this pregnancy with his child relies on embodied chronology:

> The fact is, Jude, that, though I have never informed you before, there was a boy born of our marriage, eight months after I left you, when I was at Sydney, living with my father and mother. All that is easily provable. As I had separated from you before I thought such a thing was going to happen. (215)

Necessarily vague with Jude about timing during the "pregnancy" that prompts their marriage, Arabella is specific here: The child was born eight months after she left. If this is true, then Arabella would have been very early in her pregnancy when she and Jude separated. When she says that she left "before [she] thought such a thing was going to happen," it seems that Arabella is suggesting that she left before the embodied signs of pregnancy, most notably a missed menstrual cycle, were apparent.

As it happens, any well-founded doubts we might have about Arabella's truthfulness in the matter of this child's paternity seem to be laid to rest by the heightened similarity of Old Father Time, little Jude, to "big" Jude. Sue, who has perhaps the most cause to doubt, declares, "What Arabella says is true—true! I see [Jude] in him!" (219). Just as the child argues that Arabella is not really his mother, neither Jude, Sue, nor the reader seems to find her anywhere in him. After Sue's marriage to Phillotson, Jude regrets "the willfulness of Nature in not allowing issue from one parent alone" (141). But Old Father Time seems somehow the child only of the imagination of a father who did not know he existed, the child of his father's unconscious. Old Father Time is an impossible creature who works on the novel like a dangerous force of nature on human lives, a force about which we can only try and fail to make rational sense.

The resemblance between Jude and Old Father Time seems to be more impressionistic than literal. The child embodies and intensifies nothing so much as Jude's sense of futurelessness, his fears about the doomed fate of Fawley marriages, his decadent sense of living without possibility, out of joint with time:

> [Old Father Time] was Age masquerading as Juvenility, and doing it so badly that his real self showed through crevices. A ground swell from ancient years of night seemed now and then to lift the child in this his morning-life, when his face took a back view over some great Atlantic of Time, and appeared not to care about what it saw. (217)

The language of a "real self show[ing] through crevices" and "a ground swell from ancient years" surfacing to haunt the present calls to mind the vocabulary of a psychoanalytic practice emerging, not across an "Atlantic of Time," but in Vienna across a channel of water and some little mass of land. Old Father Time is an embodiment of the uncanny, of the unseen and unspeakable pasts that threaten to rise from the depths of the mind and write themselves on the surfaces of the body:

> On that little shape had converged all the inauspiciousness and shadow which had darkened the first union of Jude, and all the accidents, mistakes, fears, errors of the last. He was their nodal point, their focus, their expression in a single term. For the rashness of those parents he had groaned, for their ill-assortment he had quaked, and for the misfortunes of these he [dies]. (265)

Old Father Time here is not a child but rather a "shape," the form and "expression" of Jude's troubles, strangely untethered to any natural explanation. His shape is not formed primarily, it seems, by Arabella as a mother nor even by an evolutionary understanding of Jude's literal, physical genetics but rather by the strange force of Jude's ill-fated marriages. So he functions as a kind of force of nature unto himself, a "shadow" that cannot be anticipated or understood but that has the power to "darken[ ]" everything in its path. The haunting possibility that Old Father Time is the dangerous embodiment of Jude's pregnant unconscious is confirmed with gothic intensity when, in reaction to a recognition of the significance of Sue's pregnant body—he murders his little siblings and kills himself. Here again—as in *The Heavenly Twins*—suicide, the most literal threat the mind poses to futurity, is prompted by and disruptive of the only "real" pregnancy narrated by the novel as an embodied condition.

Old Father Time demonstrates how the world functions beyond our control and understanding but with a strangely perceptible, haunting, and ominous force. In more realist Victorian novels, there often functions a more or less rational universe in which the things that happen to people correspond to who they are. In such a universe, visible and invisible pregnancies make sense insofar as they mark behaviors and personalities. But in Hardy's naturalistic universe, "other forces and laws than theirs were in operation," and pregnancy functions as the driving unconscious force of paternal impression (164).

Neither Old Father Time nor Sue seems to read her third pregnancy as a specter of a fin de siècle unconscious. They approach it, rather, in the Victorian mode with which the earlier chapters of this book are most concerned;

little Jude and Sue read her final pregnancy as evidence of maternal immorality and transgression. Sue's pregnant body is inconveniently legible as she and Jude try to find lodgings for their large family in Christminster. Disapproving landladies "scrutinize [the] figure" that Sue tries to conceal by "pull[ing her] cloak more round" herself (259). Despite her efforts at concealment, her pregnant body seems somehow to give her technically immoral unmarried condition away to potential hosts, despite the presence of Jude and their still-intact family. In the conversation that seems to prompt his murder/suicide, Old Father Time realizes the threat that Sue's pregnancy poses and ascribes to her the blame for it:

> "How *ever* could you, Mother, be so wicked and cruel as this, when you needn't have done it till we was better off, and father well!—To bring us all into *more* trouble! No room for us, and father a-forced to go away, and we turned out tomorrow; and yet you be going to have another of us soon! . . . 'Tis done o' purpose!—'tis—'Tis!" He walked up and down sobbing.
>
> "Y-you must forgive me, little Jude!" she pleaded, her bosom heaving now as much as the boy's. "I can't explain—I will when you are older. Is does seem—as if I had done it on purpose, now we are in these difficulties! I can't explain, dear! But it—is not quite on purpose—I can't help it!" (262; ellipsis in original)

Sue's pregnancy seems to Old Father Time a "wicked" thing that she has done to her family, a willful betrayal that drives his father away. Sue seems to acknowledge that the pregnancy is something for which she must be "forgive[n]," but convention requires that she avoid giving an explanation for her fault or explaining her own lack of control over the matter. The reader knows, of course, that Sue would much rather have always lived platonically with Jude and that, if blame is to be given anyone for her having "another one," it not unlikely lies with him.

Old Father Time rights what he feels to have been the wrongs of the births of himself and the two siblings, "because [they were] too menny" and in so doing, rights also Sue's final "cruel" pregnancy. Following the deaths of her children, this last baby is "prematurely born and . . . it, like the others, [is] a corpse" (268). All of the familiar signals of immodest Victorian reproduction mark the narration of this ill-fated pregnancy: a (technically) adulterous mother, a narratively legible reproductive body that takes too much space, and a premature birth. Though the reader may not learn a Charlotte Yongian lesson of feminine modesty from this tale, Sue certainly does. She reads these events as a sign from God, a message that she must abandon her marriage in all but law to Jude, whom she loves, and return to live with her legal husband, Phillotson, whom she finds physically repulsive.

Jude seems to absorb the even bleaker lesson of his dead son: that all pregnancy and all birth is ill-fated. On his deathbed he whispers words from Job like a prayer:

> Let the day perish wherein I was born, and the night in which it was said, There is a man child conceived. . . .
> Why died I not from the womb? Why did I not give up the ghost when I came out of the belly? (318)

Jude's final pronouncement is clearly writ in the language of dangerous pregnancy ("born," "conceived," "womb," and "out of the belly"). He has learned to fear the "shapes like our own selves hideously multiplied" that he augured earlier in the novel (225). And the reader has learned . . . what, exactly? That pregnancy can be most real when it is not real? That metaphors are bodies and bodies are metaphors? That when we see a pregnant body in the late-Victorian novel, it may not be the mother who has done something wrong, but her body nonetheless spells serious danger to the "civilized" future?

•

The History of Sir Richard Calmady stages the anxiety of mind/body transgression in a direct narrative deployment of maternal impression theory that works in concert and tension with specters of paternal impression. In Malet's underread magnum opus, Katherine Calmady—young, beautiful, kind, and loyal—witnesses the violent maiming and subsequent death of her lawful husband. Her son is, in turn, born similarly maimed, his body a reflection of his father's. Katherine's mind is struck by the impression of her husband's accident and exercises an unconscious power to shape the contents of her womb. As we have seen in *The Heavenly Twins* and *Jude*, the ultimate danger of pregnancy no longer lies in maternal immorality at the fin de siècle. Furthermore, as in *The Heavenly Twins* and *Jude*, it is paternal decadence—writ in *Richard Calmady* as a curse on the degenerate aristocratic lineage of the Calmady family—that seems to filter through the impressions of the maternal mind and body.

A vocabulary of pregnancy and birth pervades *Richard Calmady*, particularly in the novel's opening sections. Indeed, that ancient theory of conception impression—not quite synonymous with maternal impression but a close cousin—is evoked in these first chapters. The Calmadys' Renaissance manor is said to be beautiful "as the child of true lovers is said to bear through life, in a certain glad beauty of person and of nature, witness to the glad hour of its conception" (3). And, after the birth of the titular Richard, known as Dickie, the doctor who diagnoses maternal impression as a cause for the maiming of his lower body "put[s] a good deal of faith in [the] notion [that Richard's face is] beautiful as a child only can be who is born of the passion of true lovers" (57). The novel's opening chapters are heavily marked not only with a vocabulary of reproductive bodies—a vocabulary of "conception," "birth" and "still-birth," "born" and "unborn," fullness and emptiness—but also with an "old-fashioned" emphasis on myth and curse.

In the novel's second chapter, we see Katherine Calmady directly thinking about her pregnancy in a way that we almost never do in Victorian fiction prior to the fin de siècle. Katherine Calmady gives birth in March of 1843. Assuming that the pregnancy runs the standard course, she likely conceives in July of 1842, two or three months after her marriage. The novel's reader is first introduced to Katherine at the end of August of that year, when she would be almost two months into her first trimester. We meet her on the night she tells her husband that he "[has given her] a child" (15). But before making this revelation to her husband, the twinned hold of her awareness of pregnancy on her mind and body is narrated:

> Another order of emotion arose in her. She became sensible of a necessity to take counsel with herself. . . .
>
> There were things to think of, things deep and strange. . . .
>
> [There] came an instinct to rid herself of all small impeding conventionalities, even in the matter of dress. . . . A sweet seriousness filling all her mind[,] . . . she felt wholly in sympathy with the aspect and sentiment of the place. Indeed it appeared to her, just then, that the four months of her marriage, the five months of her engagement . . . were a prelude merely to the present hour and to that which lay immediately ahead. (9–10)

This passage is notable for the way it positions Katherine's sense of a need to think "things deep and strange" as both a mental and physical process. Two months into a pregnancy, Katherine would likely be experiencing certain strange and deep bodily signs and sensations: the cessation of her menstrual cycle, swollen or tender breasts, possibly nausea or exhaustion, and as women sometimes mention, a dislike of tight clothing, a desire to cast off impeding "convention[al]" items of "dress." It strikes me also that this passage's direct thinking of pregnancy includes an indirect thinking of pregnancy's chronology. Katherine's tally of her relationship with her husband (four months married, five months engaged) encodes the nine-month chronology of the pregnancy on which she now dwells.

The implacable march of chronology, the inescapability of the future marks Katherine's thoughts about her impending motherhood. Though she is a doting wife and will be a doting mother, she experiences some private resistance to her pregnancy that the reader accesses through this new narration of pregnant interiority. Katherine's mind articulates a sense of embodied experience that the novel narrates in psychological detail:

> One train of thought, which she had been busy enough by day and honestly sleepy enough at night, to keep at arm's length during this time of homecoming and entertaining, now invaded and possessed her mind filling it at once with a new and overwhelming movement of tenderness, yet for all her high courage with a certain fear. She cried out for a little space of waiting, a little space in which to take breath. She wanted to pause, here in the fullness of her content. But no pause was granted her. She was so happy, she asked nothing more. But something more was forced upon her. And so it happened that, in realizing the ceaseless push of event on event, the ceaseless dying of dear today in the service of unborn tomorrow, her gentle seriousness touched on regret. (13–14)

The pressing vocabulary employed in the description of these thoughts speaks indirectly to Katherine's pregnant body, "invaded and possessed" by an "unborn tomorrow" that she does not quite want just yet. Though she feels some emotional "tenderness" (along with some physical tenderness, we might assume), her mind "cries out for a little space" from this "fullness," space and fullness being the things that her fetus will only take more of as the "ceaseless push" of time passes and, eventually, reaches a physical push. This other kind of push hints at what that "certain" vague and imprecise fear might be, especially for a young woman whose own mother died in childbirth, as did Katherine's.

Though we've seen how suggestive of the pregnant body Katherine's thoughts are, they are not explicit. Katherine's mind names her somatic experience only indirectly, so that her pregnant embodiment functions in a liminally conscious space—the more a reader knows about the physical workings of pregnancy, the more fully the narration of Katherine's interiority seems to evoke such embodiment and the more directly Katherine's thoughts seem to reference it. The deployment of tropes of modesty and immodesty surrounding the concealment and revelation of pregnancy in Victorian literature always already create these receding bodies: Modesty requires an awareness of that which it conceals, of the confirmedly sexual body, of the swelling breasts and belly, of the uncertain future. "A certain modesty" we learn—in a self-aware deployment of the vocabulary of Victorian representation of pregnancy—makes Katherine "shrink" even from telling her husband that he will be a father. This "certain modesty" signals Katherine's direct thinking of her pregnant body as well as a desire to control the effects of that body in the world.

Indeed, that Katherine shrinks from revealing her pregnancy to her husband points to a broader struggle for control: "To know something in the secret of your own heart, or to tell it, thereby making it a hard concrete fact, outside yourself, over which in a sense, you cease to have control, are two such very different matters!" (15). This tension between what is "in" Katherine, both in her body and in "the secret" of her mind, and what is "outside"—not only her husband but a larger world over which she has little control—resonates with the decadent threat of decaying boundaries that troubles fin de siècle literature. In *Calmady*, these decaying boundaries seem to write their threats directly onto the body of Katherine's child, Dickie. His disability is represented as the result of a confluence of impressions, the maternal impressions of his mother's disordered mind following his father's death, certainly, but also the impressions of medical treatment, and the impressions of a curse that runs along the paternal line.

About six months after his marriage, Katherine's husband has an accident that first demands the surgical removal of his legs below the knee and then results in his death. Katherine, now in the second trimester of her pregnancy, paces outside the room in which his surgery is performed. In the days that follow the surgery and precede her husband's certain passing, it is the memory of this pacing outside the amputation room that haunts Katherine most, and her traumatic replaying of the scene eventually repeats itself on the body of her child. We can see the replay of this surgery in Katherine's mind most strongly as her husband dies some days later:

> Katherine's over-wrought nerves began to play cruel tricks upon her, carrying her back in imagination to that other hideous hour of waiting, in the dining room, four evenings ago. Again she seemed to hear the short peremptory tones of the surgeons, and those worse things, the stifled groans of one in the extremity of physical anguish, and the grate of a saw. These maddened her with pity, almost with rage. She feared now, as then, she might lose her self-mastery and do some wild and desperate thing. She tried to keep her attention fixed on the quick irregular rise and fall of the linen sheet expressing the broad, full curve of the young man's chest, as he lay flat on his back, his eyes closed, but whether in sleep or in unconsciousness she did not know

> . . . all the mouldings of the ceiling, all the crossing bars and sinuous lines of the richly-worked pattern, all the deepening bosses and roses of it, all the foliations of the deep cornice, sprang into bold relief, outlined, splashed, and stained with living scarlet. And this universal redness of carpet, curtains, furniture, and now of ceiling, even of white-draped bed, suggested to Katherine's distracted fancy another thing, unseen, yet known during her other hour of waiting, namely blood. (38–39)

Here, we see that danger lies in that bodily thing that is "unseen, yet known," as Katherine's own pregnancy was in the preceding passages. In dwelling on the unseen violence of surgery to her husband's body, Katherine's "imagination" becomes a "wild," "rage[ful]" site at which she might do—and later feels that she has done—"some desperate thing." The figurative blood that seems to be coursing through her memories and the house itself ("splash[ing] and stain[ing]") seems to be coursing, too, through the literal legs that Richard loses in surgery and also the blood moving between Katherine's and Dickie's shared bodies. What seem to be discrete circulatory systems, discrete bodies and minds, bleed together disorderedly as Katherine tries "to keep her attention fixed" on her barely alive husband. Of course, the discrete circulatory systems of mother and fetus always bleed together during pregnancy. Pregnancy is the nexus of decadent circulatory disorder in *Calmady*, suggesting that when fears about the breakdown of coherent boundaries are psychologically and textually central, pregnancy serves as an apt textual nexus of disorder.

In *Calmady*, these heightened problems of decadent circulation seem attributable, at least in part, to a lack of anesthesia:

> It must be remembered that in 1842 anesthetics had not robbed the operating room of half its horror. The victim went to execution wide-awake, with no mercy of deadened senses and dulled brain. And so Katherine had paced the dining-room, hearing at intervals, through the closed doors, the short peremptory tones of the surgeons, fearing she heard more and worse sounds than those. (38)

Because her husband's surgery is being performed without effective painkillers, Katherine knows that he is suffering extreme physical pain from which she "fear[s]" she hears him crying out. The "deadened senses and dulled brain" of anesthesia use common to surgical and obstetric practice by the fin de siècle but still only on the horizon of common usage in 1842 offer a disconnect between impractical circulations between body and mind that isn't afforded to Richard during his surgery. The inability to cordon off his body from his mind seems to extend to an inability to cordon off Katherine's mind and body from her husband, and by extension Dickie's from his father. When Dickie is born without legs below the knee, the local doctor offers maternal impression as a diagnosis and Katherine, marked by her pacing outside the dining room, recognizes without having to be told "the truth" that "she was herself, in a sense, accountable. That the greatness of her love of the father had maimed the child" (65).

But that which has impressed itself upon the body of Dickie is both more complicated and less knowable than this. Maternal impression, shaped by the father's body and the medical context, works in collusion with another paternal impression, manifest through ancestral curse. This curse—cast on the family in the seventeenth century by a woman scorned, a woman whose illegitimate Calmady-fathered child was killed by a carriage that severed his legs from his body just above the knee—decrees that the sins of the fathers will visit themselves upon a future Calmady "fatherless babe." This child is destined, in an echo of the illegitimate child's death, to have "a foot that will never know stocking or shoe" (26). This curse locates prevalent fin de siècle fears about the diseases and mutilations to which the bodies of the future are subject on the paternal line. These fears might extend beyond the empirical reach of medical science and operate like the bodies on which they fixate, as much in the realm of the unknown and subjective as the known.

"THE DARK MIRROR OF THE FUTURE"

Another novel published in 1901, even more remarkable than *Calmady* in its frank depictions of sexuality and its degenerative vision of reproduction, is Victoria Cross's *Anna Lombard*. The novel hinges on the titular character's radical lack of conscious bodily agency. Narrated in the first person by Gerald Ethridge, an Englishman working in the Indian Civil Service of Kalatu, the plot picks up following his first encounter with Anna shortly after her arrival in India. Anna is a "fair-skinned, light-haired Saxon girl . . . thoroughly English in every look and gesture"; the whiteness of her body is repeatedly emphasized (78). At their first meeting, Anna and Gerald fall in love, but the next day Gerald learns of a five-year posting to Burma that he feels would be dangerous for a woman. So, he leaves without proposing marriage. He returns only a year later after inheriting a large fortune that gives him more professional and personal freedom. He finds Anna apparently unchanged, and they shortly become engaged. But during his absence, Anna has fallen in "passion, not love" with and married Gaida Khan, an Indian servant in her household

(55). Gerald, hiding unbeknownst to Anna under the floor of her room, overhears her lovemaking with Gaida and learns of their Muslim marriage ceremony. Anna describes the marriage as both physically irresistible and also morally repugnant, "one horrible imprisonment and degradation" (55). Gerald, though similarly repulsed by his perception of the racialized unfitness of Gaida as a husband for Anna, considers himself responsible for her "degradation" because he didn't propose to her before leaving for Burma. So, he remains engaged to Anna, and Anna continues, with his knowledge, to receive Gaida in her rooms every night. When this holding pattern makes him physically ill, Gerald escapes Kalatu, only to return upon news that cholera has arrived in that city. There, he nurses Anna back to health and attempts to do the same for Gaida. When Gaida nonetheless dies, seemingly as the result of a steadfast refusal to accept alcohol as treatment, Gerald is overjoyed to be rid of the impediment to his marriage, as is Anna, after a few weeks of mourning and recovery. Soon, however, Anna realizes herself to be pregnant. She and Gerald move ahead with their wedding to protect her from social stain, but they do not consummate their marriage. Anna's pregnancy is unwanted and unpleasant to her, and she and Gerald plan to send the child away. When it is born, however, Anna's embodied passion for Gaida repeats itself for his child. Much to Gerald's disgust, she dotes on the infant. He informs her that this feeling is an impediment to the happiness of their marriage and she—after a week of sad contemplation—kills the baby. Anna sends Gerald away while she grieves her child but calls him back after a year, once again "the same Anna Lombard [he] had left a maiden" when he first left for Burma, her body "expanding and dilating with the force of her nervous joy" (137). Through the murder of the mixed-race child who elicits "insensate idolatry" from Anna, the novel achieves its deeply unsettling happy ending. As Gail Cunningham notes in her introduction to the only edited edition of the novel in print, the novel frames "Anna's decision to kill her own baby, her one independent act of will in the novel, [as] the single act by which she can reclaim her own body and later offer it freely to Gerald" (xx).

Pregnancy works in *Anna Lombard* to indicate Anna's lack of bodily agency. This lack cannot be fully communicated in Anna's sexual obsession with Gaida or her subsummation into mothering his child once born because she remains a very willing participant in those relationships. She does not, however, desire her pregnancy, which is marked by discomfort and fears of death in childbirth as it enters its later stages. In a novel in which "interiority [is written] mainly through bodies," Anna's distaste for her own pregnancy manifests in a lack of language (Cunningham xx). While she is able to articulate her desires regarding her marriage to Gaida and her maternal role very directly, in attempting to tell Gerald about her pregnancy, she cannot name it: "I can't say it. I can't breathe it." In fact, she cannot even "understand it," assuming it to have been impossible given her recent bout of cholera (108). And early in pregnancy as she still is at this point, she "can't be absolutely sure . . . [but thinks that she is pregnant] from several things, and especially [from fainting] last night." Despite Anna's ongoing disinclination to speak of her pregnancy ("Oh, don't ask me about it, it's so dreadful!"), these several things seem to reference bodily specificities much more directly than do revelations of pregnancy in earlier Victorian fiction (109). A reader of *Anna Lombard* is very likely to assume a reference to the cessation of menstruation here, if nothing else.

The relative frankness with which both Anna's sexual and pregnant bodily specificities are narrated in *Anna Lombard* seems to place this novel, as well as its heroine, ahead of its time. Again and again, Gerald describes Anna as belonging to the future, "not fitted to this humdrum nineteenth century," and Anna herself wonders whether she is "perhaps . . . a product of the twentieth [century] come too soon" (41, 114). It is Anna's role in this novel as futurity embodied that frames her reclamation of independence from the "degradation" of physical ties to Indian bodies as particularly important. Anna herself perceives her first husband to be her racial inferior. She sees the marriage as a degradation on the basis of her husband's racialized baseness, and she positions herself again and again alongside Gerald as "us" in the face of a "them" that includes her husband, as when she notes that "it doesn't matter if [Gaida] does see us together. He knows that I am openly engaged to you. What do these blacks not know? It is useless to try to keep anything from them" (56). It is Anna's desire to incorporate her child into the "us" that most repulses Gerald after its birth. In the infant, he sees "that curious hideousness of aspect that belongs usually to the fruit of Eurasian marriages" despite his acknowledgment that "to no eyes but those that knew the secret of its birth, would it have seemed different from a European's" (127, 128). Anna herself had expected before the birth to "hate it" and planned to have it sent away to make room for her to become "all Gerald's own" (128). It is her powerlessness in the face of the maternal relationship to her child that suggests she risks embodying "the dark mirror of [a] future" that serves as a "threat to the stability of racial categories (132; Brittain 90).[10]

---

10. For more on Victorian fears about bodily permeability and race, see Anne McClintock's *Imperial Leather*. McClintock identifies fears of bodily permeability as particularly located in women's sexual bodies. Dara Rossman Regaignon's *Writing Maternity* places these dangers in direct conversation with the anxieties of imperial maternity.

Not only does Anna's pregnancy shift her body into a fun-house mirror that distorts the future by multiplying it and its racial valences, but her pregnancy also pauses Gerald's "possession" of the future he desires in the sexual possession of Anna's body, a possession he believes to be impossible while she carries another man's child (120). Her pregnant body is impressed by Gaida. Laboring "in such horrible pain," Anna, too, frames her pregnancy as belonging to another man, wishing that she were instead "bearing [the pain] for [Gerald]" (124–25). That she does eventually decide to bear the pain of killing the child she loves to be able to give Gerald the future he wishes to possess seems a tacit acknowledgment of the child as an embodied impression of his father rather than any expression of herself.

Though reviews upon the publication of *Anna Lombard* tended to note its questionable morality, these seem to have had as much to do with a perceived laissez-faire approach to female sexuality and interracial relationships as with infanticide.[11] I find infanticide to be a pretty inescapable plot point in this novel, complicated by narrative endorsement. Melissa Purdue has demonstrated how the work of Victoria Cross tends to view maternal ties as weak and easily dissolved, though Purdue notes that Anna does not murder her child due to any weak maternal feeling but rather as a corrective to an overly passionate interracial connection. Furthermore, there is a pretty clear moral difference between even the most casual child abandonment, such as that which Purdue explores in Cross's 1914 *Hilda against the World,* and murder. That that moral difference is collapsed in this novel is the result of a racism expressed as paternal impression: Anna's baby is affectively indistinguishable from his father and is, like that father, disposable in the interests of a bright, white future. Much as Gerald contemplates killing Gaida earlier in the novel and decides not to *not* on the basis of it being wrong to do so but because doing so would hurt Anna, Anna decides to murder the baby on the basis of it being something that will serve Gerald's happiness. This overthrowing of the "natural law and the natural destiny of women" is framed as terrible, certainly, but also emancipatory (132).

If the "natural destiny of woman" is understood as the bearing of children, then both *Anna Lombard* and fin de siècle literature more broadly express a resistance that can be imagined only as death, the threat of maternal and fetal death in *The Heavenly Twins,* a murderous explosion of child and infant death in *Jude the Obscure,* and a carefully calculated infanticide in *Anna Lombard.* Somatic readings of Anna's pregnancy are complicated by a narrative perspective that expresses the unwantedness of Anna's pregnancy through a

---

11. For an overview of reviews, see Cunningham xvi–xvii.

husband who believes it to signal her physical possession by another man and a "dark" miscegenated future. But the unwantedness remains, as inescapable and irresolvable as the racist infanticide. In 1901 Cross can write a novel that imagines a masculine acceptance of woman's sexual license and tacitly endorses the infanticide of mixed-race babies, but—despite medical advances that had made possible the separation of maternal mind from fetal body and the ongoing historical practice of fertility control, including but not limited to abortion—she can't write a novel that imagines abortion as a viable option for people who don't want to be pregnant. In 2023 I can't read this pregnancy without imagining that option and the somatic stakes of its lack. Pain is pain, but the pain of a wanted pregnancy and labor is different from the pain of an unwanted one, as Anna herself indicates in wishing she were bearing pain for Gerald. I close this final chapter of *Pregnancy in the Victorian Novel* troubled by a future of somatic readers much more attuned to the pain of bearing unwanted pregnancies than I am.

A VERY SHORT CONCLUSION

The Very Long Nineteenth Century

> As thou knowest not... how the bones do grow
> in the womb of her that is with child: even so thou
> knowest not the works of God who maketh all.
> —Ecclesiastes 11:5, KJV

For most of human history, pregnancy and childbirth were encounters with the unknown: not only "how the bones do grow in the womb of her that is with child" but also whether pregnancy might be possible for any given person; how—exactly—pregnancy occurred; when pregnancy began; whether clots of blood were an early miscarriage or a late menstrual cycle; whether physical symptoms indicated pregnancy, some physical condition other than pregnancy, or the power of the mind to imagine itself on the canvas of the body; whether a placenta was dangerously positioned over the cervix; whether a pregnancy was likely to be viable; whether reduced fetal movement later in pregnancy meant that labor would deliver a baby who was already dead; whether a fetus had the typical number of umbilical arteries; whether a pregnant person was likely to develop a life-threatening condition particular to pregnancy; whether there were twins; whether a baby was head down; when a baby might reasonably be expected; whether a laboring person's blood pressure was spiking; whether a baby's heart rate was dropping with each contraction; whether the amount of postpartum maternal bleeding was normal; what might cause postpartum infections; whether the people who cared for the sick and dying were optimal caregivers for sweeping a uterus for an undelivered placenta and whether they should wash their hands first.

In 2023, for many privileged white Americans like myself, people with access to health insurance and regular prenatal care, many of these mysteries have been—largely—solved. Though the pregnancy outcomes for any given individual remain uncertain, data gestures toward answers in the aggregate: We can measure hormone levels and egg reserves to estimate the likelihood of successful conception; we know not only what the mechanisms of conception are but how to track the hormone spikes and temperature shifts that signal impending and completed ovulation; we know about optimal pH levels for vaginal mucus when people are trying to conceive and about shortcuts for slower sperm trying to get to an egg. We can begin to spot the shadow of a second line on an at-home pregnancy test nine days after conception, before a first missed period; because many women know they are pregnant so early in pregnancy, many also know that early miscarriage is miscarriage rather than late menstruation—if they aren't sure, an ultrasound and lab work can usually provide conclusive answers. We know how to diagnose the molar pregnancies, cancers, and hormonal conditions that can mimic pregnancy. An ultrasound will provide conclusive answers about whether there is any stage of pregnancy in a uterus, will indicate whether a person is pregnant with multiples, will diagnose the location of the placenta and pick up the heartbeat of a living fetus, will enable care providers to spot many fetal anomalies halfway through a pregnancy, and will confirm whether a baby is head-down at the end of pregnancy. Fetal anomalies (as well as fetal sex) are also indicated in bloodwork taken as early as eight weeks into a pregnancy; bloodwork and urinalysis later in pregnancy can help to diagnose gestational diabetes and preeclampsia in time to treat for these conditions, which can be deadly when untreated. Standard hospital procedures for fetal and maternal monitoring during labor and immediately following—though not perfect and not always necessary—can spot dangerous conditions and indicate interventions like cesarian sections, which became relatively common in the twentieth century; birth workers follow basic hygiene practices that make postpartum infections much less likely. Pregnancy in twenty-first-century America can be an encounter with knowing too much as often as it is an encounter with knowing too little.

Although America has systemic problems with maternal and infant mortality, privileged white women and their fetuses have never been more likely to survive pregnancy and childbirth than today, though more pregnant people will die following the enactment of near-total abortion bans in parts of America. These abortion bans, sometimes extending even to the treatment of deadly conditions like ectopic pregnancy, evidence the degree to which the threat of death as an ever-present companion to the creation of life has receded from popular view. Nonetheless, roughly one in four women will experience miscarriage over the course of their reproductive lives. And in 2006, "1 out of every 167 [American] pregnancies that made it to the 20th week ended with the death of the fetus before birth (that is, stillbirth before delivery)" ("How Common"). These ever-present losses are often mysterious. There were no clear-cut answers about my own miscarriages and stillbirth, which trained me in an acute awareness of embodied uncertainty.

But this book did not grow out of those experiences; most of it—including the deep investment in uncertainty as a critical attitude—predated them. The majority of this project was imagined, researched, written, and revised before my pregnancies, though, of course, my experiences, evolving cultures of scholarship, and major social events since then have informed revisions and expansions to the book. I remember suspecting, in the long months after the stillbirth of my first child, that this book had impressed a dangerous, guilty pregnancy plot onto my body; I remember suspecting that narrative tendencies for the representation of pregnancy in Victorian novels were working in real ways on the canvas of my body. I suppose I don't suspect that any longer. I've moved further away from that idea on a personal level, but I've moved closer to it critically. Narrative tendencies for the representation of pregnancy in the Victorian novel are working in real ways in the twenty-first century, not least in the choice America is making as I write to erase narratives that imagine reproductive choice from the scripts of real people's lives. Our culture has shifted the chronologies of pregnancy concealment and revelation, but Victorian frameworks for judging reproductive bodies and their potential guilt remain very much with us. So, too, do ostensibly objective assessments of maternal guilt and somatic experience, primarily diagnostic approaches to embodiment, and lurking fears about the horror and death maternal imaginations can cause. Certainly, some of these similarities (like a system of beliefs in maternal impression) are common to cultures of pregnancy more generally. There's no magical umbilical cord connecting America in the 2020s directly to the Victorian novel. But the particular intersection of the medicalization of pregnancy and childbirth—a process in which eighteenth- and nineteenth-century Western Europe and Britain in particular played outsized roles and which twentieth-century America then largely assumed—was plotted and paved in the nineteenth century and is more heavily trafficked today that anyone could have imagined even 50 years ago, much less 150.

Though this book sometimes looks warily at diagnostic approaches to the body, I suspect I might have died in pregnancy or childbirth without advanced medical care. Like Rachel Feder thinking about the stubborn placenta she and Mary Wollstonecraft had in common, I find it "hard not to remember that, had I lived [in the nineteenth century], I would be dead, too" (21). Diagnosis of and treatments for preeclampsia postdate the Victorian period. So, if I were a character in a Victorian novel, I guess I would hope to be like the first wife of Trollope's Phineas Finn, quietly lost to childbirth between novels, safe from blame. But it's more likely that I would be exposed to the kind of judgment I turned so easily on myself: The list of things I should have done differently, the ways I should have behaved better ran through my mind like constant subtitles to my experience. In living my "real" life as I have, clearly, I haven't slipped the bonds of Victorian plots. They are with me—they live *in* me—as they are with and in America. Even before the Supreme Court overturned *Roe v. Wade*, American maternal mortality rates were rising, and women of color are more likely to die as a result of pregnancy than are white women (MacDorman et al.; "Infographic"). Maternal mortality rates that reflect death during childbirth and the postpartum period but that exclude data on women who die during pregnancy also demonstrate significant disparities among white and Black women (Hoyert). And Black women in America are significantly more likely to experience miscarriage and stillbirth (Pruitt et al). Indeed, Black women in America are more than twice as likely as white women to experience stillbirth ("How Common"). And yet these vulnerable bodies are also those most likely to be assigned legal and social blame for pregnancy loss and will be more statistically significantly impacted by abortion bans. Death and guilt in cultures of pregnancy are not artifacts of the past; they are alive and well. Contemporary critical approaches to cultures of pregnancy should foster modes, like somatic reading, outward from the uncertainty that allows us to approach reproductive bodies modestly and to feel alongside representations of bodily experience without requiring affinity or even sympathy.

I am completing this book in the shadow of a loss of reproductive rights that I couldn't have imagined when I began writing about pregnancy more than a decade ago. This context makes the challenge of *Pregnancy in the Victorian Novel* more inescapable: In arguing for the explicit inclusion of personal embodied knowledge and uncertainty in analytical modes of reading, I am arguing that we should bring more of the present into literary criticism than it can bear. I cannot apply what I know about moralization, pregnancy, and loss in the twenty-first-century American reproductive landscape without acknowledging violence exacted on Black bodies and the rise of extremist positions on the bodily autonomy of pregnant people. These contexts shape the range of somatic experience and cultural meaning possible in our culture and, in so doing, haunt the edges of the legible in Victorian novels where Black pregnancy and abortion never appear. Reading pregnancy in Victorian novels somatically demands a closing acknowledgment of all of the pregnancies, miscarriages, stillbirths, abortions, and maternal deaths that it's impossible to find in these texts but that we are obligated to attend to in our own cultural context.

WORKS CITED

Ablow, Rachel. *The Marriage of Minds: Reading Sympathy in the Victorian Marriage Plot.* Stanford UP, 2007.

———. *Victorian Pain.* Princeton UP, 2017.

"Adam Bede." *The Saturday Review of Politics, Literature, Science, Art, and Finance.* Vol. 7, 1859, pp. 250–51. *Google Books,* https://www.google.com/books/edition/The_Saturday_Review_of_Politics_Literatu/FS8_AQAAIAAJ?hl=en&gbpv=0.

Allison, Sarah. *Reductive Reading: A Syntax of Victorian Moralizing.* Johns Hopkins UP, 2018.

———. *The Way We Argue Now: A Study in the Cultures of Theory.* Princeton UP, 2005.

Anderson, Amanda. *The Powers of Distance: Cosmopolitanism and the Cultivation of Detachment.* Princeton UP, 2001.

Armstrong, Isobel. *Victorian Glassworlds: Glass Culture and the Imagination 1830–1880.* Oxford UP, 2008.

Armstrong, Nancy. *Fiction in the Age of Photography: The Legacy of British Realism.* Harvard UP, 2002.

Auerbach, Nina. *Woman and the Demon: The Life of a Victorian Myth.* Harvard UP, 1982.

Auyoung, Elaine. *When Fiction Feels Real: Representation and the Reading Mind.* Oxford UP, 2018.

Bailin, Miriam. *The Sickroom in Victorian Fiction: The Art of Being Ill.* Cambridge UP, 2007.

Banet-Wieser, Sarah. *Empowered: Popular Feminism and Popular Misogyny.* Duke UP, 2018.

Bardos, Jonah, et al. "A National Survey on Public Perceptions of Miscarriage." *Obstetrics and Gynecology,* vol. 125, no. 6, 2015, pp. 1313–20.

Barrett Browning, Elizabeth. "The Runaway Slave at Pilgrim's Point." *The Norton Anthology of Literature by Women,* edited by Sandra M. Gilbert and Susan Gubar, 3rd ed., Norton, 2007, pp. 533–40.

Bathurst, Bella. "The Lady Vanishes: Victorian Photography's Hidden Mothers." *The Guardian,* 2 Dec. 2013, https://www.theguardian.com/artanddesign/2013/dec/02/hidden-mothers-victorian-photography.

Beer, Gillian. "'Authentic Tidings of Invisible Things': Vision and the Invisible in the Later Nineteenth Century." *Vision in Context: Historical and Contemporary Perspectives on Sight,* edited by Teresa Brennan and Martin Jay, Routledge, 1996, pp. 83–98.

———. *George Eliot.* Indiana UP, 1986.

Belling, Catherine. "Editor's Foreword." *Literature and Medicine,* vol. 31, no. 1, 2013, pp. vii–xii.

Bérubé, Michael. "The Audacious Argument for Modesty." *PMLA,* vol. 135, no. 5, 2020, pp. 970–75.

Best, Stephen. "Well, That Was Obvious." "Two Responses to 'Denotatively, Technically, Literally'" [special issue of *Representations*], 21 Apr. 2014, http://www.representations.org/two-responses-to-denotatively-technically-literally/.

Best, Stephen, and Sharon Marcus. "Surface Reading: An Introduction." *Representations,* vol. 108, no. 1, 2009, pp. 1–21.

"Beyonce's Baby Bump Blooper." *ABC News,* https://abcnews.go.com/blogs/entertainment/2011/10/beyonces-baby-bump-blooper.

Blackwell, Elizabeth. *Human Element in Sex: Being a Medical Inquiry into the Relation of Sexual Physiology to Christian Morality.* Churchill, 1894.

Bordo, Susan. *Unbearable Weight: Feminism, Western Culture, and the Body.* U of California P, 2003.

Boswell, Parley Ann. *Pregnancy in Literature and Film.* McFarland, 2014.

Boumelha, Penny. *Thomas Hardy and Women: Sexual Ideology and Narrative Form.* U of Wisconsin P, 1985.

Briggs, Laura. "The Race of Hysteria: 'Overcivilization' and the 'Savage' Woman in Late Nineteenth-Century Obstetrics and Gynecology." *American Quarterly,* vol. 52, no. 2, 2000, pp. 246–73.

Brittain, Melisa. "Erasing Race in the New Woman Review: Victorian Cross's *Anna Lombard.*" *Nineteenth-Century Feminisms,* vol. 4, 2001, pp. 75–95.

Brontë, Emily. *Wuthering Heights: An Authoritative Text, with Essays in Criticism,* edited by William Merritt Sale, Norton, 1972.

Brooks, Peter. *Body Work: Objects of Desire in Modern Narrative.* Harvard UP, 1993.

———. *Realist Vision,* Yale UP, 1998.

Budge, Gavin. *Charlotte M. Yonge: Religion, Feminism and Realism in the Victorian Novel.* Peter Lang, 2007.

Bull, Thomas. *Hints to Mothers for the Management of Health during the Period of Pregnancy and in the Lying-in-Room.* Longman and Co., 1837. *Google Books,* https://www.google.com/books/edition/Hints_to_Mothers_for_the_management_of_h/TowEAAAAQAAJ?hl=en&gbpv=1.

Byrne, Katherine. *Tuberculosis and the Victorian Literary Imagination.* Cambridge UP, 2011.

Caldwell, Janis McLarren. *Literature and Medicine in Nineteenth-Century Britain: From Mary Shelley to George Eliot.* Cambridge UP, 2008.

Cameron, Lauren. "Infertility and Darwinian Anthropology in Anthony Trollope's Phineas Novels." *Studies in English Literature 1500–1900,* vol. 59, no. 4, 2019, pp. 893–912.

Capuano, Peter J. *Changing Hands: Industry, Evolution, and the Reconfiguration of the Victorian Body.* U of Michigan P, 2015.

Carpenter, Mary Wilson. *Health, Medicine, and Society in Victorian England.* Praeger, 2010.

Cartwright, Lisa. *Screening the Body: Tracing Medicine's Visual Culture.* Minnesota UP, 1995.

Carroll, Alicia. *Devouring Anxiety: Victorian Breastfeeding and the Modern Individual.* ProQuest, 2009.

Chamberlain, Geoffrey. "British Maternal Mortality in the 19th and Early 20th Centuries." *Journal of the Royal Society of Medicine,* vol. 99, no. 11, 2006, pp. 559–63.

Charon, Rita. *Narrative Medicine: Honoring the Stories of Illness.* Oxford UP, 2008.

Chavasse, Pye Henry. *Advice to Wives on the Management of Themselves: During the Periods of Pregnancy, Labour, and Suckling.* From the 2nd London ed. D. Appleton, 1844. *National Library of Medicine Digital Collections,* https://collections.nlm.nih.gov/catalog/nlm:nlmuid-101562725-bk.

Chishty-Mujahid, Nadya. "Scarred and Healed Identities: Fallenness, Morality, and the Issue of Personal Autonomy in Adam Bede and Ruth." *Victorian Review,* vol. 30, no. 2, 2004, pp. 58–80.

Chodorow, Nancy J. *The Reproduction of Mothering: Psychoanalysis and the Sociology of Gender.* 2nd ed., U of California P, 1999.

Cixous, Hélène. "The Laugh of the Medusa." Translated by Keith Cohen and Paula Cohen, *Signs,* vol. 1, no. 4, 1976, pp. 875–93.

Cody, Lisa Forman. *Birthing the Nation: Sex, Science, and the Conception of Eighteenth-Century Britons.* Oxford UP, 2008.

Cohen, William A. *Embodied: Victorian Literature and the Senses.* U of Minnesota P, 2009.

———. "Interiors: Sex and the Body in Dickens." *Critical Survey,* vol. 17, no. 2, 2005, pp. 5–19.

Cohn, Elisha. *Still Life: Suspended Development in the Victorian Novel.* Oxford UP, 2015.

Coombs, David Sweeney. "Does Grandcourt Exist?: Description and Fictional Characters." *Victorian Studies,* vol. 59, no. 3, 2017, pp. 390–98.

———. *Reading with the Senses in Victorian Literature and Science.* U of Virginia P, 2019.

Crais, Clifton, and Pamela Scully. *Sara Baartman and the Hottentot Venus: A Ghost Story and a Biography.* Princeton UP, 2008.

Crary, Jonathan. *Techniques of the Observer: On Vision and Modernity in the Nineteenth Century.* MIT Press, 1992.

Cross, Victoria. *Anna Lombard,* edited by Gail Cunningham. Continuum, 2006.

Cunningham, Gail. Introduction. *Anna Lombard* by Victorian Cross, Continuum, 2006, pp. vii–xxv.

Dabashi, Pardis. "Introduction to 'Cultures of Argument': The Loose Garments of Argument." *PMLA,* vol. 135, no. 5, 2020, pp. 946–55.

Davis, Isabel. "The Experimental Conception Hospital: Dating Pregnancy and the Gothic Imagination." *Social History of Medicine,* vol. 32, no. 4, 2019, pp. 773–98.

Dickens, Charles. *Our Mutual Friend,* edited by Adrian Poole. Penguin Classics, 1998.

Donaghy, Paige. "Miscarriage, False Conceptions, and Other Lumps: Women's Pregnancy Loss in Seventeenth- and Eighteenth-Century England." *Social History of Medicine,* vol. 34, no. 4, 2021, pp. 1138–60.

Doyle, Nora. *Maternal Bodies: Redefining Motherhood in Early America.* North Carolina UP, 2018.

Duden, Barbara. *Disembodying Women: Perspectives on Pregnancy and the Unborn.* Harvard UP, 1993.

Ehrenreich, Barbara, and Deirdre English. *Witches, Midwives, and Nurses: A History of Women Healers.* 2nd ed., The Feminist Press at CUNY, 2010.

Eliot, George. *Adam Bede,* edited by Mary Waldron. Broadview, 2005.

———. *Middlemarch,* edited by Bert G. Hornbach. Norton, 2000.

Epstein, Julia. *Altered Conditions: Disease, Medicine, and Storytelling.* Routledge, 1994.

Esmail, Jennifer. *Reading Victorian Deafness: Signs and Sounds in Victorian Literature and Culture.* Ohio UP, 2013.

Evans, Jennifer, and Sara Read. "'Before Midnight She Had Miscarried': Women, Men and Miscarriage in Early Modern England." *Journal of Family History,* vol. 40, no. 1, 2015, pp. 3–23.

Feder, Rachel. *Harvester of Hearts: Motherhood under the Sign of Frankenstein.* Northwestern UP, 2018.

Fisk, Catriona. "Looking for Maternity: Dress Collections and Embodied Knowledge." *Fashion Theory,* vol. 23, no. 2, 2019, pp. 401–39.

Fitzpatrick, Katherine F. *A Document in Madness: Representations of Ophelia as Lovesick Madwoman in the Mid-Eighteenth and Nineteenth Centuries.* 2011. Mount Holyoke College, BA senior thesis.

Flint, Kate. *The Victorians and the Visual Imagination.* Cambridge UP, 2000.

Foucault, Michel. *The Birth of the Clinic: An Archaeology of Medical Perception.* Vintage, 1994.

Fournier, Lauren. *Autotheory as Feminist Practice in Art, Writing, and Criticism.* MIT Press, 2021.

Fox, Douglas. *The Signs, Disorders and Management of Pregnancy: The Treatment to Be Adopted during and after Confinement; and the Management and Disorders of Children.* Henry Mozley and Sons, 1834. *Google Books,* https://www.google.com/books/edition/The_signs_disorders_and_management_of_pr/-h9HwOP1_P4C?hl=en&gbpv=1&dq=Fox,+Douglas.+The+Signs,+Disorders+and+Management+of+Pregnancy:+the+Treatment+to+Be+Adopted+during+and+after+Confinement%3B+and+the+Management+and+Disorders+of+Children.+Henry+Mozley+and+Sons,+1834.&pg=PR1&printsec=frontcover.

Fraser, Hilary, and Carolyn Burdett, editors. "The Victorian Tactile Imagination." *19: Interdisciplinary Studies in the Long Nineteenth Century,* no. 19, 2014.

Freidenfelds, Lara. *The Myth of the Perfect Pregnancy: A History of Miscarriage in America.* Oxford UP, 2020.

Freud, Sigmund. *Studies in Hysteria.* Translated by Nicola Luckhurst, 1st printing ed., Penguin Classics, 2004.

Fulford, Roger, editor. *Dearest Child: Private Correspondence of Queen Victoria and the Princess Royal, 1858–1861.* Evans, 1977.

Garbes, Angela. *Like a Mother: A Feminist Journey through the Science and Culture of Pregnancy.* HarperWave, 2018.

Garland-Thomson, Rosemarie. *Staring: How We Look.* Oxford UP, 2009.

Gaskell, Elizabeth Cleghorn. *Ruth,* edited by Angus Easson. Penguin Books, 1997.

Gilbert, Pamela K. *Disease, Desire and the Body in Victorian Women's Popular Novels.* Cambridge UP, 1997.

———. "'A Nation of Good Animals': Popular Beliefs and the Body." *A Cultural History of the Body,* 6 vols, edited by Michael Sappol and Stephen Rice, Berg/Palgrave Press, 2010, pp. 125–48.

———. *Victorian Skin: Surface, Self, History.* Cornell UP, 2019.

Gilbert, Sandra M., and Susan Gubar. *The Madwoman in the Attic: The Woman Writer and the Nineteenth-Century Literary Imagination.* Yale Nota Bene, 2000.

Gilmartin, Sophie. "'Within the Figure and Frame and Clothes and Cuticle': Trollope and the Body." *Routledge Research Companion to Anthony Trollope,* edited by Deborah Denenholz Morse et al., Routledge, 2017, pp. 120–33.

Goldberg, Michelle. "When a Miscarriage Is Manslaughter." *New York Times,* 18 Oct. 2021, https://www.nytimes.com/2021/10/18/opinion/poolaw-miscarriage.html.

Grand, Sarah. *The Heavenly Twins.* U of Michigan P, 1992.

Hall, Lesley. "Abortion." *Pregnancy and Childbirth in the Age of Victoria,* Great Expectations Pregnancy Project, *The Victorian Web,* 15 July 2022, https://www.victorianweb.org/science/maternity/uvic/4.html.

Halperin, John. *Trollope and Politics: A Study of the Pallisers and Others.* Harper & Row, 1977.

Hanson, Clare. *A Cultural History of Pregnancy: Pregnancy, Medicine, and Culture, 1750–2000.* Palgrave Macmillan, 2004.

Hardy, Thomas. "An Imaginative Woman." *The Pall Mall Magazine,* Apr. 1894, pp. 951–69. *Internet Archive,* https://archive.org/stream/artofthomashardyoojohniala/artofthomashardyoojohniala_djvu.txt.

———. *Jude the Obscure,* edited by Norman Page. 2nd ed., Norton, 1999.

———. *Tess of the D'Urbervilles,* edited by Scott Elledge. 3rd ed., Norton 1990.

Harper, Douglas. "Etymology of Cervix." *Online Etymology Dictionary,* https://www.etymonline.com/word/cervix. Accessed 2 Apr. 2023.

Hartman, Saidiya. "Venus in Two Acts." *Small Axe,* vol. 12, no. 2, 2008, pp. 1–14.

Hayles, Katherine N. *Unthought: The Power of the Cognitive Nonconscious.* U of Chicago P, 2017.

Hirsch, Marianne. *The Mother/Daughter Plot: Narrative, Psychoanalysis, Feminism.* Indiana UP, 1989.

Homans, Margaret. *Bearing the Word: Language and Female Experience in Nineteenth-Century Women's Writing.* U of Chicago P, 1989.

"How Common Is Stillbirth?" National Institutes of Health, last reviewed 25 Oct. 2022, https://www.nichd.nih.gov/health/topics/stillbirth/topicinfo/how-common.

Howe, Irving. "A Distinctively Modern Novel." *Jude the Obscure: An Authoritative Text: Backgrounds and Contexts Criticism,* edited by Norman Page, Norton, 1999, pp. 393–404.

Hoyert, Donna L. "Maternal Mortality Rates in the United States, 2019." NCHS Health E-Stats, 4 Apr. 2020, Centers for Disease Control and Prevention, https://dx.doi.org/10.15620/cdc:103855.

Huebel, Anne. "Managing Victorian Reproduction: Medical Authority over Childbirth in British Advice Literature." *Remedia,* 23 Aug. 2017, https://remedianetwork.net/2017/08/21/managing-victorian-reproduction-medical-authority-over-childbirth-in-british-advice-literature/. Website discontinued.

Huet, Marie-Hélène. *Monstrous Imagination.* Harvard UP, 1993.

Hughes, Kathryn. *Victorians Undone: Tales of the Flesh in the Age of Decorum.* Johns Hopkins UP, 2018.

"Infographic: Racial/Ethnic Disparities in Pregnancy-Related Deaths—United States, 2007–2016." Centers for Disease Control and Prevention, last reviewed 13 Apr. 2022, https://www.cdc.gov/reproductivehealth/maternal-mortality/disparities-pregnancy-related-deaths/infographic.html.

Irigaray, Luce. "Body against Body: In Relation to the Mother." *French Feminism Reader,* edited by Kelly Oliver, Rowman & Littlefield, 2000, pp. 241–52.

Jacobus, Mary, et al. *Body/Politics: Women and the Discourses of Science.* Psychology Press, 1990.

Jaffe, Audrey. *Scenes of Sympathy: Identity and Representation in Victorian Fiction.* Cornell UP, 2000.

———. *The Victorian Novel Dreams of the Real: Conventions and Ideology.* Oxford UP, 2019.

James, Henry. "Can You Forgive Her? Review." *Nation,* vol. 1, 28 Sept. 1865, 409–10. Reprinted in *Notes and Reviews,* 1921.

Jensz, Felicity. "Miscarriage and Coping in the Mid-Nineteenth Century: Private Notes from Distant Places." *Gender & History,* vol. 32, 2020, pp. 270–85.

Jordanova, Ludmilla. "The Social Construction of Medical Knowledge." *Social History of Medicine,* vol. 8, no. 3, 1995, pp. 361–81.

Keen, Suzanne. *Thomas Hardy's Brains: Psychology, Neurology, and Hardy's Imagination.* The Ohio State UP, 2014.

Kennedy, Meegan. *Revising the Clinic: Vision and Representation in Victorian Medical Narrative and the Novel.* The Ohio State UP, 2010.

———. "Syphilis and the Hysterical Female: The Limits of Realism in Sarah Grand's *The Heavenly Twins.*" *Women's Writing,* vol. 11, no. 2, 2004, pp. 259–80.

———. "The Victorian Novel and Medicine." *The Oxford Handbook of the Victorian Novel,* edited by Lisa Rodensky, Oxford UP, 2013, pp. 259–82.

Knott, Sarah. *Mother Is a Verb: An Unconventional History.* Sarah Crighton Books, 2019.

Kramnick, Jonathan Brody. *Paper Minds: Literature and the Ecology of Consciousness.* U of Chicago P, 2018.

Kristeva, Julia. *Desire in Language: A Semiotic Approach to Literature and Art.* Columbia UP, 1980.

———. "Stabat Mater." Translated by Arthur Goldhammer. *Poetics Today,* vol. 6, no. 1/2, 1985, pp. 133–52.

Kucich, John. *The Power of Lies: Transgression, Class, and Gender in Victorian Fiction.* Cornell UP, 1994.

Langridge, Rosemary. "The Tearful Gaze in Elizabeth Gaskell's Ruth: Crying, Watching and Nursing." *Journal of International Women's Studies,* vol. 12, no. 2, 2013, pp. 47–60.

Lavery, Grace. "Generation and Class Antagonism." *PMLA,* vol. 135, no. 5, 2020, pp. 976–81.

Law, Jules. *The Social Life of Fluids: Blood, Milk, and Water in the Victorian Novel.* Cornell UP, 2010.

Leighton, Mary Elizabeth, and Lisa Surridge. "From 'A Piece of Grossness' to 'Minute Particularity': Queen Victoria's First Pregnancy in the British Press." *Journal of Victorian Culture,* vol. 27, no. 3, 2022, pp. 424–46.

———, editors. *Pregnancy and Childbirth in the Age of Victoria.* Great Expectations Pregnancy Project, *The Victorian Web,* 15 July 2022, last modified 18 Oct. 2022, https://www.victorianweb.org/science/maternity/uvic/index.html.

Levine, George. *Dying to Know: Scientific Epistemology and Narrative in Victorian England.* U of Chicago P, 2002.

Lewis, Judith Schneid. *In the Family Way: Childbearing in the British Aristocracy, 1760–1860.* Rutgers UP, 1986.

Liggins, Emma. "Writing against the 'Husband-Fiend': Syphilis and Male Sexual Vice in the New Woman Novel." *Women's Writing,* vol. 7, no. 2, 2000, pp. 175–95.

Litvak, Joseph. *Caught in the Act: Theatricality in the Nineteenth Century.* U of California P, 1992.

Love, Heather. "Close but Not Deep." *New Literary History,* vol. 41, no. 2, 2010, pp. 371–91.

———. "Close Reading and Thin Description." *Public Culture*, vol. 25, no. 3, issue 71, 2013, pp. 401–34.

———. "Ecologies of Deviance: Autism, Impersonal Sex, and the Observational Social Sciences." English Department Friday Forum, 2014, CUNY Graduate Center, New York City.

MacDorman, Marian F., et al. "Recent Increases in the U.S. Maternal Mortality Rate: Disentangling Trends from Measurement Issues." *Obstetrics and Gynecology*, vol. 128, no. 3, 2016, pp. 447–55.

Malet, Lucas. *The History of Sir Richard Calmady*, edited by Talia Schaffer. U of Birmingham P, 2003.

Malone, Cynthia Northcutt. "Near Confinement: Pregnant Women in the Nineteenth-Century British Novel." *Dickens Studies Annual*, vol. 29, 2000, pp. 367–85.

"Manifesto of the V21 Collective: Ten Theses." *V21*, http://v21collective.org/manifesto-of-the-v21-collective-ten-theses/.

Mangham, Andrew. *Violent Women and Sensation Fiction: Crime, Medicine, and Victorian Popular Culture*. Palgrave Macmillan, 2007.

Markle, Meghan. "The Losses We Share." *New York Times*, 25 Nov. 2020, https://www.nytimes.com/2020/11/25/opinion/meghan-markle-miscarriage.html.

Marland, Hilary. *Dangerous Motherhood: Insanity and Childbirth in Victorian Britain*. Palgrave Macmillan, 2004.

Matus, Jill L. *Unstable Bodies: Victorian Representations of Sexuality and Maternity*. Manchester UP, 1995.

Mazzoni, Cristina. *Maternal Impressions: Pregnancy and Childbirth in Literature and Theory*. Cornell UP, 2002.

Mears, Martha. *The Midwife's Candid Advice to the Fair Sex; or the Pupil of Nature: On . . . Pregnancy; Childbirth; the Diseases Incident to Both, Etc*. Crosby & R. Faulder, 1805. *Wellcome Collection*, https://wellcomecollection.org/works/wmgtckqm.

"Medical Evidence Relative to the Duration of Human Pregnancy, as Given in the Gardner Peerage Cause, before the Committee for Privileges of the House of Lords in 1825–6 / With Introductory Remarks and Notes by Robert Lyall." *Wellcome Collection*, https://wellcomecollection.org/works/gcg8jp7k.

Mervosh, Sarah. "Alabama Woman Who Was Shot While Pregnant Is Charged in Fetus's Death." *New York Times*, 27 June 2019, https://www.nytimes.com/2019/06/27/us/pregnant-woman-shot-marshae-jones.html.

Meyer, Susan. *Imperialism at Home: Race and Victorian Women's Fiction*. Cornell UP, 1996.

Michie, Helena. *The Flesh Made Word: Female Figures and Women's Bodies*. Oxford UP, 1987.

———. "Under Victorian Skins: The Bodies Beneath." *A Companion to Victorian Literature and Culture*, edited by Herbert F. Tucker, Blackwell, 1999, pp. 407–24.

"Miscarriage." *Mayo Clinic*, 16 Oct. 2021, https://www.mayoclinic.org/diseases-conditions/pregnancy-loss-miscarriage/symptoms-causes/syc-20354298.

Mitchell, David T. *Narrative Prosthesis: Disability and the Dependencies of Discourse*. U of Michigan P, 2001.

Morgan, Rosemarie. *Women and Sexuality in the Novels of Thomas Hardy*. Routledge, 1988.

Morgan, Susan. "Gaskell's Heroines and the Power of Time." *Pacific Coast Philology*, vol. 18, no. 1/2, 1983, pp. 43–51.

Morse, Deborah Denenholz. *Women in Trollope's Palliser Novels*. UMI Research P, 1987.

Moscucci, Ornella. *The Science of Woman: Gynaecology and Gender in England, 1800–1929.* Cambridge UP, 1993.

Mulvey, Laura. "Visual Pleasure and Narrative Cinema." *Film Theory and Criticism: Introductory Readings,* edited by Leo Braudy and Marshall Cohen, Oxford UP, 1999, pp. 833–44.

Nash, Jennifer C. *Birthing Black Mothers.* Duke UP, 2021.

Nelson, Maggie. *The Argonauts.* Graywolf, 2015.

Newman, Beth. "'The Situation of the Looker-On': Gender, Narration, and Gaze in Wuthering Heights." *PMLA,* vol. 105, no. 5, 1990, pp. 1029–41.

Oakley, Ann. *The Captured Womb: History of the Medical Care of Pregnant Women.* Blackwell, 1985.

Oberman, Michelle. "Understanding Infanticide in Context: Mothers Who Kill, 1870–1930 and Today." *The Journal of Criminal Law and Criminology,* vol. 92, no. 3/4, 2002, pp. 707–38.

Oliver, Kelly. *Knock Me Up Knock Me Down: Images of Pregnancy in Hollywood Film.* Columbia UP, 2012.

Oren-Magidor, Daphna. *Infertility in Early Modern England.* Palgrave Macmillan, 2016.

Orlemanski, Julie. "Scales of Reading." *Exemplaria,* vol. 26, nos. 2–3, 2014, pp. 215–33.

Oster, Emily. *Expecting Better: Why the Conventional Pregnancy Wisdom Is Wrong—And What You Really Need to Know.* Penguin, 2014.

Otter, Chris. *The Victorian Eye: A Political History of Light and Vision in Britain, 1800–1910.* U of Chicago P, 2008.

Owens, Deirdre Cooper. *Medical Bondage: Race, Gender, and the Origins of American Gynecology.* Georgia UP, 2018.

Paltrow, Lynn M., and Jeanne Flavin. "Arrests of and Forced Interventions on Pregnant Women in the United States, 1973–2005: Implications for Women's Legal Status and Public Health." *Journal of Health, Politics, Policy and Law,* vol. 38, no. 2, 2013, pp. 299–343.

Petersen, Emily E., et al. "Vital Signs: Pregnancy-Related Deaths, United States, 2011–2015, and Strategies for Prevention, 13 States, 2013–2017." *Morbidity and Mortality Weekly Report,* vol. 68, no. 18, 2019, pp. 423–29.

Peterson, Mildred Jeanne. *Family, Love, and Work in the Lives of Victorian Gentlewomen,* Indiana UP, 1989.

———. *The Medical Profession in Mid-Victorian London.* U of California P, 1978.

Pratt, Mary Louise. *Imperial Eyes: Travel Writing and Transculturation.* Routledge, 1992.

"pregnant,pregnancy." *Google Books NGram Viewer,* https://books.google.com/ngrams/graph?corpus=26&smoothing=3&content=pregnant%2Cpregnancy&year_end=2019&year_start=1800&direct_url=t1%3B%2Cpregnant%3B%2Cco%3B.t1%3B%2Cpregnancy%3B%2Cco#t1%3B%2Cpregnant%3B%2Cco%3B.t1%3B%2Cpregnancy%3B%2Cco.

Pruitt, Shannon M., et al. "Racial and Ethnic Disparities in Fetal Deaths—United States, 2015–2017." *Morbidity and Mortality Weekly Report,* vol. 69, no. 37, 2020, pp. 1277–82.

Purdue, Melissa. "'I Have Expatiated My Sins to You at Last': Motherhood in Victoria Cross's Colonial Fiction." *Writing Women of the Fin de Siècle: Authors of Change,* edited by Adrienne E. Gavin and Carolyn W. de la L. Oulton, Palgrave Macmillan, 2012, pp. 125–36.

Pykett, Lyn. *The Nineteenth-Century Sensation Novel.* 2nd ed., Liverpool UP, 2011.

Regaignon, Dara Rossman. *Writing Maternity: Medicine, Anxiety, Rhetoric, and Genre.* The Ohio State UP, 2021.

Rich, Adrienne Cecile. *Of Woman Born: Motherhood as Experience and Institution.* Norton, 1995.

Rollins, H. E., editor. *The Letters of John Keats.* Vol. 1, Cambridge UP, 1958.
Rothfield, Lawrence. *Vital Signs: Medical Realism in Nineteenth-Century Fiction.* Princeton UP, 1992.
Ruddick, Sara. *Maternal Thinking: Toward a Politics of Peace.* Beacon Press, 1995.
Ryan, Vanessa L. *Thinking without Thinking in the Victorian Novel.* Johns Hopkins UP, 2012.
Saint-Amour, Paul, editor. "Weak Theory/Weak Modernisms." *Modernism/Modernity,* vol. 3, no. 3, 2018, pp. 1–40.
Sanger, Charles Percy. "The Structure of Wuthering Heights." *Wuthering Heights: An Authoritative Text, with Essays in Criticism,* edited by William Merritt Sale, Norton, 1972, pp. 286–98.
Schwan, Anne. "The Limitations of a Somatics of Resistance: Sexual Performativity and Gender Dissidence in Dickens's *Dombey and Son.*" *Critical Survey,* vol. 17, no. 2, 2005, pp. 92–106.
Scott, Walter. *The Heart of Midlothian,* edited by Tony Inglis. Penguin Classics, 1994.
Semmelweis, Ignaz. *Etiology, Concept and Prophylaxis of Childbed Fever (1861).* Translated by K. Codell Carter, U of Wisconsin P, 1983.
Senf, Carol A. Introduction. *The Heavenly Twins.* U of Michigan P, 1992, pp. vii–xxxvii.
Shakespeare, William. *Hamlet: Text of the Play, the Actors' Gallery, Contexts, Criticism, Afterlives, Resources,* edited by Robert S. Miola. Norton, 2011.
Shonfield, Zuzanna. "The Expectant Victorian, (Late 19th Century Maternity Clothes)." *Costume,* vol. 6, no. 1, 1972, pp. 36–42.
Simmons, LaKisha Michelle. "Black Feminist Theories of Motherhood and Generation: Histories of Black Infant and Child Loss in the United States." *Signs,* vol. 46, no. 2, 2021, pp. 311–35.
Smellie, William. *A Treatise on the Theory and Practice of Midwifery.* Printed for T. and J. Whitehouse, 1764. *The Embryo Project Encyclopedia,* https://embryo.asu.edu/pages/treatise-theory-and-practice-midwifery-1752-1764-william-smellie.
Sparks, Tabitha. *The Doctor in the Victorian Novel: Family Practices.* Ashgate, 2009.
Spampinato, Erin. "'Never Punch Down'; or, How We Disagree (Online) Now." *PMLA,* vol. 135, no. 5, 2020, pp. 963–69.
Steinlight, Emily. "We Have Always Been Presentist." *Victorian Studies,* vol. 59, no. 1, 2016, pp. 105–08.
Stone, Pamela K., and Lise Shapiro Sanders. *Bodies and Lives in Victorian England: Science, Sexuality, and the Affliction of Being Female.* Routledge, 2021.
Stoneman, Patsy. *Elizabeth Gaskell.* Indiana UP, 1987.
Thierauf, Doreen. "The Hidden Abortion Plot in George Eliot's *Middlemarch.*" *Victorian Studies,* vol. 56, no. 3, 2014, pp. 479–89.
Teigen, Chrissy. "Hi." *Medium,* 27 Oct. 2020, https://chrissyteigen.medium.com/hi-2e45e6faf764.
——— [@chrissyteigen]. Photo of stillbirth delivery, photographed by John Legend. *Instagram,* 30 Sept. 2020, https://www.instagram.com/p/CFyWQLWpJ3u/?utm_source=ig_embed&ig_rid=de604a32-bd77-44e3-a1eb-a6d609dba0c9.
Tougaw, Jason. *Strange Cases: The Medical Case History and the British Novel.* Routledge, 2006.
Trollope, Anthony. *Barchester Towers.* Oxford UP, 1998.
———. *Can You Forgive Her?* Oxford UP, 2008.
———. *Thackeray.* English Men of Letters series, Macmillan, 1879. *Project Gutenberg,* e-text prepared by Barbara Tozier et al., 4 Aug. 2013.
Tuana, Nancy. "Coming to Understand: Orgasm and the Epistemology of Ignorance." *Hypatia,* vol. 19, no. 1, 2004, pp. 194–232.

Turner, Sasha. *Contested Bodies: Pregnancy, Childrearing, and Slavery in Jamaica*. U of Pennsylvania P, 2017.

Van Niel, Maureen Sayres, and Jennifer L. Payne. "Perinatal Depression: A Review." *Cleveland Clinic Journal of Medicine*, vol. 87, no. 5, 2020, pp. 273–77.

Vrettos, Athena. *Somatic Fictions: Imagining Illness in Victorian Culture*. Stanford UP, 1995.

Ward, Megan. *Seeming Human Artificial Intelligence and Victorian Realist Character*. The Ohio State UP, 2018.

Waterhouse, Harriet. "A Fashionable Confinement: Whaleboned Stays and the Pregnant Woman." *Costume: Journal of the Costume Society*, vol. 41, 2007, pp. 53–65.

Waugh, Norah. *The Cut of Women's Clothes: 1600–1930*. Routledge, 1968.

Wheatley, Kim. "Death and Domestication in Charlotte M. Yonge's *The Clever Woman of the Family*." *Studies in English Literature, 1500–1900*, vol. 36, no. 4, 1996, p. 895–915.

Williams, Jeffrey J. "The New Modesty in Literary Criticism." *The Chronicle of Higher Education*, 15 Jan. 2015, pp. B6–9.

Willis, Martin. *Vision, Science and Literature, 1870–1920: Ocular Horizons*. Pickering & Chatto, 2011.

Wilson, Philip K. "Eighteenth-Century 'Monsters' and Nineteenth-Century 'Freaks': Reading the Maternally Marked Child." *Literature and Medicine*, vol. 21, no. 1, 2002, pp. 1–25.

———. *The Medicalization of Obstetrics: Personnel, Practice and Instruments*. Routledge, 1996.

Withycombe, Shannon. "Happy Miscarriages: An Emotional History of Pregnancy Loss." *Nursing Clio*, 12 Nov. 2015, https://nursingclio.org/2015/11/12/happy-miscarriages-an-emotional-history-of-pregnancy-loss/.

———. "How Did We Get Here? An Interview with Lara Freidenfelds." *Nursing Clio*, 1 Jan. 2020, https://nursingclio.org/2020/01/01/how-did-we-get-here-an-interview-with-lara-freidenfelds/.

———. *Lost: Miscarriage in Nineteenth-Century America*. Rutgers UP, 2018.

Wood, Ellen. *East Lynne*, edited by Elisabeth Jay. Oxford UP, 2008.

Woods, Livia Arndal. "Flashes of Light." *The Rambling*, 21 Oct. 2022, https://the-rambling.com/2022/10/21/issue14-woods/.

———. "Generations in, Generations Of: Pregnancy in Jane Austen." *Women's Writing*, vol. 26, no. 2, spring 2019, pp. 1–17.

———. "Hints to Mothers, 1837/2018." *Synapsis: A Health Humanities Journal*, 9 Apr. 2018, https://medicalhealthhumanities.com/2018/04/09/hints-to-mothers-1837-2018/.

Woods, Robert. *Death before Birth: Fetal Health and Mortality in Historical Perspective*. Oxford UP, 2009.

Wright, Erika. *Reading for Health*. Ohio UP, 2016.

Yonge, Charlotte M. *The Clever Woman of the Family*, edited by Clare A. Simmons. Broadview Press, 2001.

Young, Iris Marion. "Pregnant Embodiment: Subjectivity and Alienation." *Journal of Medicine and Philosophy*, vol. 9, no. 1, 1984, pp. 45–62.

INDEX

Ablow, Rachel, 8, 15, 55
abolition, 12
abortion, 83, 115, 155, 157; ban on, 159; late-term, 4; rights, 88
Adam Bede (Eliot), 11n8, 18, 22, 23, 50, 52, 56, 64, 65, 66, 69, 70, 72, 115; bodily specificity and, 52n4; immorality and, 49; pregnancy in, 54, 55; reproductive bodies and, 51
adultery, 78, 145; possibilities of, 30, 46, 80, 105, 118, 133
Affinities (Goethe), 55
Allison, Sarah, 17, 50n2
anesthesia, 98, 129, 150
Anna Lombard (Cross), 126–27, 131, 133, 151, 154; pregnancy in, 152–53
anxiety, 29, 34, 42, 78, 84, 100, 103, 125, 126, 146; expression of, 101, 140; maternal, 21; perinatal, 32; reproductive, 81
Argonauts, The (Nelson), 16
Austen, Jane, 18, 19, 106n20
autotheory, 8, 16
Autotheory as Feminist Practice in Art, Writing, and Criticism (Fournier), 8
Auyong, Elaine, 15

Baartman, Sara, 12
Bailin, Miriam, 51, 92
Banet-Weiser, Sarah, 84
Barchester Towers (Trollope), 35
Bardos, Jonah, 88
Barrett Browning, Elizabeth, 11, 11n8, 12
Battiscombe, Georgina, 46, 54
Beale, Edith: death of, 136, 137; Monteith and, 134; syphilis and, 133, 135, 136, 139; syphilitic decline of, 133
Bellingham, Mr., 57; as Mr. Donne, 62, 63; Ruth and, 58, 59, 60, 61, 62; sexual body of, 62
Bentham, Jeremy, 79
Bérubé, Michael, 15
Best, Stephen, 9, 17, 53, 54
Between Women (Marcus), 17
Beyoncé, 89
big with child, 18, 99
bigamy, 80
Birth of the Clinic, The (Foucault), 95
Birthing Black Mothers (Nash), 88
Bitzer, Lloyd, 35n8

172 • INDEX

Black bodies: knowing reproductive body through, 12; racism and, 90; reproduction and, 1; violence on, 159; vulnerability of, 12

"Black Feminist Theories of Motherhood and Generation" (Simmons), 75

Black Lives Matter, 16

Black women: enslavement of, 98; miscarriage and, 90; spectacularized bodies of, 88

Black/Brown people, subjugation of, 3n3, 76

Blackwell, Elizabeth, 128

bodies: cultural significance of, 1, 127; diagnostic approaches to, 158; imagined, 55; mind and, 135; nonnormative, 96; sexual, 27, 55, 62, 149, 153n10; social, 5, 134. *See also* Black bodies; pregnant bodies; reproductive bodies

Bodies and Lives in Victorian England (Stone and Sanders), 7

Bridehead, Sue, 3; Jude and, 139, 145; Phillotson and, 143; pregnancy of, 144–45

Brontë, Emily, 11n8, 25

Brooke, Dorothea, 100, 102, 109, 114; Casaubon and, 122; influence of, 103; marriage of, 122; singularity of, 101; Will and, 118

Brooks, Peter, 91

Budge, Gavin, 42n9

Bull, Thomas, 20, 21

Byrne, Katherine: tuberculosis and, 19, 28n2

Calmady (Malet), 131, 149, 150, 151

Calmady, Katherine, 146; in childbirth, 147; interiority of, 148; maternal impression and, 151; mental illness for, 149–50; motherhood and, 148; pregnancy of, 149, 150; pregnant body of, 148

Calmady, Richard, 149, 150–51

Calmady, Richard (Dickie), 147, 149, 150

Cameron, Lauren: on Trollope plotline, 38

Can You Forgive Her? (Trollope), 22, 25, 35, 36, 37, 42

Capuano, Peter J., 7

Carlyle, Barbara Hare, 80, 82, 84, 85

Carlyle, Mr., 80, 84, 85, 86

Carroll, Alicia: infanticide and, 70n12

Casaubon, Mr., 100, 122

Changing Hands (Capuano), 7

Charlotte, Princess, 97, 98

Chettam, Celia, 101, 102, 104, 120; indisposition of, 108; pregnancy of, 103; sexual body of, 103

Chettam, Sir James, 103, 108

childbirth, 32, 159; anesthesia and, 129; data on, 76; death in, 29, 148; as encounter with unknown, 156; intervention in, 29; medicalization of, 22, 97, 158; mortality in, 29; recovery from, 135; surviving, 157

Clark, Charles Mansfield, 79

class, 74, 81; divides, 29; norms, 64; treatment of, 23; working, Victorian femininity and, 12

Clever Woman of the Family, The (Yonge), 22, 25, 41, 42, 43, 46, 47n10, 56, 63–64

Cohen, William, 4, 5, 7

Cohn, Elisha, 125n1

Colquhoun, Colonel, 133, 137

Complete British Housewife, 6

concealment, 22, 48, 62, 66, 67, 68, 71, 72, 98, 99, 145, 158; inadequate, 52; revelation and, 26–34, 46, 56, 75, 79, 92, 93, 148

conception, 147, 157

confinement, 20, 32

consumption. *See* tuberculosis

Contested Bodies (Turner), 16

Coombs, David Sweeney, 8, 10, 11, 15

COVID, 15, 90

critical fabulation, 3n3, 10

croquet fever, 44

Cross, Victoria, 126–27, 131, 151, 154, 155

"Cross Line, A" (Egerton), 125

Cultural History of Pregnancy (Hanson), 17, 21, 94

culture, 10, 23, 39, 74, 98; medicine and, 95n11; pregnancy, 24, 88, 159

"Cultures of Argument" (*PMLA*), 15

Cunningham, Gail, 152

Curtis, Rachel, 41, 42, 43, 45, 46, 47; charity and, 44; domestication of, 48; femininity of, 48

Cut of Women's Clothes, The (Waugh), 7

Dabashi, Pardis, 2, 3, 15, 26

INDEX • 173

Darwin, Erasmus, 129n3

Davis, Isabel, 79

Deans, Effie, 79

deaths, maternal, 29n4, 90, 159

diagnosis, 21; free indirect, 22, 23, 37, 41, 93–100, 105, 107, 111, 121, 123

Dickens, Charles, 92n4; Bella and, 9, 10, 11; pregnancy in works of, 4–14

disability studies, 24, 93n7, 124, 126

discourse: cultural, 93, 94; moralizing, 25–26, 50n2, 114; pregnancy, 94, 99, 114, 118–19, 120, 121, 122; public, 83

diseases, 126, 134; knowledge of, 136; social, 125; venereal, 136. *See also* illnesses

divorce, 78, 80, 85

Doctor in the Victorian Novel, The (Sparks), 98

"Does Grandcourt Exist?" (Coombs), 11

Dombey and Son (Dickens), 9

Donnithorne, Arthur: Hetty and, 65, 66, 68–69, 69n10, 71, 72–73

Doyle, Nora, 13, 16

drugs, 98, 131

Duden, Barbara, 95, 95n12

Durbeyfield, Tess: pregnancy of, 139; pregnant body of, 140; rape of, 139

Earnshaw, Frances, 32, 54; body of, 30; as consumptive, 28, 29; hysterical state of, 27–28; pregnancy of, 26, 27, 29, 31

East Lynne (Wood), 42n9, 77–87, 86n6; narration of, 80; pregnant characters in, 84; scholarship on, 87–90; somatic reading and, 23

ectopic pregnancy, 157

Egerton, George, 125

Elective Affinities (Goethe), 55

Elias, Norbert: in Gilbert, 38–39

Eliot, George, 1, 11n8, 18, 23, 49, 54, 64, 91; criticism of, 52n4; "pregnant" and, 120; *Ruth* plot and, 51

Embodied (Cohen), 7

embodiment, 2, 8, 43, 72, 73, 144, 158; animalistic, 38; female, 12, 140n9; narration of, 51; pregnant, 3, 19, 49, 97, 101, 149

Enlightenment, 97, 130, 131–32

Ethridge, Gerald, 152; Anna and, 151, 153; bearing pain for, 155; future and, 154; Gaida and, 154

euphemisms, 6, 13, 52, 69, 74, 85

"Expectant Victorian, The" (Shonfield), 7

Expecting Better (Oster), 16

experience, 15, 79; Black, 12; embodied, 3, 120–21; lived, 4–5, 4n4; pregnancy, 2, 79; social, 9; somatic, 6, 37, 39, 63–64, 86, 93, 118, 158, 159; "truth" of, 121

"Experimental Conception Hospital, The" (Davis), 79

"Fashionable Confinement, A" (Waterhouse), 7

Fawley, Arabella Donn: imaginary pregnancy of, 142; Jude and, 139, 141, 142, 143; Vilbert and, 140–41

Fawley, Jude, 132, 133, 146; Arabella and, 139, 141, 142, 143; imaginary pregnancy and, 142; Old Father Time and, 139; Sue and, 139, 145

Feder, Rachel, 5, 55, 158

Feeling of Reading, The (Ablow), 8

femininity, 3, 4n4, 36, 48, 94, 114; innate, 67; normative, 117; working class and, 12

feminism/feminist, 5, 8, 16n11, 17, 47n10, 53, 66n9, 75, 97

Fielding, Henry, 130, 130n5

fin de siècle: literature at, 24, 127, 147, 149, 154; maternal impression at, 131; pregnancy at, 13, 22, 76, 124, 125, 126, 127, 128, 131, 144, 147

Fisk, Catriona, 7, 17

Fitzpatrick, Katherine F., 33n7

Floyd, George, 90

Foucault, Michel, 92, 95, 96; discursive practices and, 94; medical gaze and, 53; medicine/culture and, 95n11

Fournier, Lauren, 8

Frayling, Evadne, 133; marriage of, 137; Monteith and, 134; pregnancy of, 139; pregnant body of, 138; suicide attempts by, 138

Freidenfels, Lara, 83, 84

Freud, Sigmund, 125

future: civilized, 146; dark mirror of, 151–55

174 • INDEX

futurity, 13–14, 24, 125, 132, 133, 134, 138, 139, 144, 153

Galbraith, Dr., 133, 137, 138
Garbes, Angela, 16
Gardner Peerage Clause (1825–26), 78, 80, 85
Gaskell, Elizabeth, 18, 49, 52, 56n7, 60, 62
gaze, 6, 13, 53n6, 61, 63, 68, 92n3; critical, 18, 102; diagnostic, 54; literal, 55; male, 53; medical, 53, 95, 121, 138; moralizing, 25; readerly, 27, 53, 55, 95; sympathetic, 121
gender, 16, 64, 75, 94, 125; ideology of, 124; theories of, 125; treatment of, 23; Victorian ideology of, 2n2
Gilbert, Pamela K., 7–8, 8n5, 38–39
Gillie, Annis, 47n10
Gilmartin, Sophie, 38, 39
Goethe, Johann Wolfgang von, 55
Grand, Sarah, 126, 131, 134
gynecology, 12, 93

Hallijohn, Afy, 86n6
Hamilton-Wells, Angelica, 135, 136
Hanson, Clare, 7, 17, 21, 33n7, 94n10, 129n3
Hardy, Thomas, 125, 126, 127, 131, 144; criticism of, 139n8; *Tess* and, 139; women/sexuality and, 140n9
Hare, Richard, 80, 82
Hartman, Saidiya, 3n3, 10, 75
Harvester of Hearts (Feder), 5
Hastings, Lady Flora, 2, 2n1
Heart of Midlothian, The (Scott), 51n3, 79
Heathcliff: Earnshaw and, 26; last meeting with Cathy and, 34; poison of, 69; return of, 30, 31; sexualized relationship with, 22
Heathcliff, Catherine Linton, 26n1, 31; birth of, 26, 27
Heathcliff, Isabella Linton, 26
Heathcliff, Linton: birth of, 26
Heavenly Twins, The (Grand), 126, 127, 131, 132, 134, 139, 144, 146, 154; syphilis and, 133
"Hi" (Tiegen), 89
"Hidden Abortion Plot in George Eliot's *Middlemarch*, The" (Thierauf), 17

Hilda against the World (Cross), 154
Hilton, Ruth, 18, 70; Bellingham and, 58, 59, 60, 62; death of, 63; identity of, 60; illness of, 55–56, 63, 64; immorality of, 61; interiority of, 57; as Mrs. Denbigh, 61, 62; pregnancy of, 23, 49–50, 51, 52, 57, 58, 59–60, 61, 63, 72–73, 99; pregnant body of, 53, 55; reproductive body of, 57–58; sexual body of, 62; visibility of, 60, 62
Hints to Mothers for the Management of Health during the Period of Pregnancy and the Lying-in-Room (Bull), 20
Hirsch, Marianne, 18, 70n11
History of Sir Richard Calmady, The (Malet), 24, 126, 127, 133, 146
Howe, Irving, 132, 133
Huebel, Anne, 20n18
Huet, Marie-Helene, 130
Hughes, Kathryn, 7
Human Element in Sex (Blackwell), 128

identity, 36, 58, 60, 81, 101, 130n5; individual, 56n7
illnesses, 19, 55–56; embodied, 49; pregnancy and, 29; representation of, 50; social, 133; vocabulary of, 54. *See also* diseases
"Imaginative Woman, An" (Hardy), 125
immodesty, 42–43, 44, 45, 46, 48, 56, 62, 68, 95, 145, 148; concealing, 43; ideology of, 19; immorality and, 104, 117, 120, 125; maternal, 92; shadow of, 30
immorality, 61, 138; immodesty and, 104, 117, 120, 125; masculine, 133; maternal, 146; pregnancy and, 49; premature birth and, 31n6. *See also* morality
impression, 21, 128, 132–39; histories of, 127; theories, 131; vocabulary of, 129
In the Family Way (Lewis), 37
Incidents in the Life of a Slave Girl (Jacobs), 11n8
Indian Civil Service, 151
infant mortality, 76, 77, 157, 159
infanticide, 11, 49, 64, 70, 70n12, 74, 155
infertility, 25, 35, 36, 37, 38, 41
Interdisciplinary Studies in the Long Nineteenth Century (Fraser and Burdett), 7

interiority, 14, 51, 64, 65, 67, 69, 73, 96, 102, 103, 104, 110, 117, 118, 148; development of, 57; limited, 54; notions of, 123; psychic, 57, 65; singular, 121; troubled, 13; writing, 152

Isabel, Lady, 77, 80, 84, 86n6; children of, 82; flight of, 81; jealousy of, 85; as Madame Vine, 82; maternity for, 23; night of pain for, 87; wages of sin and, 86

Jacobs, Harriet, 11n8

Jaffe, Audrey, 54, 75, 77

James, Henry: on *Can You Forgive Her?*, 36

Jensz, Felicity, 83–84

Jones, Marshae, 88

Jude the Obscure (Hardy), 126, 127, 131, 132, 146, 154; pregnant unconscious in, 140

judgment, 21; medical, 1, 92, 92n5; moralizing, 22, 23, 26, 34, 41, 48, 81, 92, 92n5; narrative, 2, 3, 22, 23, 128; sympathy as, 51

Keats, John, 50

Keen, Suzanne, 139n8, 140

Keith, Alick, 42, 43, 45, 48; Bessie's pregnancy and, 46; masculine authority of, 47, 47n10

Keith, Bessie, 43, 54; Cathy and, 44–45; childbirth of, 44; death of, 42, 46, 47n10; double-mindedness of, 47; fall of, 45, 46; immodesty of, 45, 46–47; pregnancy of, 25, 45, 46, 47, 56, 63, 99; somatic experience of, 63–64; Touchett and, 44

Kennedy, Meegan, 96, 96n13, 133, 133n7

Khan, Gaida, 151–52, 153, 154

Knock Me Up, Knock Me Down (Oliver), 16

Knott, Sarah, 10

Langridge, Rosemary, 61

Law, Jules, 70n12

Leighton, Mary Elizabeth, 6, 17n14

Levison, Francis, 77, 80, 85

Lewis, Judith Schneid, 37

Like a Mother (Garbes), 16

Linton, Catherine. *See* Heathcliff, Catherine Linton

Linton, Cathy Earnshaw, 3; Bessie and, 34, 44–45; childbirth of, 44; confinement of, 32; Heathcliff and, 26; illness for, 31, 33; marriage of, 30; pregnancy of, 22, 25, 30, 31, 32, 34, 56, 63, 115; recovery of, 34; somatic experience of, 63–64

Linton, Edgar, 34; Cathy and, 26; marriage of, 26, 30

Lombard, Anna: bodily agency and, 152; Gerald and, 151, 153; pregnancy of, 153, 154; sexual obsession and, 152; sexual possession of, 154

"Looking for Maternity" (Fisk), 7

"Losses We Share, The" (Markle), 89

Lost (Freidenfels), 83

Love, Heather, 11, 17, 50n2

Loving Literature (Lynch), 8

Lyall, Robert, 79

Lydgate, Rosamond: abortion and, 115; childbirth of, 108; disappointment of, 107; experience of, 4, 120–21; hyperinclusion and, 121; immodesty and, 117; interiority of, 96, 102, 104, 110, 117, 118; marriage of, 104, 105; mental process of, 105; miscarriage of, 1, 93, 117; as Miss Vincy, 119; oppositional opinion of, 116–17; pregnancy loss of, 3–4, 24, 100, 101, 104, 106, 107, 108, 113, 114, 115–16, 118; pregnancy of, 93, 99, 101, 103, 105, 111, 117, 121, 123; premature birth and, 113, 117; somatic expression of, 113; Tertius and, 109–10, 111, 112, 113, 114, 117, 120, 121; Will and, 109

Lydgate, Tertius, 93, 100, 109; financial difficulties for, 104, 106, 121, 123; interiority of, 102, 103, 104; medical authority of, 108, 112, 115, 117, 121; medical opinion of, 108; moral authority of, 107, 110, 112, 113, 115; personal/professional crisis for, 116; pregnancy and, 105; Rosamond and, 109–10, 111, 112, 113, 114, 117, 120, 121; scientific view of, 121

Lynch, Deirdre, 8

Malet, Lucas, 126, 131

Malone, Cynthia Northcutt, 7, 17, 18, 99, 104

Mangham, Andrew, 32, 82, 130

Marcus, Sharon, 17, 53, 54

Markle, Meghan, 77, 88; miscarriage of, 90; Sensation fiction and, 90; on suffering of others, 89–90

Martin Chuzzlewit (Dickens), 18

Mary Barton (Gaskell), 56n7
masculine authority, 42, 46, 47, 47n10, 48
Maternal Bodies (Doyle), 16
maternal guilt, 81, 158
maternal imagination, 129, 158
maternal impression, 24, 130; as diagnosis, 151; understandings of, 131
maternal mortality, 29, 76, 77, 157, 159
maternity, 10, 11, 58, 154; culture of, 88; disembodied, 49; hybrid responses to, 5; imperial, 153; loss/guilt/repentance and, 87; representations of, 127; sublimation of, 81
Matrimonial Causes Act (1857), 78, 78n2, 80
Matus, Jill L., 19, 52n4, 70, 92n3, 105n19, 128
Mazzoni, Cristina, 128, 129, 129n4, 130
McClintock, Anne, 153n10
medical authority, 20, 41, 74, 95, 99, 107, 112, 115, 117, 140
medical diagnosis, 99, 102, 132
medical humanities, 7, 8n6, 23, 96
medical knowledge, 136; advances in, 97, 126
medical practice, 92; discursive, 93–100
medicalization of pregnancy and childbirth, 22, 79, 91, 92, 96, 97, 128, 129, 158
medicine, 18–21, 94, 97, 130, 151; culture and, 95n11
Mellor, Anne, 5
menstrual cycle, 5, 58, 62, 142, 143, 147, 156, 157
mental illness, 29, 32, 59, 133, 134, 149
metaphorical approach to pregnancy, 14, 121–22, 127
Middlemarch (Eliot), 1, 93, 94, 96, 103, 107, 112, 128; approach to, 4; free indirect diagnosis in, 23; narration of, 122; pregnancy discourse in, 114, 118–19, 120, 121, 122; pregnant bodies and, 101, 102, 122; prelude to, 100
mind-body separation, 129, 130, 135, 146
miscarriage, 1, 34, 76, 82, 86, 93, 106, 117, 142, 158; Black women and, 159; chromosomal abnormalities and, 83; criminalization of, 88; early/late, 83, 88, 156; experiencing, 83, 90, 157; fake, 89; history of, 84; misunderstanding of, 83; social, 99; stillbirth and, 106n20

"Miscarriage and Coping in the Mid-Nineteenth Century" (Jensz), 83–84
modernity, 1, 8, 94, 127
modesty, 18, 37, 43, 56, 68, 99, 119, 148–49; as critical practice, 2, 10n7, 14, 15; feminine, 46, 145
molar pregnancy, 157
mommy memoirs, 16
mommy wars, 16
Monteith, Sir Mosely, 133, 134, 136
moral authority, 95, 96, 107
morality, 19, 108, 122, 128; maternal, 76; teaching, 25. *See also* immorality
Morgan, Rosemarie, 140n9
Morris, Dinah, 51, 54, 56, 70, 114; Hetty and, 67, 68; Ruth and, 64; Seth and, 66; sympathy and, 65
Morse, Deborah, 36
Moscucci, Ornella, 93, 94
Mother Is a Verb (Knott), 10
"Mourning Glencora" (Morse), 36

narrative authority, 22, 114
narrative voice, 25, 36, 42, 107
Nash, Jennifer C., 88, 90
National Institutes of Health, 76
"Near Confinement" (Malone), 17
Nelson, Maggie, 16
neonaticide, 70
"New Modesty in Literary Criticism" (Williams), 14
New York Times, 88, 89
Newman, Beth, 53n6
Nineteenth-Century Sensation Novel, The (Pykett), 78
North and South (Gaskell), 56n7
Nursing Cleo (Withycombe), 10n7

Oakley, Ann, 129, 129n4
Old Father Time, 139, 142–43, 144
Oliver, Kelly, 16
Ophelia, 33, 33n7
Orlemanski, Julie, 8
Oster, Emily, 16

Otherness, racial, 24
Our Mutual Friend (Dickens), 5, 6
Owens, Deidre Cooper, 12
Oxford movement, 25

Palliser, Lady Glencora, 25, 39, 41; infertility of, 38; narration of, 35; pregnancy of, 36–37, 40
Palliser, Plantagenet, 36, 37, 38, 39, 40, 41
paternal impression, 24, 127, 128, 129, 131, 139
pathologization, 11n8, 49, 50, 50n1, 93, 96
people of color, 12; death/murder of, 127; maternal, 87; spectacularized bodies of, 88; violence against, 10
Peregrine Pickle (Smollett), 130
Persuasion (Austen), 18, 106n20
Poolaw, Britany, 88
postcritique/postcriticism, 11, 14, 17, 50n1; surface reading as, 9
postpartum period, 29, 32, 82, 133
preeclampsia, 157, 158
Pregnancy and Childbirth in the Age of Victoria, 17n14
pregnancy cravings, 130
pregnancy loss, 24, 81, 82, 84, 87, 100–102, 104, 106, 107, 108, 111, 113, 114, 115–16, 118; cultural visibility of, 88; experiencing, 77; impact of, 3–4; public discourse and, 83; social blame for, 159
pregnancy revelation, 75, 95, 117–18, 119–20; chronologies of, 158; concealment and, 26–34
pregnancy tests, 73, 74, 157
pregnant bodies, 30, 36, 45, 72, 74, 95, 114, 120, 124, 127, 138, 139, 140, 146, 148; articulation of, 91; engagement with, 54; experiential space of, 115; moralizing judgment of, 34; plot and, 135; possibilities of, 73; representation of, 21, 101, 102, 122, 137
pregnant unconscious, 125, 126, 140
premature birth, 44, 106, 113, 145; immodesty and, 117; immorality and, 31n6
prenatal care, 98, 156
professionalization, masculine processes of, 91–92
Propper Daley summit, 89

psychoanalysis, 54, 140
psychology, 125
punishment, 41–48, 49, 50
Purdue, Melissa, 154
Pykett, Lyn, 78

Rabuzzi, Kathryn Allen, 94n9
racism, 74, 125; anti-Black/anti-Brown, 76, 90
rape, 11, 139
Reading with the Senses in Victorian Literature and Science (Coombe), 8
real/reality, 4–6, 9–10, 19, 56, 98, 144, 146, 158
Reductive Reading (Allison), 17, 50n2
Regaignon, Dara Rossman, 21, 35
Representations, 17, 53
reproduction, 10, 16, 35, 94; cultures of, 9; experiencing, 93, 116–17; vision of, 151; vocabulary of, 101, 122, 147
reproductive bodies, 6, 10, 37, 51, 57–58, 93, 103, 120, 123, 141, 145; depiction of, 2–3; exclusion/objectification of, 23; judging, 158; knowing, 12; medicalization of, 91, 92; mind/body relationship and, 16; vocabulary of, 147
reproductive imagination, 74
Revising the Clinic (Kennedy), 96
Roe v. Wade (1973), 89, 159
"Runaway Slave at Pilgrim's Point, The" (Barrett Browning), 11
Russell, John, 105
Ruth (Gaskell), 18, 22, 50, 52, 54, 55–56, 59, 62; bodily specificity and, 52n4; Eliot and, 51; fallen-woman plot of, 64; immorality and, 49; pregnancy in, 55; reproductive bodies and, 51
Ryan, Vanessa L., 125n1

Saint-Amour, Paul, 17
Sanders, Lise Shapiro, 7
Sanger, Charles Percy, 27
Scenes of Sympathy (Jaffe), 54
Schreiner, Olive, 11n8
Schwan, Anne, 9
Scott, Sir Walter, 51n3
Sedgwick, Eve Kosofsky, 50n2

self-knowledge, 64–65, 70, 97

sensation, 21n20, 32, 74, 76, 80, 87, 89, 118, 120; physical, 81, 91, 95, 100; somatic, 75, 77, 105

Sensation fiction, 21, 21n20, 23, 75, 77, 78, 90; dangerous women and, 82; plots associated with, 80

Sense and Sensibility (Austen), 18–19

sentimental motherhood, ideology of, 13–14

"seven-month child," 31, 31n6

sexual symbols, 43

sexuality, 37, 58, 138, 141; female, 61; ideology of, 124; moral, 57; notions of, 16, 127; representations of, 127; sublimation of, 81, 81n3; theories of, 125; treatment of, 23

Shelley, Mary, 55

Shonfield, Zuzanna, 7

short stories, pregnancies in, 125

Sickroom in Victorian Fiction, The (Bailin), 92

SIDS. *See* Sudden Infant Death Syndrome

Simmons, Clare A., 46

Simmons, LaKisha Michelle, 75, 76

Sims, James Marion, 12, 98

slavery, 75, 76, 98

Smellie, William, 20, 130n5

Smollett, Tobias, 130, 130n5

social norms, 11, 36

somatic reading, 7, 8, 9, 11, 14, 15, 16, 24, 50, 51, 53, 56, 61, 78, 90, 154, 159; space for, 3–4, 100; stakes of, 21; texture of, 23; value of, 1–2

Sorrel, Hetty, 3, 18, 96, 114, 121; acknowledgment of guilt by, 64; Adam and, 71, 73; Arthur and, 65, 66, 68–69, 69n10, 71, 72–73; beauty of, 68, 69; body of, 55; Dinah and, 67, 68; dread/terror for, 71, 72; hypervisibility of, 23, 67; interiority of, 64, 65, 67, 73; pregnancy of, 23, 49, 51, 52, 52n4, 65, 66, 71–73; pregnant body of, 53, 54, 74, 115; reproductive knowledge and, 70; self-knowledge and, 64–65, 70; somatic unknowing of, 74; sympathy with, 49, 64

Sparks, Tabitha, 98

Staring (Garland-Thomson), 53

Steinlight, Emily, 77, 77n1

stereotypes, 29; sex/reproduction, 93–94

Sterne, Lawrence, 130, 130n5

stillbirth, 76, 86, 97, 106, 115, 116, 147, 158; Black women and, 159; criminalization, 88; experiencing, 88, 90; grief about, 89; miscarriage and, 106n20

Stone, Pamela K., 4n4, 9

Stoneman, Patsy, 61

Story of an African Form (Schreiner), 11n8

Studies of Hysteria (Freud), 125

Sudden Infant Death Syndrome (SIDS), 82

suicide attempts, 137, 138, 144, 145

Surridge, Lisa, 6, 17n14

sympathy, 56–64, 89; bodily, 75; limits of, 23, 64–65, 70, 74

syphilis, 134, 135, 139; knowledge of, 136; pregnancy and, 133, 138

"Syphilis and the Hysterical Female" (Grand), 133

Taylor, Breonna, 90

Teigen, Chrissy, 77, 88, 89

Tess of the D'Urbervilles (Hardy), 139

Thackeray (Trollope), 35

"Theories and Methodologies" (*PMLA*), 15

Thierauf, Doreen, 17, 105n19, 115

Thinking without Thinking in the Victorian Novel (Ryan), 125n1

Tom Jones (Fielding), 18

Touching Feeling (Sedgwick), 50n2

Tougaw, Jason, 19n16, 50

trans pregnancy, 2n2

Treatise on the Theory and Practice of Midwifery (Smellie), 20, 130n5

Tristam Shandy (Sterne), 130n5

Trollope, Anthony, 25, 35, 38–39, 159

"Trollope and the Body" (Gilmartin), 38

tuberculosis, 19, 28, 28n2, 29

Turner, Sasha, 11–12, 16

ultrasounds, 2, 14, 74, 157

umbilical cord, 156, 158

unconscious mind, 131, 149–50

Unstable Bodies (Matus), 54n2, 70, 127, 128

unwanted pregnancy, 74, 155

US Supreme Court, 89, 159

V21 Collective, manifesto of, 50n1
Vavasor, Alice, 35, 36, 37, 39
venereal disease, 136
Victoria, Queen, 2, 2n1, 32; in childbirth, 97, 98; reproductive body of, 6
Victorian Pain (Ablow), 15
Victorian Skin (Gilbert), 7–8, 8n5
Victorians Undone (Hughes), 8
Vilbert, Dr.: Arabella and, 140–41
Violent Women and Sensation Fiction (Mangham), 32, 81
visibility, 42, 53, 61, 67, 69, 72, 73, 90, 114, 122; cultural, 88; external, 91; language of, 63, 119; narrative, 86, 103, 104, 132; physical, 62; sexualized, 104; vocabulary of, 66, 68
visuality, 53, 75, 84
vocabulary, 54, 66, 68, 129; pregnancy, 101, 146, 149; reproduction, 101, 122, 147
Vrettos, Athena, 10, 11, 13

Waterhouse, Harriet, 7
Waugh, Norah, 7

weak theory/thought, 17, 23, 50, 50n2, 77
"Weak Theory/Weak Modernisms" (Saint-Armour), 17
Wheatly, Kim, 47n10
Wilfer, Bella, 5, 6, 9, 10, 11, 12, 13
Williams, Jeffrey J., 14
Wilson, Philip, 129–30, 130n5
Withycombe, Shannon, 10n7, 83, 84
Wollstonecraft, Mary, 158
Women and Sexuality in the Novels of Thomas Hardy (Morgan), 140n9
women of color, 1, 159; spectacularized bodies of, 88
Writing Maternity (Regaignon), 21, 35n8
Wuthering Heights (Brontë), 11n8, 22, 25, 31, 34, 44, 53n6, 56, 60, 63, 69, 115; "human cuckoo" of, 26; timeline of, 27

Yonge, Charlotte Mary, 25, 42n9, 46, 54; anti-feminism of, 48; feminine modesty and, 145; moralizing judgments of, 48
Young, Iris Marion, 5

Zoonomia (Darwin), 129n3

www.ingramcontent.com/pod-product-compliance
Lightning Source LLC
Chambersburg PA
CBHW020739230426
43665CB00009B/489